Motherhood in the Old South

Motherhood in the Old South

PREGNANCY, CHILDBIRTH, AND INFANT REARING

Sally G. McMillen

LOUISIANA STATE UNIVERSITY PRESS
Baton Rouge and London

06 05 04 03 02 01 00 99 98 97   5 4 3 2 1

Designer: Laura Roubique Gleason
Typeface: Bembo
Typesetter: The Composing Room of Michigan, Inc.
Printer and binder: Thomson-Shore, Inc.

Portions of this book have appeared in a slightly different form in "Mothers'
Sacred Duty: Breast-Feeding Patterns Among Middle- and Upper-Class
Women in the Antebellum South," *Journal of Southern History,* LI (1985),
333–56.

Library of Congress Cataloging-in-Publication Data

McMillen, Sally G., 1944–
    Motherhood in the Old South : pregnancy, childbirth, and infant
  rearing / Sally G. McMillen.
        p.   cm.
    Bibliography: p.
    Includes index.
    ISBN 0-8071-1517-7 (cloth)   ISBN 0-8071-2166-5 (pbk.)
      1. Motherhood—Southern States—History—19th century.
    2. Pregnancy—Southern States—History—19th century.
    3. Childbirth—Southern States—History—19th century.   4. Infants—
  Care—Southern States—History—19th century.   I. Title.
  HQ759.M43   1989
  306.874'3'0975—dc20   89-34679
                                                                   CIP

To Blair and Carrie

Contents

Acknowledgments

This study grew from my curiosity and interest in the South and in the role of women. As a Californian transplanted to the South, I perceived differences in gender expectations and roles, which made me want to understand the historical reasons for women's position in southern society. As the mother of two children, I also wondered how southern women survived their numerous pregnancies and their confinements, breast-feeding, and infant rearing in a period of limited medical knowledge and a well-defined role for women. My graduate education let me explore the conceptual and historical framework of these questions. Moreover, I was fortunate to have access to the manuscript collections in several southern university libraries. There I spent long but happy hours intruding upon the intimate lives of southern mothers. As they described their daily activities, reactions, concerns, joys, and despair, I gained enormous admiration for their fortitude and sensitive perceptions and became convinced that their lives were complex, difficult, and demanding. I hope that this study does southern mothers justice and provides a glimpse of the hardships, demands, and infirmities that beset a role glorified by nineteenth-century America.

No historical work can claim to be the product of only its author, and this book is no exception. I am especially grateful to Robert Durden, who served as doctoral adviser to a dissertation that certainly extended beyond his own political expertise in southern history; to Peter English, who fostered my interest in medical history, gave endless encouragement to this project, and read and commented on numerous drafts; and to Paul Escott, who directed me through a master's degree and continued to provide support and friendship beyond the call of duty.

I would also like to thank a number of people who read and commented on all or part of this manuscript or who offered valuable advice and criticism. These include Anne Firor Scott, whose critical evaluation was immensely helpful, and Carole Haber, who started the entire project by suggesting an investigation of southern breast-feeding habits. They include, as well, Julia Blackwelder, David Patterson, Elisabeth Perry, Paul Nitsch, Sydney Nathans, Carl Fisher, Bill McDonald, Beth Curry, David McKnight, the anonymous readers for LSU Press, and my mother, Elizabeth Gregory. In giving credit, however, I by no means hold others accountable for my errors or omissions, or for my conclusions. They are mine.

Librarians—archivists especially—and other manuscript specialists have been helpful in easing the research process. I am especially grateful to Robert Byrd, Ellen Gartrell, and the late Mattie Russell, of the Manuscript Department of the William R. Perkins Library, at Duke University, who always seemed to discover another letter for me to read; to Robin Brabham, in the Special Collections section of the J. Murrey Atkins Library, at the University of North Carolina at Charlotte, who drew my attention to the Jane Woodruff Diary; to Betty McFall, at the Andrew L. Todd Library, of Middle Tennessee State University, Murfreesboro, who was unfailingly supportive in tracking down interlibrary-loan material; to Mary Teloh, Head of Special Collections at the Vanderbilt University Medical Center Library, who informed me of the hundreds of medical dissertations there and locked me in a room to read them; to Terry Cavanagh, Archivist at the History of Medicine Library of the Duke University Medical Center Library, who photocopied material and tolerated numerous requests for rare books; and to Edwina Walls, of the History Archives at the University of Arkansas Medical Sciences Library, in Little Rock. I would also like to thank the general and archive staffs of the Southern Historical Collection, in the L. R. Wilson Library, at the University of North Carolina at Chapel Hill; of the Ida Jane Dacus Library, at Winthrop College, in Rock Hill, South Carolina; of the Archives and Manuscripts Collection at the Tennessee State Library and Archives, in Nashville; of the South Caroliniana Library, at the University of South Carolina, in Columbia; of the South Carolina Historical Society Library, in Charleston; of the Waring Historical Library and Annex, at the Medical University of South Carolina, in Charleston; and of the Arkansas State History Commission Archives at the Arkansas State Library, in Little Rock.

I wish also to thank Judy Mullins for collating and photocopying material and for providing valuable hours of assistance. I am grateful to

Middle Tennessee State University for awarding me a research grant to assemble background information on the subjects of this study.

Finally, it is to my two children, Blair and Carrie, that I dedicate this book. Without them, I would not have experienced the challenges or overriding joys of motherhood.

Manuscript Repositories

Manuscript Collection, Arkansas State History Commission Archives, Arkansas State Library, Little Rock

Special Collections, J. Murrey Atkins Library, University of North Carolina at Charlotte

Archives and Special Collections, Ida Jane Dacus Library, Winthrop College, Rock Hill, South Carolina

Manuscript Department, William R. Perkins Library, Duke University, Durham, North Carolina

South Carolina Historical Society Library, Charleston

South Caroliniana Library, University of South Carolina, Columbia

Southern Historical Collection, L. R. Wilson Library, University of North Carolina at Chapel Hill

Manuscripts Collection, Tennessee State Library and Archives, Nashville

Special Collections, Vanderbilt University Medical Center Library, Nashville

Waring Historical Library and Annex, Medical University of South Carolina, Charleston

Motherhood in the Old South

Introduction

In 1848, Lydia Sigourney emoted over the benefits she and others perceived in motherhood, writing that each birth brought married women to a "higher place in the scale of being."[1] Mrs. Sigourney was a popular lady of letters during a period of history when American women were most admired for submissiveness, piety, domesticity, and silence. Since she was also a wife and mother, though, one might have expected her comment to give a truer picture of the realities of maternal life. But even Mrs. Sigourney publicly embraced the popular belief that the "sacred occupation" of nineteenth-century women was a condition to envy. Her voice was merely one of thousands in the period before the Civil War that glorified the rewards of motherhood. Few people acknowledged the difficulties inherent in achieving and fulfilling that role. Yet, belying pronouncements such as hers was the fact that no other occupation of the antebellum period was as hazardous or as demanding.

As a woman living in urban New England, Mrs. Sigourney had perhaps escaped the difficulties that many mothers faced in bearing and rearing children. Thus there may have been some justification for her cheerfulness. But in a period of dramatic and often unsound medical practices, success in achieving and fulfilling motherhood could not be assured. Not only was there an unsettled medical profession but epidemic and endemic illnesses plagued nineteenth-century America, frequent confinements were the rule, and the whole country experienced high maternal and infant mortality. The prospects for southern women were more perilous still. The disease environment of the antebellum South threatened women's and infants' health. The rural nature of plantation society implied lonely lives for many and, sometimes, the absence of a support system to help in difficult moments. Southerners favored especially large families, and frequent confinements increased

1. Lydia Sigourney, *Letters to Mothers* (New York, 1848), 9.

the risks. Despite the dangers, though, most southern mothers shared Mrs. Sigourney's perception. They would probably have added a strongly worded postscript noting the risks, but they felt ennobled by their sacred profession.

Until recently, historians had largely neglected the importance of the maternal experience and had scarcely investigated either the impact of motherhood on women or the recorded reactions of women to motherhood. Southern motherhood had escaped analysis. That is curious, for no other experience had such a significant effect on the way married women in the South conducted their daily lives. Perhaps scholars, like most observers in the nineteenth century, deemed the events surrounding childbirth too ordinary to be important. Or perhaps the difficulty of seeing events in this case from the perspective of those most involved made research too discouraging. Antebellum mothers rarely chronicled the intimate details of their lives.

This study focuses on the experiences of privileged southern women in childbirth and infant rearing between 1800 and 1860. It concentrates on health and medical concerns. Since the topic was hidden from the public eye, the best sources for understanding maternal behavior are the words of the women themselves and of their families. This monograph presents a personal view, relying heavily on thousands of pages of letters and journals written by women and family members living in different regions of the antebellum South. Middle- and upper-class women who were literate and who bothered to record their experiences supply the basis for my conclusions. Their husbands' occupations—as planters, merchants, educators, ministers, lawyers, and physicians—suggest that family income provided opportunities for these mothers to write during their busy child-rearing years. Most of the women lived in rural areas, and the majority were part of slave-owning families. Class bias is therefore unavoidable, for the study covers only southern women who had the time, energy, and education to leave a record of their maternal experiences. The monograph ends in 1860, a year perhaps more critical to political and social than to obstetric history. Historians have studied the antebellum period from a host of perspectives, but the emphasis here on childbirth and infant rearing means to add a new dimension by focusing on women's sacred occupation. The outbreak of the Civil War is also a convenient demarcation point in that it symbolizes the possibility of a changing perception of women with the end of plantation society in the South.

Central to the study is the shifting role of the antebellum medical profession in obstetrics and infant care. The descriptions of medical therapy and of the professional preoccupations of southern physicians are culled at times from a few private account books but primarily from southern medical journals. The attitudes and medical ideas of the region's doctors are evident in these periodicals as well as in antebellum medical dissertations.

All these sources prove that the realities surrounding childbirth for an antebellum southern woman were a far cry from the mythical image of her gliding through days of leisure and from Mrs. Sigourney's uplifting judgment. More likely the typical privileged southern woman bore and reared several children, suffered poor health, exhaustion, and a variety of physical ailments, grieved over the death of at least one child, and was either pregnant or nursing a newborn in every year until her midforties. Married women in the Old South found their lives defined by their duties. Pronouncements ostensibly elevating their status tied them to the home and did not raise them to a plane beyond domestic functions.

The Old South provides a particularly interesting context in which to examine childbirth and infant rearing, their implications for women, and the role of the medical profession. Southern women's lives were circumscribed in the public sphere and scrutinized in the private. Biological and maternal functions determined daily existence. Since Mrs. Sigourney was an urban woman living in a region that was beginning to concede additional options to women, she escaped some of the constraints women lived under in the South. In a way, she was an exception, but she also reflected the possibilities unfolding for at least some women in the urban Northeast. In the South, however, gender placed a strong restriction on public involvement. At least until the Civil War, the region remained patriarchal and prided itself on being a society with well-defined gender roles. Living in a hierarchical, rural, plantation society, southern wives had few choices besides motherhood. Southern men glorified the maternal role and criticized as masculine northern women who stepped beyond it. Families in the antebellum South tended to be larger than the national norm, for few social or economic constraints limited fertility. A positive attitude toward having large numbers of children reflected the vigor of the patriarchy, the importance of the southern family, and the prosperity of the region. But women were left to bear and raise the young.

At the core of this study is concern with women's physical and emotional well-being. The unhealthful climate of the antebellum South had negative and often fatal repercussions on both mothers and infants. The maternal mortality rate was greater for southern women than for women living in the other settled regions of the country. Women not only endured the normal discomforts of pregnancy but also experienced them repeatedly and suffered debilitating encounters with diseases endemic to their part of the nation. Unsound or dramatic remedies that remained an integral part of the southern medical profession's approach could cause a lifetime of ill health for the parturient woman or the newborn. An alarmingly high infant mortality rate marked southern society before the Civil War. Mothers spent endless days and even weeks nursing young children who were susceptible to contagious diseases, suffered severe and often fatal illnesses, and sometimes endured heroic therapeutics.

Changes in the perceptions of medical responsibility that occurred during this period affected the middle- and upper-class southern women who chose to use male doctors. Mothers gradually accepted male accoucheurs in the birthing room and began to consider medical attendants for infant health problems. The nation's heightened interest in health, professional training, and scientific solutions encouraged a growing employment of trained male doctors during childbirth. Traditionally, parturition had been a natural, though painful, event. Women customarily had monitored their own pregnancies, using female midwives and attendants for assistance during labor, and they had relied on domestic remedies for infant diseases.

In the late eighteenth century and increasingly during the antebellum period, male doctors reconceived childbirth as pathological. They argued that male doctors trained in the use of instruments and drugs had become essential during labor. Childhood illnesses might require similar professional attention. Throughout the period, doctors tried to convince mothers that male authority, scientific answers, and professional medical advice could best ensure a successful delivery and a healthy child. Midwives and home medical remedies, they argued, had been superseded. Southern women gradually put their faith in male accoucheurs, pleased with the status they brought to the birthing chamber and the attention they focused on motherhood. It is doubtful that the doctors deserved such trust. Even with professional attendants, maternal and infant mortality rates remained high, and improved health in the region was imperceptible before the Civil War.

Southern doctors approached obstetrics and infant care in the same way they dealt with most diseases. Dramatic therapy was the order of the day. But southern medical professionals clung to traditional remedies long after their northern colleagues had begun to explore other possibilities. Despite an exposure to northern medical ideas, southern physicians reflected the conservative nature of their society and often resisted change. Thus many were reluctant to apply methods that could ease women's experiences during confinement and to question the soundness of extensive bleeding, purging, and drugging. They looked to the past rather than the future for scientific ideas and generally remained wedded to dramatic therapeutics. And as midcentury approached, some Southerners became convinced that any idea—or even cautious warning—emanating from the North was suspect. Just as important, though, was the profession's belief in the geographical specificity of disease. Because it saw that the unhealthy southern climate caused unique medical problems, it concluded that heroic remedies were well justified. But the commitment of southern doctors to dramatic therapies for women and children was often unsound in practice, exacerbating ailments rather than curing them.

In the area of obstetrics and infant care, the antebellum period was one of transition and inconsistency, reinforcing the perception that history rarely moves steadily forward. Despite a growing professionalism surrounding childbirth, traditional practices lingered in the South. The personal side of childbirth remained, and southern women continued to rely on the support of other women during labor, breast-feeding, child care, and periods of mourning. Such support was crucial for women facing the hazards and uncertainties of their maternal experience. Shared concerns promoted a special sense of female unity among married women. Their experiences heightened their dependence on religion as well. Women accorded God responsibility for a safe delivery and for the recovery of an infant from a long illness. The frequency of infant and maternal death engendered a special appreciation of religion and provided women with the strength to handle their grief and share their emotions with others.

The antebellum South is also a particularly interesting arena in which to examine maternal commitment. The presence of nearly four million black slaves offered privileged Southerners a labor source lacking in other regions of the country. Middle- and upper-class women could have turned to black women for child rearing and wet-nursing. Although mistresses occasionally used black midwives, and slave women and children often served as assistants and child-sitters, the majority of healthy white women accepted their maternal role with commitment and love. They rarely delegated their motherly duties to others but assumed principal responsibility for breast-feeding and the care of infants during illnesses.

The study of childbirth and infant rearing gives a clearer under-standing of the devotion of antebellum mothers to what they perceived as their sacred and singular occupation. For most women, bearing and rearing children brought tangible rewards in a society that offered few alternatives. Despite the risks and demands, mothers took their duties seriously and rarely faltered. They must have found satisfaction in the role. Out of deep affection and the acceptance of their maternal duties, southern mothers devoted their health, energy, and even their lives to bearing and rearing children. The South glorified this occupation, and southern mothers apparently responded. Ultimately they achieved a sense of self-esteem within the family and often the joy of close, affec-tionate ties to their children. What they sacrificed in physical and emo-tional health and in the breadth of female roles apparently was less important. Perhaps the idea of expanding their ambit beyond the home would have challenged too much before the Civil War. Most women probably never imagined possibilities beyond their own lives. The pa-triarchy vigorously encouraged and celebrated the maternal focus. Southern women, who loved their children deeply and who had been raised to align themselves with male perceptions, embraced their do-mestic role. They hoped that the investment of energy, affection, and good health would bring credit to themselves, to the family, and to the nation. What follows is their story, telling of their dedication to a pro-fession that occupied the most significant years of their married lives. It was southern women's sacred, but also demanding and perilous, occupation.

1 *To Physicke and Comfort*

THE ANTEBELLUM MEDICAL PROFESSION

In 1804, Peter Miller, a young medical student, described a mother's experiences in bearing and rearing children, noting that when she "reflects upon the dangers attending the puerperal state, the slow and difficult recovery of some, the death of others: when she considers that half of the human race do not attain the age of seven years, . . . it may truly be said that in sorrow does she bring forth." Without a shred of optimism, he analyzed the situation that most women faced in becoming mothers. He noted that all were "subject to a train of suffering and distress in consequence of complying with a duty imposed upon them by the great author of nature, for the purpose of propagating the human race." Miller urged his colleagues to sympathize with the condition of women and to exert every effort to alleviate their sorrows. As an observer and future professional, Miller, like other physicians, realized that childbirth and infant rearing defined women's lives but were dangerous, taxing, and often painful experiences for most mothers. The intercession of male professionals was, he thought, the best expedient for lessening their suffering.[1]

The nineteenth century has often been called the century of the child. Americans focused not only on the importance of children within individual families but also on their critical role in the nation's future. The new republic could not progress without healthy, vigorous citizens. A millennial vision of the country's potential and a new interest in reform during the antebellum period heightened the concern surrounding children. Each child became a socially significant being—a reflection of the perceived vigor of the republic.[2] The hope for a greater

1. Peter Miller, *An Essay on the Means of Lessening the Pains of Parturition* (Philadelphia, 1804), 14.
2. For a discussion of the significance of the child in recent history, see Phillipe Aries, *Centuries of Childhood: A Social History of Family Life,* trans. Robert Baldick (London, 1962); Carl Degler, *At Odds: Women and the Family in America from the Revolution to the*

nation rested upon its youngest citizens. Improving children's character, their mind, behavior, and physical being could create a better
citizenry and a more nearly flawless society. The majority of Americans
no longer believed in predestination and a child's inherently sinful
nature. Instead, many thought that children were born in innocence,
ready to be molded into superior persons. The possibility existed of the
lofty attainment of near-perfection. But theories alone could not ensure
that outcome. A careful nurturing of each child and a close attention to
its health, along with a sound education and an instilling of strong
religious values, were critical to achieving the ideal.

Mothers stood at the center of these perceptions. Obviously there
was nothing new about motherhood, but the significance of the maternal role grew. Women could guide and influence the country's future
from within their domestic sphere by focusing their time and energy on
bearing and rearing children. This was a serious responsibility, to be
undertaken not lightly but rather with dedication, sacrifice, vigilance,
and deep affection. From the pulpit, the published volume, and polite
conversation came an endless stream of comments magnifying the role
that mothers were to assume. Women's duties as childbearers and nur-
turers became the linchpin of the nation's future.

Doctors like Miller gradually became aware of the role that this
exalted perception of motherhood permitted them. If children and
mothering were important, the bearing and rearing of children were
now publicly seen as complex and demanding activities—an idea that
women had undoubtedly accepted for thousands of years. To Miller
and his progressive colleagues, it was apparent that mothers could not
handle the full range of their responsibilities single-handedly. The
achievement of motherhood was, they thought, still too reliant on
traditional ideas and natural processes. The nineteenth century was a
new world, capable of scientific and enlightened visions and rational
answers to age-old problems. Too much was at stake to allow women

Present (New York, 1980), 72–74; Linda K. Kerber, "Daughters of Columbia: Educating
Women for the Republic, 1787–1805," in Linda K. Kerber and Jane DeHart Mathews
(eds.), *Women's America: Refocusing the Past* (New York, 1982), 82–94; Anne Louise Kuhn,
The Mother's Role in Childhood Education: New England Concepts, 1830–1860 (New Haven,
1947); Edward Shorter, *The Making of the Modern Family* (New York, 1975); and Bernard
Wishy, *The Child and the Republic: The Dawn of Modern American Child Nurture*
(Philadelphia, 1968). The standard study on the changing concepts toward English children is Lawrence Stone's *The Family, Sex, and Marriage in England, 1500–1800* (New York,
1980).

sole charge of their significant tasks. Rather, male doctors could rescue women from "suffering and distress" and improve mothers' and infants' chances. Drawing on humanitarian concerns, an increasing interest in scientific solutions, progressive ideas for a better nation, and their own self-interest in expanding individual practices and enhancing the medical profession, physicians gradually took an active role in assisting parturient and nurturing women. Professional medicine and motherhood gradually intertwined during the antebellum period.

For thousand of years, women had regarded childbirth as a natural though painful event and relied on midwives and female friends and relatives to assist in birthing. Infant health care had traditionally fallen within the province of domestic medicine and homemade cures. All this began to alter by the late eighteenth century. Doctors wishing involvement came to consider childbirth a pathological condition. By viewing the situation of expectant women as diseased, they could argue that science rather than nature should assume a primary role during labor. And by appealing to the nation's interest in the health of its children, they could argue for a role in infant nurturing. Popular medical procedures such as bleeding, purging, medicating, and employing instruments defined the medical profession's approach to obstetrics and infant care. As middle- and upper-class Americans became accustomed to placing weight on training, education, and male expertise, doctors rather than midwives gradually assumed the leading role in maternal and infant medicine.[3]

Nineteenth-century medical practice was still largely empirical. The most widely accepted method of treatment was based on traditional heroic, or antiphlogisitic, therapy. Dr. Benjamin Rush, a noted Phila-

3. The change from female midwives to male doctors has been widely studied. See Irving S. Cutter and Henry R. Viets, *A Short History of Midwifery* (Philadelphia, 1964); Jane B. Donegan, *Women and Men Midwives: Medicine, Morality, and Misogyny in Early America* (Westport, Conn., 1978); Donegan, "The Midwife Throughout History," *Journal of Nurse-Midwifery*, XXVII (1982), 3–11; Richard W. Wertz and Dorothy C. Wertz, *Lying-In: A History of Childbirth in America* (New York, 1977); Catherine M. Scholten, *Childbearing in American Society, 1650–1850* (New York, 1985); Scholten, "'On the Importance of the Obstetrick Art': Changing Customs of Childbirth in America, 1760–1825," *William and Mary Quarterly*, XXXIV (1977), 426–45; Sylvia Hoffert, *Private Matters: American Attitudes Toward Childbearing and Infant Nurture in the Urban North, 1800–1860* (Urbana, Ill., 1989); and Judith Walzer Leavitt, *Brought to Bed: Childbearing in America, 1750–1950* (New York, 1986). Scholten, Hoffert, Leavitt, and others show that the trend toward a dependence on male accoucheurs began in the urban Northeast among middle- and upper-class women.

delphia physician, popularized this form of allopathic medicine in the late eighteenth century. Introducing ideas learned at the University of Edinburgh, Rush hypothesized that vascular tension caused disease. The most effective way to ease that tension and rid the body of undesirable substances, he argued, included the drastic measures of venesection, leeching, cupping, blistering, purging, and extensive medication. Negative results often followed well-intended efforts. Doctors reacted to visible symptoms rather than causes, for they lacked the medical acumen that would have encouraged them to look beyond the obvious. Allopathic doctors who emulated Rush believed the body's blood supply to be twice its actual volume, and sometimes energetic lancing of an artery or the jugular vein resulted in death. If one dose of medication was insufficient, heroic therapeutics called for several. In difficult cases, when doctors found one method ineffective, they intensified their efforts and experimented with a variety of techniques until they achieved success or the patient died. Only luck or a strong constitution allowed a patient to withstand extreme remedies.[4]

By the 1840s and 1850s, some northern allopaths began to question the effectiveness of heroic therapy. But with the exception of a handful of physicians associated with regional medical institutions, the greater number of southern doctors remained dedicated to it at least until the Civil War. Active purging and bleeding were prescribed for most diseases and health problems in the antebellum South. The relatively static character of medicine in the region was due in part to Southerners' devotion to received ideas. To some doctors with limited training and few effective cures, heroic remedies seemed the clear answer, for invariably they generated some response. It took little skill to lance an artery or apply a mustard plaster, but in patient and bystanders alike there was little doubt that the doctor was making a difference, even if the remedies attempted did not promote better health.[5]

4. For discussions of heroic medicine, see Alex Berman, "The Heroic Approach in Nineteenth-Century Therapeutics," in Judith Walzer Leavitt and Ronald L. Numbers (eds.), *Sickness and Health in America: Readings in the History of Medicine and Public Health* (Madison, Wis., 1978), 77–86; William G. Rothstein, *American Physicians in the Nineteenth Century: From Sects to Science* (Baltimore, 1972); Joseph Waring, "The Influence of Benjamin Rush on the Practice of Bleeding in South Carolina," *Bulletin of the History of Medicine*, XXXV (1961), 230–37; and John Harley Warner, *The Therapeutic Perspective: Medical Practice, Knowledge, and Identity in America, 1820–1885* (Cambridge, Mass., 1986).

5. A. Clair Siddell, "Bloodletting in American Obstetric Practice," *Bulletin of the History of Medicine*, LIV (1980), 101–102; James H. Cassedy, *Medicine and American Growth, 1800–1860* (Madison, Wis., 1986), 102–104. Siddell argues that southern doctors used heroics in obstetrics, a form of therapy unknown when midwives presided.

When northern doctors criticized the South's fixation upon heroic techniques, its physicians had their response ready. After seeing southern therapies flayed, a doctor defended his colleagues' approach: "Their reason is obvious: the diseases with which they have to contend are rapid and dangerous to a degree entirely unknown further north and their remedial measures have to be pursued with an energy and decision that northern diseases seldom require." He continued his argument by noting that the South's unhealthful climate was hospitable to diseases foreign to other areas. Doses of medicine, he asserted, that might prove effective in northern cities "would be wholly insufficient in New Orleans."[6]

The defense by southern doctors rested partly on the important tenet of specificity. Diseases could alter, antebellum medicine maintained, with race, age, gender, environment, and region. No climate, the physicians imagined, could be more disease-ridden than that of the South. Therefore, strong medical actions were essential to counteract the environment and its miasmic conditions. According to Erasmus Darwin Fenner, a New Orleans physician and the publisher of *Southern Medical Reports,* the "most destructive diseases" prevailed in the South. Malaria was consequently an important exhibit in building the case for heroic answers.[7]

Physicians' ledgers and account books, detailed cases in southern medical journals, and even personal letters attest to the widespread use of dramatic remedies. Since heroic therapy remained the most popular medical approach, it shaped the way the majority of southern doctors addressed obstetrics and infant care. But there was a problem. The new republic desired vigorous citizens, but it was apparent that allopathic remedies had a poor record of success. And in the 1820s and 1830s, health concerns became a national priority and competing medical theories such as phrenology, botanic medicine, and Grahamism arose to challenge the accepted methods.

Home remedies and herbal cures had stood the test of time and continued in use throughout the antebellum period, especially in rural southern and western households. A few published volumes offered

6. The doctor arguing for heroics was answering the criticism of a Dr. Chapman, at the University of Pennsylvania. See *Western Journal of Medicine and Surgery,* n.s., VI (1842), 474.

7. For a discussion of specificity, see Warner, *The Therapeutic Perspective,* 58–80. Erasmus Darwin Fenner, "Introductory Address," *Southern Medical Reports,* I (1849), 8; "Practical Suggestions to Young Physicians," *Stethoscope and Virginia Medical Gazette,* IV (1854), 211–18.

such cures to the public. One of the most popular guides in the South, *Gunn's Domestic Medicine; or, Poor Man's Friend,* included a compilation of southern herbal recipes. First published in Tennessee in 1830, the book received high praise from its readers. In a typical testimonial, Polly Summey, of Asheville, North Carolina, urged her sister to consult Gunn's medical advice because it would provide a "full description" of her health problem. To many like Polly, Gunn's volume was a valued friend. Another guide, by Richard Carter, a self-styled doctor from Virginia, printed a curious compilation of herbal recipes based upon his Indian mother's methods of self-diagnosis and -cure.[8]

Although home-produced medicines were not in direct competition with allopathic practice, the creation of a formalized theory based upon botanic cures seriously challenged the medical profession. The rise of a medical fad known as Thomsonianism in the 1810s and its widespread popularity by the 1820s caused regular doctors some uneasiness. Sam Thomson, a New Hampshire farmer, supposed that insufficient heat in the body produced illness. His cures included torrid baths and the ingestion of substances such as cayenne pepper and, most important, the plant lobelia, to restore the body to its proper temperature. Though Thomson's measures were often as drastic as those employed by allopaths, his sect gained a following among the middle and lower classes, especially in the South and West, where because of the tradition of domestic medicine his antielitist approach was appealing.[9]

Water cures also won converts. The ideas of European hydropaths spread to the United States by the 1830s. Cold-water remedies, regular bathing, the drinking of quantities of water, visits to sulphur springs, a sensible diet, and regular exercise constituted the regimen of hydropaths. Spas in Alabama, Georgia, Mississippi, and Virginia, as well as

8. John C. Gunn, *Gunn's Domestic Medicine; or, Poor Man's Friend, Shewing the Diseases of Men, Women, and Children* (2nd ed.; Madisonville, Tenn., 1834); Polly Summey to Selina Lenoir, December 5, 1841, in Lenoir Family Papers, Southern Historical Collection, L. R. Wilson Library, University of North Carolina at Chapel Hill; Richard Carter, *Valuable Vegetable Medical Prescriptions, for the Cure of All Nervous and Putrid Disorders* (Cincinnati, 1830). For a good view of Gunn's work and its impact on antebellum society, see Charles E. Rosenberg, "Introduction to the New Edition," in *Gunn's Domestic Medicine* (Knoxville, Tenn., 1986), v–xxi.

9. James O. Breeden, "Thomsonianism in Virginia," *Virginia Magazine of History and Biography,* LXXXII (1974), 150–80; Frederick C. Waite, "American Sectarian Medical Colleges Before the Civil War," *Bulletin of the History of Medicine,* II (1946), 148–65. In 1852, the Georgia state legislature drew five thousand dollars from the state treasury to establish a botanic school at Macon.

local institutions such as the Franklin Water Cure, in Tennessee, attest to the popularity of these ideas, particularly among middle- and upper-class southern families. Many plantation women indulged in annual pilgrimages to distant spas or gathered periodically at nearby springs for bathing and socializing. Women often traveled to spas after their confinements. Allopaths found little to criticize in these customs, for many used water as a remedy themselves.[10]

Homeopathy, developed by Samuel Hahnemann, a German, in the 1790s, achieved popularity in the United States by the 1840s and remained a threat to allopathic medicine at least until the Civil War. Homeopaths advocated the idea of *similia*—of introducing a like and minute dosage of the disease-producing agent as a cure. Homeopaths retained a following throughout the antebellum period in part because their prudent approach to medicine met with some success, and in part because their rather intellectual procedures attracted an elite and intelligent group of Southerners. Heroic doctors mocked homeopathic theory by exaggerating the usefulness the theory ascribed to minute dosages and by appealing to Americans' xenophobia and their aversion to what was of German origin.[11]

The rise of competing sects led doctors to defend their professional reputations and disparage quackery. Their criticism did little to weaken the opposition, however, or to bolster the regular medical profession. Throughout the antebellum period, allopaths decried the techniques of hydropaths, botanists, phrenologists, and quacks, and each of these sects criticized heroic therapeutics. Formal and informal debates occurred in print and in other public forums, and southern medical journals overflowed with articles taking alternative forms of medicine to task. Regional medical dissertations reflected the depth of feeling. Graduating students discussed the "abuses of medicine" and categorized their opponents as "dishonest, treacherous and gold-loving

10. James H. Cassedy, *American Medicine and Statistical Thinking, 1800–1860* (Cambridge, Mass., 1984), 139–45; Jane B. Donegan, *Hydropathic Highway to Health; Women and Water-Cure in Antebellum America* (New York, 1986); W. K. Bowling, "Hydropathy," *Nashville Journal of Medicine and Surgery,* VI (1854), 51; "Water Cure Doctor" (in Manuscripts Collection, Tennessee State Library and Archives, Nashville); "Editorials and Synopsis of Monthly Intelligence, Medical Items," *Nashville Journal of Medicine and Surgery,* VIII (1855), 80.

11. Rothstein, *American Physicians in the Nineteenth Century,* 152–74; Martin Kaufman, *Homeopathy in America: The Rise and Fall of a Medical Heresy* (Baltimore, 1971); Cassedy, *American Medicine,* 124–35.

villains" who practiced "deeds of the Devil." The intensity of feeling, unfortunately, served only to undermine confidence in a profession that needed greater credibility. The bickering indicates the depth of insecurity that existed among doctors, few of whom felt they could remain above the fracas. Quarreling and factionalism were the typical state of the medical profession.[12]

Perhaps the uneasiness was justified. Beginning in the 1830s, medical licensing virtually disappeared. Any white man could declare himself a doctor. As early as the late eighteenth century, allopaths had established state medical societies and licensing boards to upgrade standards, enhance the reputation of trained physicians, and eliminate quacks. In 1817, South Carolina required that the state examining board license all doctors. Arkansas tried to appoint a state board that would certify physicians and approve those with a medical education. But the spread of democratic ideas in the Jacksonian period caused many to question not only political but also social ideals. Medical licensing smacked of elitism in the way it seemed to restrict the field to people who could afford training or an education. By the 1830s, medical licensing disappeared in all states but New Jersey and Louisiana. Whether the formation of medical sects occurred because leaders pressured state legislatures to lower standards or whether the elimination of medical requirements was a consequence of the emergence of the sects is not clear. But a new emphasis on democratic principles and a frustration with the failure of allopathic methods were evident. All practitioners, whether botanics, eclectics, steam doctors, hydropaths, quacks, or trained allopaths, were allowed to hang out their shingles and call themselves doctors.[13]

Women and many rural practitioners were not direct participants in the heated competition. But the insecurity of the doctors, the lack of

12. Articles describing numerous debates among competing sects include "Water Cure Doctor," *Nashville Journal of Medicine and Surgery,* II (1852), 282; "Quackery," *ibid.;* and Review of James Simpson's *Homeopathy: Its Tenets and Tendencies, Theological and Therapeutical, ibid.,* VI (1854), 252. Medical dissertations denouncing sectarian medicine: G. Bivens, "Abuses of Medicine," Dissertation 93 (1854), James Perry, "The Quack," Dissertation 274 (1857), Eugene Anderson, "Honorable Medicine," Dissertation 389 (1858), all for the Department of Medicine, University of Nashville, and in Special Collections, Vanderbilt University Medical Center Library.

13. Kaufman, *Homeopathy,* 11; Breeden, "Thomsonianism in Virginia," 154; Rothstein, *American Physicians in the Nineteenth Century,* 144–45; Paul Starr, *The Social Transformation of American Medicine* (New York, 1982), 30, 57–58; W. David Baird, *Medical Education in Arkansas, 1879–1978* (Memphis, 1979), 1–3.

confidence the public felt, and the squabbling within the medical profession affected the way almost all physicians practiced medicine. To prove their competence, doctors zealously demonstrated the superiority of their techniques while maligning the opposition. As physicians came to take a larger part in obstetrics and infant care, their energetic approach to therapy owed not only to devotion to popular dramatic theories but also to insecurity. By the late 1840s and 1850s, only a handful of southern practitioners—generally those holding positions of authority in medical institutions—were still urging their colleagues to show moderation in the delivery room. These voices were the exception, for caution implied the possibility of error and of the worth of northern or other competing practices.

Readers of southern medical journals and personal accounts are struck time and again by the extent to which doctors bled, leeched, drugged, and purged. Some southern physicians believed that women —indeed, most patients—welcomed experimental or heroic efforts. One practitioner asserted that women enjoyed the opportunity to be "subjects of medical treatment" because they desired the "flush of health that they see in the opposite sex."[14] There seemed little reason to alter the efforts, and some doctors remained blind to the way that their attempts at remedies often resulted in poor health. Anyway, they had no easy or demonstrably successful therapies to offer in replacement.

The importance of science and education contributed to the founding of dozens of medical schools and journals during the antebellum period. By 1860, the United States could claim at least forty institutions for the training of doctors. With the disappearance of medical licensing, a degree in hand became the chief symbol of professional status. It was a matter of pride that the country had more medical institutions than any other nation. But quantity did not imply quality. The majority of the country's medical colleges were haphazard, and many lasted only a few years. Funding was scarce, and teachers relied on student fees for their salaries. Standards were often questionable: because institutions competed for students, struggling medical schools accepted anyone who could pay the tuition. Institutions with the least demanding curriculum often attracted the largest student body. A course of study lasted a year or two; prior experience on the job could shorten formal study. A required thesis or "dissertation," often of twenty or fewer pages, gave

14. H. S. Leigh, "Uterine Hemorrhage as Connected with Pregnancy," Dissertation 432 (1859), in Vanderbilt University Medical Center Library.

graduating students the opportunity to compile secondhand information and personal rumination on a topic of their choice. Medical colleges offered course work in obstetrics, which by the 1830s had become a requirement for graduation in many schools. Students mastered obstetrical procedures by listening to lectures rather than by attending live patients, and most doctors first saw a woman in labor when they began private practice.[15]

The North moved far ahead of the South in establishing medical schools, and the most prestigious institutions were in Philadelphia and New York. By the 1840s, it became obvious to many Southerners that their region had no reputable medical colleges to match northern and European schools. Many southern physicians seemed haunted by a sense of their inferiority and urged the region's medical profession to create its own institutions. The South acted quickly. It established at least twenty medical colleges by 1860, though many were marginal and lacked a solid reputation. But regional promoters, like James De Bow, editor of *De Bow's Review,* could point with pride to the two fine medical institutions in New Orleans. And they could note the large enrollment and sizable endowment of Transylvania University, in Lexington, Kentucky, until its demise in 1850. For the first time, southern men could receive a sound medical education on home territory. That, it was hoped, would enhance their competence to practice southern medicine.[16]

The need for a truly southern approach to medicine became a widely shared preoccupation by the 1850s, heightened by political and social concerns. Observers worried—and as early as 1838, statistics confirmed—that many southern students lacked a commitment to their region. One southern journal's tabulation disclosed that half the medical-school graduates of the University of Pennsylvania were from the South. By 1858, the situation worsened, for two-thirds of all students at the medical school of the University of Pennsylvania and at Jefferson Medical College, in Philadelphia, were Southerners. Their affinity to northern institutions kindled a sense of uneasiness, particularly as the issue of slavery sharpened sectional differences. The *Southern*

15. Waite, "American Sectarian Medical Colleges," 148–65; Starr, *The Social Transformation of American Medicine,* 43; Cassedy, *Medicine and American Growth,* 67–72.
16. Rothstein, *American Physicians in the Nineteenth Century,* 75; "Editorial Notes and Miscellany," *De Bow's Review,* XXIX (1860), 396; Cassedy, *Medicine and American Growth,* 103–104; Warner, *The Therapeutic Perspective,* 76–79.

Medical Reformer and Review issued a direct appeal. "Can any man of the South be called a friend to his home and country," asked an editor, "who gives his influence and patronage to the North?" Although his cry skirted the issue of abolition, the editor probably envisioned vulnerable southern men studying medicine amid the liberal reformers and abolitionists of Philadelphia. Couching the matter in medical terms, the *Nashville Monthly Record of Medical and Physical Sciences* argued that the region's physicians should remain at home to understand the "multiform shades and types" of southern diseases caused by the area's "most unstable climate." Indeed, there was some validity to such concerns. But it was also evident to those seeking a good education that the outstanding medical institutions were northern. Despite pleas from fire-eaters and the keepers of regional values, young men flocked northward until the Civil War, wanting degrees from esteemed institutions. Even though they constituted only a minority of southern doctors, their actions were tacit proof that southern medical training was inferior to that in the North.[17]

Still, southern doctors managed to unite on one issue: their right to take charge of obstetrics. Almost unanimously, they overcame their ideological differences and their disparities of educational background in venting wrath upon midwifery, which they perceived as a threat to their ends. The creation of medical specialties like surgery and pathology occurred with relative ease, for no entrenched interests fought the medical profession when it tried to move into those fields. Obstetrics faced midwifery. In the eyes of antebellum physicians, reliance upon midwives blocked the advancement of science and profes-

17. Rothstein, *American Physicians in the Nineteenth Century,* 75; "Medical Schools," *Western Journal of Medicine and Surgery,* 3rd ser., III (1848), 85; "Medical Education—Nashville—Shelby Medical College," *Nashville Medical Recorder,* I (1858), 59; T. C. G., "Southern Schools—Literary and Scientific," *Southern Medical Reformer and Review,* VII (1857), 309; *Nashville Monthly Record of Medicine and Physical Science,* I (1858), 58. For interesting perceptions on southern medical education, see Harold J. Abrahams, "Secession from Northern Medical Schools," *Transactions and Studies of the College of Physicians of Philadelphia,* XXXVI (1968–69), 29–45, which describes the exodus of nearly three hundred southern medical students from Philadelphia institutions; James O. Breeden, "States' Rights Medicine in the Old South," *Bulletin of the New York Academy of Medicine,* LII (1976), 348–72; John Harley Warner, "A Southern Medical Reform: The Meaning of the Antebellum Argument for Southern Medical Education," *Bulletin of the History of Medicine,* LVII (1983), 365–81; and Warner, "The Idea of Southern Medical Distinctiveness: Medical Knowledge and Practice in the Old South," in Judith Walzer Leavitt and Ronald L. Numbers (eds.), *Sickness and Health in America: Readings in the History of Medicine and Public Health* (2nd ed.; Madison, Wis., 1985), 53–70.

sionalism. The vitriol with which doctors mounted their offensive reflects their determination to assume center stage as childbirth attendants, but it also makes manifest their insecurity as they usurped what had been a predominantly female specialty.

Physicians attempted to convince female patients that masculine skills were essential in the delivery room. Because they recognized, however, that they faced an uphill battle, their effort became two pronged. Doctors touted their own professional skills at the same time that they vilified their female competition. It may seem surprising that southern doctors undertook a campaign so disproportionate to the relative powerlessness of the group they attacked. But their motives went beyond an adherence to scientific standards and a humanitarian desire to lessen women's sufferings. Medicine was not a high-paying profession in the antebellum period, and a profitable practice demanded many patients. This goal proved elusive. But one route to a large following was by earning the favor of a woman who could bring a whole family under the doctor's care. And what better means to win her good will, and even dependence, than to see her through a successful delivery? Moreover, obstetrical and gynecological procedures were relatively expensive, competing with surgery for high fees. Charges between five and twenty-five dollars for each delivery made an important contribution to a physician's income. Doctors concluded that midwives not only thwarted science but also interfered with doctors' efforts to earn a decent living.[18]

Southern doctors met the provocation. They blamed midwives for women's sufferings during childbirth. Dr. John Wilson did not mince words in castigating female practitioners. "Who has not seen mothers rendered miserable for life, by prolapsis and inversion of the uterus; rupture of the perineum; rectal and vaginal fistula, and c. & c.," he asked, "all of which have been occasioned by the ignorance and unskillfulness of the 'old grannies' to whom females are almost compelled to submit their lives?" A Tennessee doctor who performed an emergency cesarean did not blame the patient's death on his own unfamiliarity with a risky surgical procedure. Instead, he laid the responsibility on the midwife who had delivered the woman's previous infant.

18. Donegan, *Women and Men Midwives*, 67. See Benjamin Franklin Mebane Account Books, 1849–1860 (Southern Historical Collection). Mebane's prices rose from two dollars and a half to ten dollars during these years, and at one point he charged more to attend slave women in labor.

Criticizing her ignorance, he could only conclude, "It is a matter of sincere regret that there is not a statute to prohibit ignorant women from the practice of midwifery." Even the highly respected Louisiana State Medical Society declared that only "sensible, confidential persons" should attend women during parturition. The meaning was obvious. Physicians pounced on whatever they could as proof of female incompetence.[19]

During the early part of the nineteenth century, some voices in the medical profession opposed the employment of males as accoucheurs, though the resistance declined by the 1840s. A few doctors felt that male attendance outraged female modesty. Others concluded that such intimacy could lead to sexual improprieties. Samuel Gregory, an unreticent northern botanic who established the Boston Female Medical College, argued that the presence of male doctors invited adultery, violated the private relationship of husband and wife, and could end in domestic misery. Some physicians refused to attend confinements. They concluded that since the majority of births occurred without mishap, required no special expertise, and traditionally had been handled by women, obstetrics was both demeaning and a waste of time. Thomas Ewell, a Virginia physician, believed that doctors lost precious hours in attending childbirth, for obstetrics "required no particular skill, no superior knowledge." He even endorsed the education of female midwives, probably not to elevate women in the profession but to keep men uninvolved. Thomsonians challenged the medical conception of childbirth as a disease. They believed that labor should not be regarded as pathological, and they noted that untrained attendants had assisted women for thousands of years. Most medical men who accepted female midwives saw obstetrics as unbefitting male doctors. Nevertheless, such voices were few, and eventually the majority silenced them.[20]

Most physicians took a keen interest in obstetrics and gynecology. Advice books and journal articles concerning these fields inundated the

19. John Wilson, "Female Medical Education," *Savannah Journal of Medicine,* III (1861), 378, quoted from the *Southern Medical and Surgical Journal* (1853); John Travis, untitled, *Western Journal of Medicine and Surgery,* V (1839), 352; William P. Hort, "Report of the Committee on Midwifery and the Diseases of Children," *New Orleans Medical and Surgical Journal,* II (1854), 289.

20. Samuel Gregory, *Man-Midwifery Exposed and Corrected* (Boston, 1848), preface; Thomas Ewell, *Letters to Ladies, Detailing Important Information, Concerning Themselves and Infants* (Philadelphia, 1817), 29; Daniel Whitney, *The Family Physician, and Guide to Health, in Three Parts* (New York, 1833), 149.

public beginning in the 1820s. The shift to the written word reflected an overall interest in medical science, a more literate citizenry, a growing emphasis on professional solutions, and technological improvements in the publishing industry. But the emphasis on female and infant health, especially on problems associated with childbirth, also reflected enthusiasm, curiosity, and concern. The printed page gave male doctors another platform for proving their superior skills and for combating what they regarded as a misplaced, old-fashioned reliance upon midwives.

Physicians and advisers wrote, published, and plagiarized dozens of medical texts and advice books each decade. Some addressed the wary mother, others the rural family far from a doctor's care or those who could not afford a physician. An English doctor, William Buchan, wrote one of the most popular of these volumes, in 1769. His *Domestic Medicine* became a best seller, was reissued in numerous editions, and eventually sold more copies in America than in England. Buchan encouraged women to serve as their own physicians. The historian Charles Rosenberg claims that this book was the most popular health guide prior to the twentieth century. Its inconsistencies gave it broad appeal, and its down-to-earth tone made it accessible to all literate Americans. Other volumes, particularly those appearing in the latter part of the antebellum period, attempted to present the latest in scientific scholarship. Doctors associated with medical colleges frequently emphasized technical problems and solutions, and their books were used primarily as medical texts for colleagues or students rather than as self-help volumes in the home. No matter how knowledgeable, doctors showed scant compunction about plagiarism. Information was often repeated, and an author at a loss for words or lacking a clear explanation might copy passages verbatim from another doctor's work.[21]

The most reputable obstetrical texts came from the North and Europe, including those by Drs. Buchan, William Potts Dewees, and Charles Delucena Meigs. The foreign and northern provenience of the volumes was yet another facet of the southern medical profession's

21. Starr, *The Social Transformation of American Medicine,* 32–33; William Buchan, *Domestic Medicine; or, A Treatise on the Prevention and Cure of Diseases, by Regimen and Simple Medicines* (Boston, 1809). See also Joseph Ioor Waring, *A History of Medicine in South Carolina, 1670–1825* (Charleston, S.C., 1967), 148; and Charles Rosenberg, "Medical Text and Social Context: Explaining William Buchan's *Domestic Medicine,*" *Bulletin of the History of Medicine,* LVII (1983), 22–42 (quotation from p. 22).

feeling of insecurity. The flow from the presses was so heavy that one southern doctor observed that if obstetrics "could be learned from books alone, we doubt not our colleagues might turn at once [into] the most accomplished accoucheurs."[22]

Southern physicians rarely made an effort to compete by writing their own works. Instead, they confined themselves nearly exclusively to articles in regional medical journals. An editor of the *New Orleans Medical and Surgical Journal* confirmed this. "It is seldom that we meet with books of southern birth," he noted. "Upon the practice of medicine two or three physicians of the South have written or published." Erasmus Darwin Fenner concurred, lamenting that southern doctors were "bereft of all the customary stimulants to ambition, have spent their toilsome lives in obscurity, and carried with them to the tomb whatever useful knowledge they may have gathered from the lessons of experience." Only a handful of men, including Dr. Henry Miller, at the University of Louisville, produced scholarly and sound obstetrical texts, and Miller's publisher went bankrupt shortly after his book's publication.[23]

Why doctors in the South were so remiss excited considerable discussion. Richard Arnold, a highly regarded physician from Savannah, and first secretary of the American Medical Association, decided that southern doctors had little time for extraclinical activities. He believed that they were too busy dealing with the maladies harbored by the unhealthful southern climate to have time to write. Others conjectured that doctors were more consumed with growing cotton than with their profession. For many southern physicians had dual occupations and regarded their medical endeavors as stepping-stones to a more lucrative

22. William Potts Dewees, *A Treatise on the Physical and Medical Treatment of Children* (Philadelphia, 1825); Dewees, *A Compendious System of Midwifery* (Philadelphia, 1828); Charles Delucena Meigs, *Obstetrics: The Science and the Art* (1st ed.; Philadelphia, 1849). Dewees (1768–1841), born in Pennsylvania, briefly occupied the chair of obstetrics at the Medical College of Philadelphia. His *Treatise* was the nation's best seller on infant and women's medical care. Meigs (1792–1869) was Dewees' successor as the expert on infant and female concerns. He taught at Jefferson Medical College, in Philadelphia, and was known for his conservative views, which often appealed to southern physicians. The quotation is from the *New Orleans Medical and Surgical Journal*, I (1845), 357.

23. *New Orleans Medical and Surgical Journal*, VII (1850), 789; Fenner, "Introductory Address," 8. Southern efforts include Henry Miller's *A Theoretical and Practical Treatise on Human Parturition* (Louisville, Ky., 1849). This text might have been used more often if the publisher had not gone bankrupt shortly after the book's appearance. It was reissued just before the Civil War as *The Principles and Practice of Obstetrics* (Philadelphia, 1858).

future exclusively in agriculture. After all, owning a successful plantation was the key to economic and social power in the antebellum South. Perhaps, too, southern doctors felt diffident about writing since, as rural practitioners, they were out of touch with medical advances. There was also the difficulty of publishing in a region of the country with few urban centers. Establishing a publishing industry with a sustaining clientele proved difficult for the South in all fields of study, not just in medicine. Many southern doctors had received their training in the North and no doubt felt comfortable using familiar texts in their classrooms and private practices and about recommending them to others. The Louisiana State Medical Society sanctioned Dewees' and Buchan's texts as the most reliable works on obstetrics and domestic health problems. From the number of advice books still to be found in private and public collections, the degree to which many southern doctors and individual families relied on northern or European efforts is clear.[24]

Infant health care generated less curiosity than infant delivery and prenatal care, and it lacked the challenges the male practitioners discovered in obstetrics. The medical profession readily admitted that doctors often paid little attention to child-care concerns and left their resolution, as well as the very treatment of the young, to mothers, nurses, and quacks. Unlike obstetrics, which achieved recognition as a medical specialty during the antebellum period, pediatrics did not gain such distinction until the 1880s. During the antebellum period, the study of infant diseases at medical institutions fell under the title of women's health. The practitioners who attended children were family doctors, and their procedures were those of the period. Bloodletting, purging, and drugging figured in infant therapy no less than in adult, despite the dawning realization that small bodies required gentler treatment. Heroic therapy remained the order of the day, and it did little to better the health of southern infants.[25]

The movement of the medical profession into obstetrics and infant care during the antebellum period was a change from tradition. Whether it was an advance for maternal and infant health will be a

    24. Richard H. Shryock (ed.), *Letters of Richard D. Arnold, M.D., 1808–1867* (New York, 1929), 19, 58; Hort, "Report of the Committee," 472–79, 567–78. For a discussion of the problems of the southern publishing industry, see John McCardell, *The Idea of a Southern Nation: Southern Nationalists and Southern Nationalism, 1830–1860* (New York, 1979), 157–58.

    25. Thomas E. Cone, *History of American Pediatrics* (Boston, 1979), 69–98.

question for the chapters to come. Prior to 1860, the limited under-standing physicians had of basic medical problems, of the causes of disease, and of proper therapy led to a good deal of guesswork, experi-mentation, and reliance upon the untested. When doctors involved themselves in childbirth and infant care, their uncertainties created a chancy experience for their new patients. Professional attendance often increased the serenity of the patient, but the insecurities felt by southern doctors often bred overreaction and defensiveness. Medicine was in a state of flux, and doctors were attempting to expand their practices and enhance their reputations. Motherhood, they maintained, needed the involvement of science and modern medical ideas.

2 *In a Delicate Way*

PREGNANCY

"I was full of pain and much debilitated," wrote Rachel Mordecai Lazarus from her coastal home in Wilmington, North Carolina, in 1825, as she described her second pregnancy. "I rode every day for exercise and avoided fatigue as much as possible." More than twenty-five years later, a successful Alabama lawyer remarked of a pregnant friend, "Mrs. Witherspoon has had another hemorrhage this week and is very sick and weak. She has no baby yet. Dr. Witherspoon does not expect her to survive." These two upper-class southern white women, representing different generations and regions of the South, experienced what was fairly typical of pregnant women during the antebellum period: ill health. Each was preparing for her important role as a mother but, in the process, enduring a good deal of hardship and illness, as well as uncertainty about the outcome.[1]

While many expectant southern women suffered exhaustion, pain, and even life-threatening complications, medical advisers delivered a more edifying message. Motherhood was an antebellum woman's sacred occupation. Achieving it was a responsibility women had to take seriously and approach with joyful expectation, relying, when necessary, on the skills and counsel of male practitioners. In a popular advice manual, Dr. William Buchan urged his female readers to adopt a happy demeanor during their nine-month vigil. "The anticipated pleasure of presenting a fond husband with the dearest pledge of mutual love ought naturally to increase her cheerfulness," he pontificated.[2] Yet probably

1. Rachel Mordecai Lazarus to her sister Caroline Mordecai Plunkett, October 13, 1818, in Jacob Mordecai Papers, Manuscript Department, William R. Perkins Library, Duke University; Henry Watson, Jr., to his mother, October 4, 1851, in Henry Watson, Jr., Papers, Manuscript Department, William R. Perkins Library.
2. William Buchan, *Advice to Mothers, on the Subject of Their Own Health; and of the Means of Promoting the Health, Strength, and Beauty of their Offspring* (Boston, 1809), in *The Physician and Child-Rearing: Two Guides, 1809–1894* (New York, 1972), 11.

few women concurred with Buchan's optimism. The reality that expectant southern women faced in an unhealthy environment created an experience far different from his cheerful vision.

Pregnancy entailed certain patterns for southern white women, including hardships and fears that neither their wealth nor their station could alleviate. Privilege did not ensure better health; many observers believed that the leisured life-style of upper-class women encouraged ills. They pointed to the more robust bodies of farming and slave women and suggested more exercise, fresh air, and sensible clothing for the advantaged. (Since most southern women, whatever their station, worked hard, other factors, such as environment and endemic diseases, may have determined their relative weakness.) In any case, personal accounts reveal that pregnancy was difficult for middle- and upper-class women. Of course, these women suffered the physical problems normally associated with pregnancy. More severe medical complications, such as convulsions, hemorrhages, illnesses, and exposure to endemic diseases, added to their woes. In the worst instances, pregnancy imposed limitations on their daily lives, for poor health could play havoc with their domestic routine, the care of their children, and their social activities. For nearly all middle- and upper-class women, a persistent fear of childbirth clouded the anticipation of a new son or daughter.

The view of pregnancy altered in the early part of the antebellum period, paralleling changes in obstetrics. Emerging from the interest doctors developed toward all aspects of childbirth was a recognition of the importance of prenatal care. With a virtual consensus and a good deal of conviction, doctors accepted the idea that the fetus was alive from the moment of conception. No longer did the majority adhere to the old-fashioned belief that quickening was the beginning of life. In 1858, a confident southern medical student argued against traditional theories. "To deny vitality as some do to the foetus prior to this period is no less absurd than to deny humanity to the infant because it is not an adult," he declared. For doctors and women who accepted the new understanding, the well-being of children depended not only on devoted mothering but on maternal and medical attention during fetal development.[3]

3. James B. Duggan, "Procreation," Dissertation 362 (1858), in Vanderbilt University Medical Center Library. James Mohr (*Abortion in America: The Origins and Evolutions of National Policy, 1800–1900* [New York, 1978], 6) argues that during most of the antebellum period, quickening marked the time when the fetus was accepted as being alive.

The interest physicians took in pregnancy reinforced their overall interest in obstetrics. Maternal attention and vigilance were essential. Dr. William Potts Dewees perceived a direct correlation between a pregnant woman's condition and that of the fetus. "The physical treatment of children should begin . . . with the earliest formation of the embryo," he stated. "The various contingencies which may affect her, as well in health, as in disease, must exert an influence upon the fetus. Let her then, in early life, convince herself that an awful responsibility is attached to the title Mother." Many southern doctors, accepting the idea of fetal viability, agreed with a Georgia physician who, in 1855, encouraged proper maternal behavior. "There is a responsibility imposed upon the mother," noted Dr. J. R. Lasseter, "which transcends all others heretofore known to her in her parental capacity." Doctors inferred that quickening was merely the first time that doctor or mother could perceive fetal motion rather than the first instant of life. From the moment of conception—or at least from the moment it was realized to be likely that a pregnancy had occurred—women needed to pay strict attention to prenatal guidelines.[4]

Despite the interest of antebellum physicians in care during pregnancy and their desire to establish a central role in childbirth, they accorded women a good deal of responsibility in normal pregnancies. The Louisiana State Medical Society was typical. "A woman who is pregnant should consider the whole affair from its inception to its termination as a natural process," remarked Dr. William Hort, the principal author of a report published by the society. Other southern physicians concurred, stating that deformities, stillbirths, and miscarriages occurred only if mothers behaved in an "unnatural" manner.[5] Presumably this meant ignoring prescribed medical guidelines. If labor was now considered a pathological condition, pregnancy was not. Yet

---

"Women believed themselves to be carrying inert non-beings prior to quickening," he says. An abortion performed before detecting fetal movement was not considered a crime by mother or doctor. Though courts may have used quickening to determine fetal viability, it seems evident from the writings of most antebellum physicians that they accepted life from the moment of conception.

4. William Potts Dewees, *A Treatise on the Physical and Medical Treatment of Children* (Philadelphia, 1825), xi; J. R. Lasseter, "A Lesson to Mothers," *Southern Medical Reformer and Review,* V (1855), 67. Dr. Lasseter was from La Grange, Georgia.

5. William P. Hort, "Report of the Committee on Midwifery and the Diseases of Children," *New Orleans Medical and Surgical Journal,* II (1845), 571.

that did not imply a professional lack of interest in it. The output of material, the speculative interpretations, and the number of dissertations dealing with the prenatal period are evidence that pregnancy was a fascinating subject to most physicians. But antebellum doctors were cautious, for they had a limited understanding of the mysteries of conception and fetal growth and of the health problems related to pregnancy. They did not encourage regular prenatal consultations, and southern women rarely visited a doctor as a matter of course. Pregnant women sought professional attention only for severe problems. But since poor health was common in the antebellum South, doctors played an active role in prenatal care more often than one might expect.

To ask why antebellum physicians consciously limited active participation during women's pregnancies is probably to ask the wrong question. That doctors were involved or concerned at all was a significant change from the past. Women had traditionally determined and monitored their own conditions and established their own patterns of activity. As male physicians increased their involvement in parturition, it was natural that their interest should extend to pregnancy. But in affirming that the nine-month vigil was natural, doctors consciously limited their participation. Expectant women who had only occasional health problems needed little medical attention beyond bed rest, bleeding, and a supply of tonics and medicines. From a practical standpoint, southern women in rural areas frequently had only difficult access to a doctor and avoided the inconvenience of consulting one unless their symptoms turned severe.

To handle effectively the normal problems as well as the more serious illnesses associated with pregnancy, antebellum physicians published a steady stream of advice. Through the written word, doctors exhibited enormous concern and reassured wary women and insecure practitioners. But there were stern warnings as well. The authors of the guidelines spoke of dire consequences for women who ignored medical advice. Mrs. J. Bakewell, in a maternal guidebook, showed distress over the inattention of expectant women to salubrious behavior. "It is to be feared," she observed, "that but few young married women are aware how much the future bodily health, mental vigour, and moral tendencies of their offspring, depend on their own conduct and state of being during pregnancy." Dewees was just as critical of mothers who neglected their responsibilities to the growing fetus. "Were every female during pregnancy to regulate her conduct as though she were accountable for the health and intelligence of her child," he noted, "it would prevent much of the mischief so constantly witnessed."[6]

Hampering an expectant mother was always the uncertainty of whether or not she was actually carrying a child. Antebellum physicians and women had as much difficulty identifying pregnancy as the historian does searching for clues of the condition. Often the researcher's only datum is a woman's notation that she has given birth, with no earlier comments of anticipation. Determining the condition was many times a matter of intuition or guesswork. In the early nineteenth century, some women spent months expecting to give birth, only to discover that they were not pregnant. Contrariwise, a few were unaware of their condition until they gave birth.

By the 1850s, southern doctors realized that advances in medical science could provide an invaluable, not to mention lucrative, service in ascertaining a woman's pregnancy. New techniques developed in Europe increased the precision of doctors' determinations and gave male accoucheurs another entrée into obstetrics. Accurately recognizing a woman's condition could honorably enhance a physician's reputation. Doctors argued that identifying a pregnancy was a professional concern, since knowing whether or not a woman was bearing a child could affect not only her family but society as well. Physicians observed that a correct evaluation could save an unmarried woman from the "fatal shafts of calumny" and could rescue a pregnant woman in prison from the immediate threat of capital punishment. Should a woman become pregnant before marriage, it would permit her to "hide from public view her secret enormities." In addition, pregnancy could influence the choice of medical therapies. "The presence or absence of pregnancy," noted W. B. Greene, a medical student, "will have an important bearing on the measures we adopt." Doctors needed to adjust specific treatments to a woman's condition.[7]

Physicians divided the signs of pregnancy into two categories, sensible and rational. Sensible signals included the symptoms that women had traditionally trusted. Many doctors, however, argued that these

6. Mrs. J. Bakewell, *The Mother's Practical Guide in the Physical, Intellectual, and Moral Training of Her Children* (3rd American ed.; New York, 1846), 22; Dewees, *A Treatise on the Treatment of Children,* 42.

7. W. B. Greene, "Signs of Pregnancy," Dissertation 421 (1859), F. H. Gaines, "The Signs of Pregnancy," Dissertation 194 (1856), John S. Pettus, "The Signs of Pregnancy," Dissertation 58 (1853), all in Vanderbilt University Medical Center Library.

were merely leftovers from a time before scientific testing. They were just impressions, and none was foolproof. Doctors considered amenorrhea, or cessation of the menses, an unreliable indicator, for irregular menstruation was commonplace among nineteenth-century women and some females menstruated well into their pregnancies. A woman's perception of quickening could also be deceiving, for other internal problems could cause abdominal movement. Morning sickness, increased salivation, a swelling and sensitivity of the breasts, fretfulness, specific food cravings, a general state of plethora, toothaches, and of course, visible growth of the abdominal area were equally suspect as signs, according to physicians and medical students.[8]

A Georgia plantation woman, Ella Clanton Thomas, recognized her own premonitory state and noted in her journal, "I have a great deal of sick stomach and headache and find that I am again destined to be a mother." Her prediction proved accurate several months later. Undoubtedly, many doctors hoped that women like Ella were part of the past, for their objective was to become indispensable and to offer a service that would enhance their authority and lessen women's dependence on nature and midwives. Scientific tests could identify pregnancy with greater certainty. Better yet, the rational signs of pregnancy— those that depended on scientific analysis—presupposed the skills of the physician: a cervical examination called a ballotement; an inspection for changes in the areola or nipple area; ausculation, or listening for fetal movement or heartbeat with the ear or stethoscope; a Jacquemin's test to measure vaginal color change; and a Kiestein test of the urine. The majority of educated allopaths wanted all practicing physicians to gain experience with these important examinations.[9]

Despite the scientific progress, southern women did not custom-

8. Greene, "Signs of Pregnancy"; Gaines, "The Signs of Pregnancy"; Pettus, "The Signs of Pregnancy"; Sylvanus Johnson, "The Signs of Pregnancy," Dissertation 320 (1857), Joseph Cowan, "Signs of Pregnancy," Dissertation 41 (1853), John K. Clarke, "Diagnosis of Pregnancy," Dissertation 198 (1856), E. G. Davis, "The Signs of Pregnancy," Dissertation 153 (1855), W. W. Crockett, "The Signs of Pregnancy," Dissertation 374 (1858), all in Vanderbilt University Medical Center Library.

9. Ella Clanton Thomas Diary, June 16, 1855 (Manuscript Department, William R. Perkins Library); Greene, "Signs of Pregnancy"; Gaines, "The Signs of Pregnancy"; Pettus, "The Signs of Pregnancy"; Johnson, "The Signs of Pregnancy"; Cowan, "Signs of Pregnancy"; Clarke, "Diagnosis of Pregnancy"; Davis, "The Signs of Pregnancy"; Crockett, "The Signs of Pregnancy"; John Wilson, "Pregnancy as a Complication of Disease," Dissertation for the Medical College of South Carolina (1843), in Waring Historical Library, Medical University of South Carolina, Charleston.

arily seek a physician to confirm their pregnancies. Doctors wrote—or read—about the new methods far more than they practiced them. Entries in personal medical accounts which record doctors' consultations several months prior to a woman's confinement may or may not indicate testing. Poor health was a likelier cause for visiting a doctor. One North Carolina physician who carefully listed each parturient woman he attended noted only one woman's visit prior to her confinement. Yet doctors who had the opportunity to use the new tests found them reliable and felt they reflected well on the profession. For instance, in 1853, a South Carolina woman who had just miscarried a five-month-old fetus called for a doctor. She had not suspected her pregnancy, and the determination was tardy, but the physician proudly noted that her areolas' altered color and formation revealed her condition.[10]

Some southern physicians refused to accept the new methods and clung to traditional ideas. Thomas Ewell, who generally supported minimal medical intervention, believed that fetal motion was the most accurate indicator of pregnancy. Another Virginia doctor, James Ewell, believed women the best judges when they sensed "uneasiness in their breasts." John Wilson, a matriculant at the Medical College of South Carolina, had perhaps the best solution. He observed how frequently southern wives bore babies and wisely concluded that all women should be considered pregnant until proved otherwise.[11]

Both physicians and women were unsure of the exact length of gestation, though doctors observed that the period usually lasted between 270 and 280 days. Southern doctors were latitudinarians in predicting due dates, with some even concluding that women might in unusual circumstances carry a child for eleven or twelve months. A few relinquished any effort to explain the process and timing and scoffed at others who tried. Dr. Alva Curtis, a botanist, criticized overzealous allopaths, declaring, "The more they write, the more clearly they exhibit their ignorance of the whole subject." A Charleston doctor con-

10. Anonymous Physician's Account, 1824–31, Anonymous Ledger, 1831–38 (both in Manuscript Department, William R. Perkins Library); "Abortion Without a Suspicion on the Part of the Mother of the Existence of Pregnancy," *Western Journal of Medicine and Surgery*, 3rd ser., XI (1853), 186; Benjamin Franklin Mebane Account Books, 1849–60, various entries (Southern Historical Collection, L. R. Wilson Library, University of North Carolina at Chapel Hill).

11. Thomas Ewell, *Letters to Ladies, Detailing Important Information, Concerning Themselves and Infants* (Philadelphia, 1817), 111; James Ewell, *The Planter's and Mariner's Medical Companion* (Philadelphia, 1807), 409; Wilson, "Pregnancy as a Complication of Disease."

ducted his own scientific survey based on eleven patients. He saw a direct correlation between a woman's age and the length of her pregnancy, and he even speculated that the husband's age could be an influence. The length of gestation has never been precise, for babies can be premature or tardy, and the predictions of birth dates by most antebellum doctors were relatively accurate if they could deduce when the child had been conceived.[12]

But the process of conception remained a mystery. Up until the Civil War, the majority of doctors believed that women were fertile immediately before and after menstruation. Some physicians hypothesized that the male sperm swam into the ovary and that agitation of the fallopian tube or sac caused the release of an egg. Two weeks then ensued before the ovum finally lodged in the uterine lining. Other ideas were equally speculative or imprecise. Perhaps to avoid possible error, Thomas Ewell commented only that conception occurred "when the circumstances have been favorable."[13]

Once pregnancy was either suspected or established, women and their families announced the forthcoming event with restraint and circumspection, if they bothered at all. Despite the Southerners' celebration of large families, silence usually surrounded a woman's pregnancy. The reticence probably made sense. Since large southern families were common, another pregnancy was unremarkable. Isaac Avery, a plantation owner near Morganton, North Carolina, expressed a typical reaction toward his wife's condition. "Harriet is not very well and hence I am writing for her," he noted, "but as her disease is one she is having, perhaps for the twelfth time, it neither excites as much sympathy or apprehension as it ought." Not even Avery could be sure how often his wife had been pregnant. A Virginia husband reacted casually: "I suppose you will exclaim again but you know babies have ceased to be a novelty in our family."[14]

12. "Length of Gestation," in *Physician's Visiting List* (Philadelphia, 1857; found in Milligan Papers, Southern Historical Collection); Duggan, "Procreation"; Alva Curtis, *Lectures on Midwifery and the Forms of Disease Peculiar to Women and Children* (2nd ed.; Columbus, Ohio, 1841), 42; Dr. Clay, "On the Laws Which Regulate the Duration of Utero-Gestation," *Charleston Medical Journal and Review*, IV (1849), 224–26.

13. Review of Charles Delucena Meigs's *Obstetrics: The Science and the Art*, in *Western Journal of Medicine and Surgery*, 3rd ser., IV (1849), 42; Thomas Ewell, *Letters to Ladies*, 16.

14. Isaac Avery to his mother-in-law, Selina Lenoir, February 18, 1835, in Lenoir Family Papers, Southern Historical Collection; [?] to Mary, December 15, 1818, in Bedinger-Dandridge Letters, Manuscript Department, William R. Perkins Library.

Infrequent pregnancies or the absence of children elicited more comment. Barren women in the antebellum South often felt at a distinct disadvantage. Mary Boykin Chesnut, the noted Civil War diarist, was unable to bear children. She referred to herself as a "childless wretch" and observed that "women have such contempt for a childless wife." Despite the freedom that childlessness brought, Mrs. Chesnut felt guilty that she could not fulfill her maternal function. She apparently yearned for the experience of bearing children and would have liked to share the experience with other women. Fortunately, she found an outlet for her maternal impulses in her nieces and nephews. Southern men believed that childbearing and child rearing were central to a woman's existence. "From time immemorial, women have regarded the barren womb as a great calamity," commented a southern medical student. "All their hopes of happiness are centered around the hope of giving birth to children." Whatever their sentiments toward the act of giving birth, both men and women regarded motherhood as the premier occupation of southern women.[15]

Letters, family accounts, and diaries show the large number of southern women who gave birth to eight, ten, or even a dozen live children. A woman frequently bore a child toward the end of her first year of marriage and continued with an infant every two to two and a half years until menopause, death, or incapacity because of poor health. Since privileged southern women often married relatively young, they lengthened their childbearing years and increased the possible number of pregnancies. More recent demographic evidence verifies the impression that diaries and letters give. Family size decreased nationwide during the antebellum period—from an average of 7.04 children per woman of childbearing age in 1800 to 5.4 by 1850—but most antebellum southern women exceeded that rate and often devoted thirty or more years of their lives to bearing, nursing, and raising children. Jane Turner Censer recently concluded that among the North Carolina plantation population, the birthrate averaged seven children per marriage in the antebellum period. Another scholar estimated that Alabama plantation wives bore an average of 5.5 live children. A demographic study

15. Mary Boykin Chesnut, *Mary Chesnut's Civil War,* ed. C. Vann Woodward (New Haven, 1981), 32; Chesnut, *A Diary from Dixie,* ed. Ben Ames Williams (New York, 1949), 25; W. B. Mills, "The Signs of Pregnancy," Dissertation 270 (1857), in Vanderbilt University Medical Center Library. See also Elisabeth Muhlenfeld, *Mary Boykin Chesnut: A Biography* (Baton Rouge, 1981).

compared birthrates in different regions of the United States and concluded that though southern families were decreasing in size, they remained larger than their counterparts in New England.[16] Since miscarriages, stillbirths, and infant deaths were common, the average number of live children recorded in any census was smaller than the mean number of times women had been pregnant and smaller also than the mean number of children born, since many infants died within a few months after birth and were never recorded. The census figures reflect the number of offspring per woman of childbearing age, and not all women married or had children. Therefore, the average number of infants born to women who actually had children would be even higher.

Expectant women often failed to mention their condition because they were ill, preoccupied with other duties, or unable to write. The sick and harried sometimes related their experiences only months after delivery, if at all. Nor did women always suspect they were pregnant. At times, too, modesty may have been behind their reticence, though that an increasing number of middle- and upper-class women were allowing male physicians to take charge of a very intimate experience shows that modesty's hold was not unbreakable. Still other women hesitated to describe a condition that could have a questionable outcome. Stillbirths and miscarriages were common, and women may have wished to avoid the possibility of public disappointment. Anyway, childbirth in the antebellum period carried the real possibility of death for mother and child, and this fear may have kept women quiet.

Any remark that revealed a woman's pregnancy was generally restrained in tone and imprecise in substance. Family members or close friends might make the announcement for her. Comments on a woman's physical form could convey the message indirectly. William Shelton, of Tennessee, proudly described Virginia, his pregnant wife. "She

16. For information on fertility, see Carl Degler, *At Odds: Women and the Family in America from the Revolution to the Present* (New York, 1980), 181; Wilson H. Grabill, Clyde V. Kiser, and Pascal K. Whelpton (eds.), *The Fertility of American Women* (New York, 1958), Table 6, p. 14; Jane Turner Censer, *North Carolina Planters and Their Children, 1800–1860* (Baton Rouge, 1984), 26–28, 91; Ann Boucher, "Wealthy Planter Families in Nineteenth Century Alabama" (Ph.D. dissertation, University of Connecticut, 1978), 84–89; Maris Vinovskis, *Fertility in Massachusetts from the Revolution to the Civil War* (New York, 1981); and Richard H. Steckel, "Antebellum Southern White Fertility: A Demographic and Economic Analysis," *Journal of Economic History,* XL (1979), 331–50. Steckel (p. 338) estimates that southern women gave birth to their last child when they were an average of 38.7 years old.

is so fat that her dresses will not meet on her by several inches," he related to the woman's uncle, "and her cheeks are so rosy and blooming that you would scarcely recognize her." The fact that Virginia was six months pregnant was implied but never stated outright. Mary Burton described a pregnant friend, noting that "her shape has enlarged very much and as large waists are not in fashion, I would advise her to try tight lacing." Expectant mothers were likely to impart information in a veiled manner. Some simply noted that their children would soon have another "companion" or "partner in our affections."[17]

Others reacted ambivalently or with less enthusiasm. Ella Clanton Thomas noted in her diary, "The sickness of stomach might indicate my being in a peculiar situation, a calamity which I would especially dread this summer for I have no disposition to renew the past unpleasant summer." Time had not yet erased the memory of the miscarriage she had suffered a year earlier. Julia Bryan, a Georgia woman, wrote that a friend "found greatly to her surprise by some symptoms which she could not misunderstand that she was considerably advanced in pregnancy. The disappointment was so great it actually made her sick." Anticipated difficulties in childbirth and the numerous responsibilities associated with a newborn were likely causes for these reactions.[18] Offsetting such costs, however, were the benefits women gained by bearing children and the enhanced status some achieved within the home. Most married women in the antebellum period desired children. Motherhood was their proclaimed duty, and in the antebellum South, what other occupation could bring them equivalent rewards?

Men usually showed more enthusiasm. Ella Clanton Thomas noted that her husband was "grateful at the prospect" of a new baby, and William Lacy, of Virginia, boasted that his wife "intends to give me another little boy, as much finer and smarter than little Ned." Having to support none of the discomforts of pregnancy nor the physical pain of parturition—and usually exempt from the direct responsibilities of infant rearing—most fathers found joy in their growing families. A large

17. William Shelton to David Campbell, January 15, 1850, in Campbell Family Letters, Manuscript Department, William R. Perkins Library; Mary Burton to Mira Lenoir, September 22, 1815, in Lenoir Family Papers.

18. Ella Clanton Thomas Diary, June 11, 1856 (Manuscript Department, William R. Perkins Library); Julia Bryan to Maria Bryan, January 11, 1827, in Hammond, Bryan, and Cummings Papers, South Caroliniana Library, University of South Carolina. For southern women's negative feelings toward pregnancy, see also Anne Firor Scott, "Women's Perspective on the Patriarchy in the 1850s," *Journal of American History,* LXI (1974), 52–64.

family reflected a husband's masculinity, and there seemed to be few economic and social constraints upon the size of southern families aside from a rare solicitude for women's physical and emotional health. Land was plentiful, and economic opportunities abounded for the motivated and privileged. A Tennessee doctor noted breezily that one patient had borne several children because she was "anxious to gratify her husband in rearing a large family." If the woman was indeed "anxious," chances are that she was so in the sense of being fearful, and not in the sense that the doctor intended. He assumed that husbands welcomed each new addition and that women courted their mate's approbation at whatever price.[19]

The antebellum South had a patriarchal structure, in that men normally held the upper hand in both the public and the domestic spheres. Some scholars have suggested that the importance of children and the family allowed nineteenth-century women opportunities to achieve greater power within the home. Associated with that idea is the control women were gradually beginning to assume over their own fertility. The suggestion may be true for some relationships, particularly in the urban Northeast, but the patriarchal structure was essential to maintaining order in a rural, slave-owning society. The larger families of the South may signify the husband's retention of power there. If southern women ever tried to control their fertility, their efforts rarely influenced the number of pregnancies.[20]

Once pregnancy was established with a degree of certainty, women were to exercise a vigilance over the growing fetus and their own behavior. Doctors carefully detailed the expectant woman's physical regimen. They stressed the importance of exercise. Advisers recommended that pregnant women engage in activities ranging in vigor from the "friction of the flesh brush," for the emaciated woman, to daily walks, carriage rides, dancing, and even hill climbing. Perhaps to

19. Ella Clanton Thomas Diary, July 16, 1856; William Lacy to Edward Graham, February 7, 1819, in Graham Family Papers, Manuscript Department, William R. Perkins Library. On Southerners' lack of constraints on family size, see also Steckel, "Antebellum Southern White Fertility," 350. Steckel argues that southern women had a higher fertility rate because more southern women married, southern women married at a younger age, many couples had sufficient assets to establish a family, and Southerners rarely used birth-control measures. Steckel (p. 350) concludes that knowledge of effective contraceptive methods was a regional phenomenon, and found less often in the South.

20. Degler, *At Odds,* 188. For arguments concerning women's power within the home, see Ruth H. Block, "Untangling the Roots of Modern Sex Roles: A Survey of Four Centuries of Change," *Signs,* IV (1978), 251.

stir females from idleness, Buchan warned that miscarriages and puerperal fever were more common among indolent women. He wisely
perceived that exercise would prepare the body for childbirth, lessen
anxiety, and promote regularity. The committee report from the Louisiana State Medical Society concluded that "those females who take the
most exercise . . . produce the most vigorous and healthy children."
Thomas Ewell concurred, noting that exercise would ensure robust
babies. He observed that domestic animals roaming in the largest pas-
tures produced the biggest offspring, and he drew from this that if
pregnant women wandered freely about the countryside, they would
have finer children than if they confined themselves indoors.[21]

Maintaining a woman's proper state of mind was critical during
pregnancy. Traditional beliefs concerning the influence of maternal impressions persisted through the antebellum period. For instance, some
people believed that if a pregnant woman saw a man lose a lower limb,
her baby might be born with only one leg. Expectant women who
craved grapes or apples or viewed a snake might find darkened images
of such objects on their infant's skin. Medical journals, despite their
emphasis on facts and science, repeated these folktales with a degree of
credulity. The mysterious and freakish aspects of human experience
have always captivated people, and stories of the grotesque convinced
even some professionals.[22]

Other doctors tried to discredit the notions as the folktales they
were. But the conviction of a close but mysterious connection between
a woman's uterus and the other parts of her body held many imagina-
tions in its grip. Respected physicians believed that anything affecting
the female brain, digestive tract, or stomach somehow had an impact on
the fetus as well. For instance, Dr. John Watson, chief of obstetrics at the
medical department of the University of Nashville, vowed that "there is

21. Samuel Kennedy Jennings, *The Married Lady's Companion; or, Poor Man's Friend*
(2nd ed.; New York, 1808); Buchan, *Advice to Mothers*, 21; Hort, "Report of the Committee," 570; Thomas Ewell, *Letters to Ladies*, 119; Nyra Maguire McGrellis, "Prenatal Care
120 Years Ago," *Journal of Obstetrics, Gynecology, and Neonatal Nursing*, V (1976), 56.
22. As examples, see T. G. Underwood, "Influence of the Mother's Mind on the
Foetus," *Nashville Journal of Medicine and Surgery*, XI (1856), 119–22; W. P. Moore, "Influ-
ence of the Mother upon the Foetus in Utero," *Nashville Journal of Medicine and Surgery*,
XII (1857), 36–37; J. R. Lasseter, "A Lesson to Mothers," *Southern Medical Reformer and
Review*, V (1855), 65–67; I. G. Braman, "Influence of the Imagination or Will upon
Pregnant Woman," *New Orleans Medical and Surgical Journal*, IX (1852), 362–63, and D. L.
Saunders, *Woman's Own Book; or, A Plain and Familiar Treatise on All Complaints and
Diseases Peculiar to Females* (Little Rock, Ark., 1858), 71. Nearly all southern medical
journals carried such articles.

some undefined nervous communication between mother and embryo." To nineteenth-century thinking, the uterus was the controlling organ of a woman's anatomy and being. Physicians thus admonished pregnant women to avoid romantic novels that filled their heads—and presumably the fetus's mind—with trivial ideas, but also to abstain from serious study, which might draw vital blood from the uterus to the brain, limiting fetal growth. Buchan warned against gaming, card playing, and any activity that could "fatigue the mind by constant exertions of the judgment and memory." Mrs. Bakewell encouraged pregnant women to read "good works on education and on parental duties," and she even included a list of suitable titles at the conclusion of her book. An important connection between the brain and uterus was widely credited well into the late nineteenth century.[23]

A proper diet was also emphasized, though doctors' conclusions were baldly empirical rather than seated in any theory of essential nutrients. Pregnant women, naturally prone to indigestion, were not to fill their stomachs "largely" nor to eat rich, constipating, or spicy foods. Coffee, tea, and liquor were to be avoided. Since nineteenth-century physicians believed in a communication between the uterus and the digestive tract, they urged pregnant women to avoid raw onions and to confine their flesh eating to immature meats, such as veal, lamb, and chicken, that would be more palatable to a developing fetus and not contribute to vascular tension. Cravings for one particular food were not to be indulged. The Louisiana State Medical Society, on the other hand, adopted a relaxed approach to eating habits, content that the "instincts of nature" would determine what pregnant women chose to consume.[24]

Just as important was a woman's duty to clear her digestive tract.

23. John M. Watson, "On the Influence of the Mother's Mind on the Fetus in Utero," *Nashville Journal of Medicine and Surgery*, XVIII (1860), 105; Buchan, *Advice to Mothers*, 24; Bakewell, *The Mother's Practical Guide*, 24. See also Carroll Smith-Rosenberg and Charles E. Rosenberg, "The Female Animal: Medical and Biological Views of Women," in Charles E. Rosenberg, *No Other Gods: On Science and American Social Thought* (Baltimore, 1976), 56; and Barbara Ehrenreich and Deirdre English, *For Her Own Good: 150 Years of the Experts' Advice to Women* (New York, 1978), 108, 112, 113. The issue of the centrality of the uterus resurfaced with vigor in the late nineteenth century when Edward Hammond Clarke, a doctor at Harvard Medical School, argued (*Sex in Education: or, a Fair Chance for the Girls* [Boston, 1873]) that women's unique physiology limited their educational capacity. He felt that serious study could interfere with the development of women's procreative organs. For an excellent discussion of this topic, see Rosalind Rosenberg, *Beyond Separate Spheres: The Intellectual Roots of Modern Feminism* (New Haven, 1982), 1–27.

24. Buchan, *Advice to Mothers*, 18; Hort, "Report of the Committee," 571.

Antebellum society had a fixation upon bowel regularity, and at no time, it judged, was attention more critical than during pregnancy. Dr. John Gunn believed that neglect of the bowels caused half of all prenatal health problems. Some doctors, such as Thomas Ewell, recommended few medicinal remedies but encouraged nature. His advice was clear-cut: "Persevere" until the bowels cleared. Other doctors recommended laxatives, purgatives, enemas, or even the use of a spoon for scooping out impacted waste. Few doubted that prolonged constipation could permanently affect a woman's constitution. Dr. E. W. Treadwell, of Cherokee County, Alabama, warned his pregnant wife, Mattie, to clear her system, for "the fecal matter and the child cause a pressure upon your nerves, and these nerves sympathize with those of your stomach and causes it to be irritable." Calomel, a mercury chloride, was the standard purgative. Often taken to the point of intense salivation or bleeding gums, it left antebellum women with dental problems and the need for false teeth while they were still young. An enema of milk and water often followed the dosage of mercury to clear the lower intestine.[25]

As part of nurturing and protecting the child to be born, southern women tried to regulate their daily behavior during pregnancy, though they had probably been doing so less self-consciously before physicians published guidelines. Evidence in personal writings indicates that middle- and upper-class southern women ate a fairly adequate diet during pregnancy, just as they seem to have done normally. Whether they consumed sufficient protein and iron is unknown, and the few studies on southern food indicate a shortage of milk, particularly during the later antebellum period. Nevertheless, most plantation families had large gardens, numerous fruit trees, and domestic animals for slaughter.[26] The rare passages on food consumption in the writings indicate that women ate ample vegetables and fruits, pork, poultry, and fish, and even several desserts at a single sitting. It is little wonder that expectant mothers often presented "large" figures.

25. John C. Gunn, *Gunn's Domestic Medicine; or, Poor Man's Friend, Shewing the Diseases of Men, Women, and Children* (2nd ed.; Madisonville, Tenn., 1834), 342; E. W. Treadwell to his wife Mattie, 1835, in E. W. Treadwell Collection, Manuscript Department, William R. Perkins Library; Thomas Ewell, *Letters to Ladies*, 120.

26. For background on antebellum southern diet, see Richard O. Cummings, *The American and His Food* (1941; rpr. New York, 1970); Lewis C. Gray, *History of Agriculture in the Southern United States to 1860* (Washington, D.C., 1933); Samuel Bowers Hilliard, *Hog Meat and Hoecake: Food Supply in the Old South, 1840–1860* (Carbondale, Ill., 1972); Edgar

Like the physicians of the time, pregnant women were obsessed with regular bowel movements. They believed that inattention could cause serious consequences. Laura Norwood, of Hillsboro, North Carolina, attributed her "sick and acid stomach, heartburn and headache" to costiveness and complained that keeping her bowels open was a "fulltime" task. Any deviation from strict regularity seemed to cause alarm. During one pregnancy, Serena Rootes Lea, of Georgia, blamed a six-week-long illness on a cold that settled in her bowels. Women found various cures for their intestinal problems, including enemas, special powders, quantities of fresh fruit, visits to healing springs, and the ever-popular cure-all, calomel.[27]

In the area of exercise, southern women seem, at least at first glance, to have ignored the counsel of the advice books. Their personal correspondence includes many descriptions of bed rest and afternoon naps. Since demanding lives left expectant women with little time for repose, what explains the repeated references to nap taking? First, many of the women may have been ill or suffering from temporary health problems connected with pregnancy. Often women require more rest during certain stages of pregnancy. Second, since women did most of their correspondence and journal writing in quiet moments, it is likely they would mention inactivity. Third, in contrast to our current view of exercise, which is colored by an emphasis on vigorous, programmed activity, exercise in the nineteenth century was less regimented and less draining, particularly since most healthy persons led physically active lives. Typical advice to a pregnant woman came from Ann Rutherfoord's aunt, who advised her niece to "take all the gentle exercise you can" but only in the "cool of the evening." Ann had probably already spent a day at hard work on her Virginia plantation. Southern doctors, who often decried the lethargy of indulged women, at the same time encouraged activities no more strenuous than those conducted "on foot or in carriage." For some plantation women, recreational exercise only

---

W. Martin, *The Standard of Living in 1860: American Consumption Levels on the Eve of the Civil War* (Chicago, 1942); Waverly Root Lewis and Richard De Rochemont, *Eating in America: A History* (New York, 1976); and Andrew Soule, "Vegetables, Fruit and Nursery Products, and Truck Farming in the South," in James C. Ballagh (ed.), *Southern Economic History, 1607–1865* (Richmond, 1909), Vol. II of Ballagh, *The South in the Building of the Nation,* 13 vols.

27. Laura Lenoir Norwood to her mother, Selina Lenoir, September 26, 1836, in Lenoir Family Papers; Serena R. Lea to Martha Jackson, March 21, 1835, in Jackson and Prince Collection, Southern Historical Collection.

added to their exhaustion, an ever-present experience for the many who led demanding lives. Rebecca Haywood Hall wrote her sister that at times physical activity "makes me sore from my head to my heels and hastens my circulation so that I have to lie down." Since Rebecca had sole care of two young children and often assumed her husband's plantation duties, her statement arouses no doubt.[28]

Daily exercise, whether during pregnancy or not, was rarely included in the regimen of most nineteenth-century women. But some observers felt that southern women were less active than European or northern women. Frances Anne Kemble, the noted British actress who observed southern life from her husband's Georgia plantations, described southern women's sedentary ways with evident distaste. "They are languid in their deportment and speech," she wrote, "and seem to give themselves up, without any effort to counteract it, to the enervating effect of their warm climate." Perhaps Fanny's remarks deserve softening. Anyone who has experienced a long southern summer can understand how not only the climate but also long dresses, layers of petticoats, tight lacing, and endemic diseases might encourage a sedentary existence even for women who were not pregnant. And some southern men preferred the delicate female. A writer for the *Southern Quarterly Review* stated that the more sturdy and athletic women were, the "less they suited our taste." Personal correspondence, however, belies the image of inactivity in the case of most privileged southern women. Beyond an afternoon nap, few healthy middle- and upper-class women made a habit of horizontal rest during their pregnancies. Southern women led a reasonably active nine months, forced by reality—even if not by inclination—to conduct their lives normally. And physical activity in myriad forms may have been so common that it was not considered worth mentioning in personal letters.[29]

In treating pregnancy as a special though natural time in women's lives, antebellum southern society set few social restrictions on women's activities. So did doctors. They agreed that pregnant women were not pathologically affected at this stage but, rather, should remain in

28. W. W. Roy to Ann Rutherford, July, 1857, in John Rutherfoord Collection, Manuscript Department, William R. Perkins Library; Rebecca Haywood Hall to Eliza Haywood, October 16, 1837, in Haywood Family Collection, Southern Historical Collection.

29. Frances Ann Kemble, *Journal of a Residence on a Georgia Plantation in 1838–1839,* ed. John A. Scott (London, 1961), 101; "Laws of Life," *Southern Quarterly Review,* XXII (1852), 478–89 (a review of Elizabeth Blackwell's *Laws of Life*).

good health. None but the truly indulged or infirm could afford to ignore her responsibilities or lead an idle existence. What southern family could survive with a mother who likened her wonted pregnancies to illness rather than to health? A recumbent mother would have been unable to garden, nurse her children, supervise slaves and household members, sew, cook, clean, or tend to the thousands of duties associated with nineteenth-century households. Mothers were essential to the smooth operation of the home and were therefore unlikely to be found at rest for a prolonged period unless truly ill. Expectant women's activities reflected their health and level of energy rather than limitations imposed or indulgences allowed as a result of their condition. As long as women remained healthy, the majority maintained an active and normal schedule. Few relinquished attendance at weekly church services or prayer meetings. Many continued their sewing, nursing, and reading, and their visiting with friends and relatives. Plantation mistresses oversaw domestic slaves and gardened. Some had no choice but to take on major responsibilities. Both the wife of one of North Carolina's wealthiest plantation owners and the wife of Arkansas' territorial governor directed annual hog butcherings during their pregnancies. Expecting a baby did not secure rest for the weary.[30]

Some expectant women traveled long distances, though health and a sensitivity about their appearance restrained others. Mrs. Hall found it confining that she could not visit her sister in Raleigh. "I know I could not travel any way," she wrote her, "without being hastened and taken down on the way." Poor health rather than embarrassment kept her housebound. On the other hand, Ella Clanton Thomas felt a degree of physical self-consciousness. When only five months pregnant, she decided to complete all her shopping in Augusta. "It will soon be so that I will be compelled to remain at home," she noted in her journal, "so I had better go while I can."[31]

Mary Boulware, of Shelby, North Carolina, kept a detailed diary in 1855, during her first pregnancy, and when ill health prevented her writing, her husband assumed the task. She attended religious camp

30. The two women were Anne Ruffin Cameron and Matilda Fulton. See Anne Cameron to Paul Cameron, January 8, 1858, in Cameron Family Papers, Southern Historical Collection; and Matilda Fulton to William Fulton, February 9, 1832, in William Savin Fulton Papers, Manuscript Collection, Arkansas State History Commission Archives, Little Rock.

31. Rebecca Haywood Hall to Eliza Haywood, October 16, 1837, in Haywood Family Collection; Ella Clanton Thomas Diary, November, 1855.

meetings, visited her parents' home, sewed, picked berries, baked, rode horses, attended several parties and a college commencement, often visited a local healing spring, and assisted her sister-in-law with her newborn. She also suffered several bouts of illness and had the local doctor visit her as often as three times a day. The doctor bled her frequently and prescribed a variety of medicines.[32]

Jane Harris Woodruff, reared in a wealthy Charleston household in the 1810s, married an army paymaster who had substantial landhold-ings in Georgia and Florida. During their first six years of marriage, Jane bore five children, four of whom died. In the winter of 1823–24, Joseph Woodruff decided to move the family to his Florida plantation. Jane must have become pregnant during the journey or shortly there-after. When the family arrived, they discovered only a small log cabin as living quarters, no neighbors, and scant food for themselves and their dozens of slaves. During the next several months, Jane had to bribe local Indians to hunt food, since the family provisions were lost at sea. A summer siege of distemper killed many of their horses, dogs, and poultry. By July, sixty of their slaves were sick. Jane, now six months pregnant, became the plantation physician, with only the medical ad-vice books to guide her. During the final few weeks of her pregnancy, her diet was reduced to maggot-infected meat and hominy. When their overseer became ill, Jane and her husband had to work in the fields and supervise the slaves. In her advanced "family way," she reported the work to be "very distressing." Jane's pregnancy was noteworthy for her poor diet and the difficult and lonely conditions of her struggle.[33]

Kate DeRosset Meares had a far different experience as the indulged daughter of a wealthy Wilmington, North Carolina, family in the 1840s. Though the evidence concerning her first pregnancy is thin, Kate seems to have taken full advantage of her situation. Because her husband's mercantile business required him to be away frequently, Kate remained in her parents' home during her prenatal period. Nervous headaches, morning sickness, and pain encouraged long daily baths. When visiting an aunt, Kate preferred to remain alone in her room instead of socializing. "I have not been able to join the family on the piazza," she reported to her husband, "but play the invalid as a sick indoors." A month later she wrote her husband that her summer's

32. Mary Boulware Journal (Boulware Family Papers, Archives and Special Collec-tions, Ida Jane Dacus Library, Winthrop College, Rock Hill, S.C.).

33. Jane Harris Woodruff Diary, 1829 (Clarkson Family Papers, Special Collections, J. Murrey Atkins Library, University of North Carolina at Charlotte).

activity had been to "indulge my lazy propensity, which you know is by no means slight. . . . I begin to think that Ma and Pa think me incapable of exerting myself." Kate's torpidity was probably not typical; her lethargy surprised even her parents. For Kate, pregnancy may have offered a welcome excuse to lead a sedentary existence or it may have truly brought her poor health.[34]

Virginia Shelton, married in her midthirties to a Baptist minister and teacher from Tennessee, was well educated and energetic. During her first pregnancy, at the age of thirty-eight, she and her husband traveled by steamboat and carriage to visit relatives. Virginia, who had little tolerance for boredom, spent her days studying Greek, reading French, sewing, visiting friends, walking, and holding long conversations with her husband. The couple attended weddings, balls, parties, and a dinner given in their honor. On several occasions when Virginia became ill, she consulted one of the town's doctors. She was no less active during her second pregnancy, keeping her mind stimulated and following a physician's advice when ill.[35]

Pregnancy did not abate the chores associated with a family, especially when there were young children. Primiparous women who, like Mrs. Meares, could pass their days in repose may have been lucky but were certainly rare. Women with children had numerous obligations, often involving the sickbed. An expectant mother in Fayetteville, North Carolina, nursed her child for several weeks through a fatal illness, watched it die on Saturday, and gave birth on Sunday. When seven months pregnant, Mary Ann Gwynn, of Wilkesboro, North Carolina, nursed her eighteen-month-old daughter, Sally, through days of convulsions. The girl did not die but was left partially paralyzed. The result was enormous demands on Mary Ann and her husband once their newborn appeared. Anne Cameron nursed a sick daughter for ten weeks. "But for her situation," she wrote, "I should most of the time been on the bed myself." Whatever their own discomfort, mothers often had no choice but to meet their family responsibilities. Most were unwilling to put a child's life into someone else's hands.[36]

34. Kate DeRosset Meares to Gaston Meares, July 30, August 29, 1850, both in DeRosset Family Papers, Southern Historical Collection.

35. William Shelton to David Campbell, January 15, 1850, Virginia Campbell Shelton to Margaret Campbell, January 15, February 6, February 22, April 21, May 5, 1850, all in Campbell Family Letters.

36. Catherine Holmes Blanks to Elizabeth Holmes Blanks, August 10, 1834, in

During the antebellum period, pregnant middle- and upper-class southern women with access to doctors often depended on professional advice concerning their own health problems or illnesses. The rhetoric in advice books trumpeted that pregnancy was normal, but blooming health was not. Expectant women could generally count on being ill at some time. For pregnancy added to their normal health woes. Morning sickness, headaches, nervousness, cramps, and exhaustion were temporary but unpleasant symptoms. Lucilla McCorkle, of Talladega, Alabama, whose introspective nature made her more sensitive to every bodily ill, wrote repeatedly of her weakness and "troublesome headaches." Mrs. Cameron's three pregnancies in as many years created physical hardship, and she admitted, "My health and spirits have both suffered by it." Others experienced headaches, stomach pains, fevers, and general debility. A visit to the local physician or a self-administered dose of calomel, morphine, or laudanum usually eased the minor sufferings. But other, less fortunate women experienced far more pain. Sally Graham Lacy, of Virginia, was in such distress that she could not write until after her illness had passed. "I know you have had many anxious moments on my account," she wrote her mother. "I often felt unwilling for you to hear how very ill I was. Yes, my dear Mama, the time of my trial is drawing near but I do not dread it as much as I once thought I should. I believe I have suffered as much as my constitution was able to bear."[37]

Adding to antebellum women's difficulties were severe disorders that could lead to prenatal or postnatal problems or even death for mother or fetus. Miscarriages and spontaneous abortions were not unusual. Dr. Charles Hentz's obstetrical records noted several occasions when he attended women after miscarriages. In one case he discovered a Mrs. J. C. Jeffries "lying on floor—cold—almost pulseless and flighty—foetus hanging by the cord." He managed to check her severe hemorrhaging with his "splendid, large linen handkerchief," and the woman survived. Ella Clanton Thomas had a miscarriage when

---

Elizabeth Holmes Blanks Letters, Manuscript Department, William R. Perkins Library; Mary Ann Gwynn and James Gwynn letters, November 10, 1843, to December 27, 1843, in Lenoir Family Papers; Anne Cameron to Paul Cameron, May 10, 1850, in Cameron Family Papers.

37. Lucilla Gamble McCorkle Diary, summer and fall, 1847 (Southern Historical Collection); Anne Cameron to Paul Cameron, May 10, 1850, in Cameron Family Papers; Sally Graham Lacy to her mother, Margaret Graham, July 21, 1817, in Graham Family Papers.

two months pregnant. "I was not very much frightened and have suffered more from extreme debility than anything else," she reported. "I have been sick two weeks and feel as though I had been ill two months."[38]

Health problems associated with pregnancy could quickly become pathological and require a doctor's intervention. The doctors middle- and upper-class southern women were likely to encounter employed dramatic remedies. Frightening illnesses required heroic responses. Puerperal convulsions, or preeclampsia and eclampsia, were potentially the most traumatic problem for pregnant women, and they required a doctor's immediate attention. These epileptic-like seizures occurring only in pregnancy were a danger during the latter months and might last for days or even weeks. Headaches, dizziness, and vomiting often accompanied them. Physicians, not knowing their cause, attributed the seizures to sensitivity of the nervous system, to a plethoric state, or to mental or atmospheric influences. All physicians feared them. Dr. Joseph Eve, professor of obstetrics at the Medical College of Georgia, declared that he had witnessed no trauma "more frequent in its occurrence, more terrific in its invasion or more truly dangerous in its results than convulsions." The only means to combat them, he found, was with "boldness and energy." His dramatic measures included cold water or ice applied to a shaven head, extensive bleeding, sinapisms on the extremities, and mustard baths followed by doses of calomel. In every case, he reported that the fetus was stillborn, but he was not inclined to alter his therapy. Dr. Josiah Brown, of Gaylesville, Georgia, treated a woman for convulsions by first extracting forty ounces of blood. When that proved ineffective, he had her inhale chloroform. Then he gave her a teaspoon of chloroform orally every two hours. Somehow she survived. The journal editors cautioned other doctors, however, that such treatment could result in death. The Louisiana State Medical Society recommended the opening of a temple artery to reduce blood pressure on the brain. Allopathic reactions to a desperate situation were drastic. Extensive bleeding did quickly lower blood pressure, but the procedure ultimately did more harm than good to the helpless patient. In the end, there was little an antebellum doctor could do to treat eclampsia apart from delivering the baby.[39]

38. Charles A. Hentz Obstetrical Records, Case 77, December 2, 1858 (Hentz Family Papers, Southern Historical Collection); Ella Clanton Thomas Diary, August 18, 1856.
39. Joseph Eve, "Cases of Convulsions and Other Nervous Affections," *Southern*

Similarly heroic remedies became standard for a variety of less frightening problems. Doctors believed that bleeding was a cure for many ills. To the antebellum physician, bloodletting appeared an obvious solution to a woman's "full" or plethoric state. The volume of blood in expectant women increases as a natural physiological reaction, preparing the body for a loss of blood during parturition. But to the antebellum doctor that seemed unnatural. To restore a balance in the body's fluids, he prescribed bleeding. Mrs. Boulware suffered several illnesses during her first pregnancy, and her doctor repeatedly cupped and blistered her side. A young medical student at the Medical College of South Carolina reflected the opinion of southern allopaths that bloodletting during pregnancy was "one of the most important remedies for the relief and prevention of disease."[40]

People outside the medical profession often appreciated the immediate reactions from bleeding. After Joseph Norwood's pregnant wife had been indisposed, the relieved husband proudly reported, "I thought it right to have her bled and she has been better ever since." In some instances, the patients insisted on heroic therapy. Mary Biddle, who suffered from headaches during one pregnancy, analyzed her problem and begged the doctor to bleed her. He reluctantly complied. Cheerfully, Mary reported to her husband that she felt better. She noted that her friends also found relief through frequent bloodletting.[41]

Certainly a dramatic and possibly painful treatment like bloodletting would have drawn attention away from the afflicted area. And having a professional perform a popular procedure could produce a placebo effect when there were no dire results. Tapping blood could cause lethargy in the patient, and that conduced to bed rest. Bleeding could give temporary relief from high blood pressure and vascular congestion. There is, however, little long-term medical justification for bloodletting, particularly for drawing large amounts, and many times it had a deleterious effect on the fetus and the woman alike. Pregnant women tend to be anemic, and bleeding exacerbated that. A removal of

Medical and Surgical Journal, III (1847), 513–15; Josiah Brown, "On Convulsions," *ibid.*, IX (1856), 464; Hort, "Report of the Committee," 574.

40. Mary Boulware Journal, 1855; George C. Newby, "A Dissertation on Blood-Letting" (1846), in Waring Historical Library, Medical University of South Carolina, Charleston.

41. Joseph Norwood to Selina Lenoir, February 19, 1837, in Lenoir Family Papers; Mary Powell Biddle to Samuel Biddle, July 1, 1847, in Samuel Biddle Papers, Manuscript Department, William R. Perkins Library.

oxygen-carrying red blood cells decreased the oxygen supply to the fetus as well. Rarely were bloodletting instruments sanitary, and infection was always a possibility.[42]

The kinds and dosages of medication administered to southern women during pregnancy were consistent with accepted nineteenth-century practice. But southern physicians were seldom overcautious. Enthusiastic about the effectiveness of many drugs, allopaths in the South especially promoted the benefits of calomel and opiates. The Charleston doctor J. Hume Simons, a typical advocate of heroic therapy, recommended calomel for nearly any illness and encouraged every plantation family to keep a box of opium pills handy. Dr. Alfred Folger declared calomel to be "quite the most important of our medicines."[43]

The excessive medication of pregnant women was common, for if a small dose of a drug proved ineffective, the rational course often seemed to be to administer more. One telling case led to long-term suffering. When Mrs. Gwynn was ill and feverish throughout most of her first pregnancy, her physician, feeling that cathartics were the answer, prescribed quantities of calomel to the point of salivation. Mary Ann's concerned mother wrote, "She is certainly, I think, suffering under the effects of the great quantity of mercury and other strong medicines that was pour'd down her in the dreadful fever she laboured under last spring." Despite the suspicion of overmedication, the family acquiesced in the doctor's judgment. Mary Ann's physical condition did not improve until long after her infant was born. Eventually she and her husband concluded that their suspicions had been correct. They publicly criticized the doctor, who responded with an angry letter, fearing for his local reputation. Whether the mercury that Mary Ann took also explained her daughter's convulsions and paralysis is unclear.[44]

Even without a doctor's advice, antebellum women often self-administered cathartics and opiates during pregnancy. Traditionally, herbs and drugs were a part of domestic medicine, and many were readily available in southern homes. Most expectant women who had malaria routinely took cinchona bark or quinine to control their chills

42. For an interesting perspective on bleeding, see Lester Snow King, *Medical Thinking: A Historical Preface* (Princeton, 1982), 227–44.

43. John Hume Simons, *The Planter's Guide, and Family Book of Medicine* (Charleston, S.C., 1848), 71; Alfred M. Folger, *The Family Physician, Being a Domestic Medical Work, Written in Plain Style, and Divided into Four Parts* (Spartanburg, S.C., 1845), 244.

44. Mary Ann Gwynn and Joseph Gwynn to her mother, Selina Lenoir, June, 1841, to January, 1842, in Lenoir Family Papers.

and fevers. Mrs. Cameron had another solution. She found that morphine and laudanum relieved the troublesome headaches that attended her bouts of malaria. Mrs. Norwood, something of a hypochondriac by nature, took laudanum during her pregnancies and on one occasion reported that it relieved her "entirely of the pain but [made her] feel sick and miserably stupid today, as it always does." Indeed, many women confessed that they felt "stupid" and languid after taking drugs, but that seemed far better than the agony that was the alternative. Few in the antebellum years were aware that drugs might injure the fetus or the expectant mother.[45]

"Fever and ague," as malaria was called in the South, was during this time the gravest health problem in every region of America outside New England. It was recognized as particularly virulent in the South. Margaret Mordecai Devereux, a wealthy North Carolina woman, referred bitterly to the southern coastland as the "land of swamps and ague," and a Charleston physician wrote that malarial fevers were endemic because of the "warm, moist climate, . . . low grounds, and stagnant waters." Almost no part of the South was spared the disease's devastating effect, though people living in the higher elevations, above the preferred breeding ground of anopheles mosquitoes, probably suffered least. Malaria occurred in seasonal waves, reaching its crests in the summer and fall. The disease was so common among southern families that cases went without mention unless they were particularly severe. One mother reported that her family was well, except for "chills and fevers," as if these were only to be expected. But serious and recurrent cases sometimes forced southern families to move.[46]

Malaria is a febrile disease caused by protozoa of the genus *Plasmodium,* carried by the female anopheles mosquito. Once the parasite is released into the bloodstream of its human host, the body reacts with alternating fevers and chills. Headaches, nausea, anorexia, dizziness, and lethargy are also symptoms. Relapses are typical. It is possible to achieve partial immunity during a season, and eventually over a lifetime, by repeated exposure to the disease. Newcomers to the South, young children, and pregnant women, however, were particularly vul-

45. Anne Cameron to Paul Cameron, December 26, 1845, in Cameron Family Papers; Laura Norwood to her mother, Selina Lenoir, June 3, 1841, in Lenoir Family Papers.

46. Margaret Devereux, *Plantation Sketches* (Cambridge, Mass., 1906), 40; David Ramsay, *The History of South Carolina, from Its First Settlement in 1670, to the Year 1808* (2 vols.; Charleston, S.C., 1809), II, 97; Mrs. Powell to her daughter Mary Powell Biddle, November 26, 1847, in Samuel Biddle Papers.

nerable to severe attacks. Malaria did not generally kill adults, though some strains did. But the disease had a particularly enervating effect on its victims, lowering resistance to other infections and causing unpleasant, debilitating responses.[47]

Women in the second half of pregnancy experience general immunosuppression. They are particularly vulnerable to malaria and to recurrences of previous malarial infection, and thus expectant women in the South suffered from malaria more frequently than other adults. Primiparous women, according to recent studies, are more likely to suffer ill effects, though antebellum plantation letters reveal that nearly anyone pregnant was vulnerable. Southern women came to dread summer and fall, particularly if they were carrying a child. "I assure you I look forward with much anxiety to our sickly month of September," Julia Pickens Howe, of Alabama, wrote her aunt. "I trust that a kind providence will bring me happily through. . . . I hope I am sufficiently accustomed to the climate now so as not to stand in so much danger of fevers." At least a few southern doctors perceived the dire impact malaria had on pregnant women. A Savannah physician commented that miscarriages were an "accident of almost daily occurrence in our malarious district." Unfortunately, limited knowledge about the disease and its causes precluded any long-term solution.[48]

Today's better understanding of the disease makes it easier to understand malaria's negative effect on pregnant women and on the unborn fetus. High fever can activate the uterus, causing spontaneous abortion or premature labor. Malarial fevers up to 104 degrees can create an environment too hot for the unborn child and lead to fetal death. By

47. For descriptions of malaria and its effect, see Erwin H. Ackerknecht, *Malaria in the Upper Mississippi Valley, 1760–1900* (Baltimore, 1945; New York, 1977); G. Robert Coatney *et al.*, *The Primate Malarias* (Bethesda, Md., 1971); William H. Deaderick and Loyd Thompson, *The Endemic Diseases of the Southern States* (Philadelphia and London, 1916); Kenneth F. Kiple and Virginia Himmelsteib King, *Another Dimension to the Black Diaspora: Diet, Disease, and Racism* (New York, 1981); Darrett B. Rutman and Anita H. Rutman, "Of Agues and Fevers: Malaria in the Early Chesapeake," *William and Mary Quarterly*, XXXIII (1976), 31–60; Todd Savitt, *Medicine and Slavery: The Diseases and Health Care of Blacks in Antebellum Virginia* (Urbana, Ill., 1978); Savitt, "Black Health on the Plantation: Masters, Slaves, and Physicians," in Judith Walzer Leavitt and Ronald L. Numbers (eds.), *Sickness and Health in America: Readings in the History of Medicine and Public Health* (Madison, Wis., 1978), 313–30; and Jill Dubisch, "Low Country Fevers: Cultural Adaptations to Malaria in Antebellum South Carolina," *Social Science Medicine*, XXI (1985), 641–49.
48. Julia Pickens Howe to Selina Lenoir, May 7, 1841, in Lenoir Family Papers; Joseph J. West, "Quinine in Pregnancy," *Savannah Journal of Medicine*, I (1858), 21.

impeding the passage of oxygen and other nutrients across the placenta, malaria can impair fetal growth and result in lower birth weight. The chance of anemia increases, for the disease destroys red blood cells. Intrauterine transmission of malaria from a mother to her child is possible. Moreover, quinine, the favored medication for malaria by the 1820s, was a known abortifacient and could stimulate the uterus and lead to a miscarriage. Endemic malaria was an important cause of miscarriages, stillbirths, neonatal deaths, and maternal health problems in the antebellum South.[49]

In the early nineteenth century, most southern doctors accepted the explanation of malaria first articulated by Giovanni Lancisi, an Italian, in the seventeenth century. Thinking that the cause of malaria—or "bad air"—was a miasma, or polluted atmosphere, and knowing nothing about carrier mosquitoes, he inferred that the disease arose from decaying vegetable matter and was carried to humans by warm winds. Southern doctors found Lancisi's account plausible and referred to the disease as "marsh fever." After a particularly unhealthy autumn in Savannah, a prominent Georgia physician, Dr. Richard Arnold, gave a recipe for fever and ague. "Mix vegetable matter with water and subject it to heat, and the most malignant malaria will be generated," he assured. Arnold recommended that his patients close windows facing low, swampy areas. His suggestion may have helped, by decreasing the number of mosquitoes entering the house.[50]

49. Most studies that discuss malaria and its effect on pregnant women deal with contemporary African women. The physiological reaction of white women living in the antebellum South could have been far different. Many blacks are born with the sickle-cell trait, which provides immunity to the vivax strain, the most common form of malaria in the South. One can safely assume, however, that the reaction of nineteenth-century southern white women, without such genetic or acquired traits, would have been every bit as severe, and probably far worse. For studies on the subject, see H. M. Gilles *et al.*, "Malaria, Anemia, and Pregnancy," *Annals of Tropical Medicine and Parasitology*, LXIII (1969), 245–63; J. D. MacGregor and J. G. Avery, "Malaria Transmission and Fetal Growth," *British Medical Journal*, III (August 17, 1974), 443–63; M. C. Reinhardt, "The Effects of Parasitic Infections in Pregnant Women," in *Perinatal Infections*, Ciba Foundation Symposium, n.s., LXXII (Amsterdam, 1980), 149–70; Tukutau Taufu, "Malaria and Pregnancy," *Papua New Guinea Medical Journal*, XXI (1978), 197–206; P. C. C. Garnham, "The Present State of Malaria Research: An Historical Study," *Experientia*, XL (1984), 1305; and Todd Savitt, "Black Health on the Plantation," 314–15.

50. Richard Dennis Arnold, *An Essay upon the Relation of Bilious and Yellow Fever*, read before the Medical Society of the State of Georgia (Augusta, 1856). Other contemporary sources that include a history of the disease: Elisha Bartlett, *The History, Diagnosis, and Treatment of Typhoid and of Typhus Fever, with an Essay on the Diagnosis of Bilious Remittent and of Yellow Fever* (Philadelphia, 1842); John MacCulloch, *An Essay on the Remittent and*

In the years before the war, some southern doctors and medical students began to notice that malaria could occur when vegetation was growing, and not only when it was decaying. The disease was also most prevalent in areas that lacked thick vegetation, such as riverfronts. Their conclusion was that a mysterious combination of heat and water was essential for creating the poison that caused such widespread illness in the South.[51]

Aware or not of the scientific explanations, expectant southern women suffered from malaria, and some cases were sufficiently discomforting or even alarming to warrant comment. Caroline Summey, of North Carolina, endured chills and fevers for seven weeks in the middle of her pregnancy. Eventually discovering that the fetus was quiet, she gave premature birth to a dead infant. Daniel Anderson, of Petersburg, Virginia, reported that his wife, who had long been indisposed with intermittent fever, lost her baby. Other pregnant women and their fetuses were more fortunate, but often the women were very sick. They described chills, fevers, incessant vomiting, and incapacitating exhaustion. Sally Lacy, who suffered three weeks of chills and fever during one pregnancy, blamed the location of their new home, for Sally and her husband had settled, in Missouri, near the "bank of a stagnant creek which has a large, rich bottom with ponds, all which smells horrid in the summer." Such a creek would have been a breeding ground favorable to the anopheles mosquito.[52]

If a pregnant woman with a severe case of malaria sought the as-

---

Intermittent Diseases, Including, Generically, Marsh Fever and Neuralgia (Philadelphia, 1830); Thompson McGown, *A Practical Treatise on the Most Common Diseases of the South* (Philadelphia, 1849); George Turner, "The Aetiology of Malaria," Dissertation 313 (1857), in Vanderbilt University Medical Center Library; Daniel Drake, *Malaria in the Interior Valley of North America: A Selection* (1850), ed. Norman D. Levine (Urbana, Ill., 1964).

51. Turner, "The Aetiology of Malaria"; John Baxter, "Malaria," Dissertation 330 (1857), Samuel English, "Malaria and Its Results," Dissertation 202 (1856), James Lewis Mitchell, "Malaria," Dissertation 230 (1857), W. A. Haynes, "Malaria," Dissertation 252 (1857), Asa W. Griggs, "Malaria," Dissertation 132 (1855), A. H. Dunarant, "Malaria," Dissertation 140 (1855), S. Fletcher, "Malaria," Dissertation 360 (1858), J. H. Dunn, "Malaria," Dissertation 381 (1855), J. F. Cook, "Malaria," Dissertation 410 (1859), James H. Hughes, "Malaria," Dissertation 483 (1858), all in Vanderbilt University Medical Center.

52. Polly Summey to Selina Lenoir, December 2, 1832, January 23, 1833, in Lenoir Family Papers; Daniel Anderson to Duncan Cameron, August 4, 1803, in Cameron Family Papers; Sally Graham Lacy to William Graham, February 2, 1821, in Graham Family Papers.

sistance of a physician, his prescription was most likely cinchona bark or quinine. Doctors knew that quinine caused contractions of the uterus and was an abortifacient. But the disease continued to puzzle them, and they could do little more than resort to known cures and traditional heroic remedies, even if in some instances the outcome was a stillbirth or a premature delivery.

Despite the commonness of ill health that encouraged a dependence by expectant mothers on doctors, not only physicians played an important role during the women's long vigil. Southern women had traditionally relied upon people outside the medical profession, and they continued to do so throughout the antebellum period. Middle- and upper-class women found a good deal of support and solace from friends and relatives. Since most women had experienced the joys and pains of pregnancy and parturition, they could provide sympathy and advice. Women often shared their concerns about pregnant friends or family members, and unsolicited advice was constantly forthcoming in personal correspondence. For instance, Caroline Mordecai Plunkett's two sisters urged her to curtail some of her activities, fearing she would endanger herself as well as the fetus she was carrying. When Caroline continued teaching, housecleaning, socializing, and boarding students, an exasperated Rachel scolded her, noting that "the state of a female at such a time is at best so precarious that too much attention cannot be paid to every particular." Mary Jones, of Liberty County, Georgia, felt little hesitancy about offering advice to Ruth, her daughter-in-law in Savannah, though she tactfully filtered her suggestions through her devoted son Charles. As Ruth's confinement approached, Mrs. Jones cautioned her to "be prudent for the next two or three weeks, living plainly and taking an occasional dose of cooling medicine." Without Ruth's replies, it is impossible to know how the young woman accepted such advice. Adelle Allston's sister, Harriet, who was childless, nevertheless felt qualified to advise her pregnant sister on several occasions. She purchased material for Adelle's maternity clothes, advised her that the proper fashion was to dress "loosely," and urged her to leave the unhealthy climate of "Middleton" plantation for the cooling breezes of Charleston. Much of the advice that women gave one another was practical in nature and welcomed as a sign of concern.[53]

53. Rachel Lazarus to Caroline Plunkett, March 9, 1823, in Jacob Mordecai Papers; Robert Manson Myers, *Children of Pride: A True Story of Georgia and the Civil War* (New Haven, 1972), 694; Harriet to Adelle Allston, September 9, 1834, October 31, 1836, both in Allston Family Papers, South Carolina Historical Society Library.

What is just as evident is the sympathetic role many husbands assumed during their wives' pregnancies. Often men expressed great tenderness, worry, and understanding during the vigils. Physicians encouraged such empathy, urging men to indulge feminine whims during the prenatal period. "No man can form an adequate idea," wrote John Peters, a homeopath, "of the manifold inconveniences, and annoyances to which a woman is subject while pregnant." It would seem that a majority of southern men sympathized with these "inconveniences." Husbands who spent a good portion of their time away from home wrote frequently and often expressed frustration at their absence. Henry Lawrence, a New Orleans merchant, sent his wife to her family home in Kentucky well in advance of her confinement. Absence did little to quell either his ardor or his concern. Daily missives to his "angel baby" urged Fanny to arrange proper care for herself, to take plenty of exercise, and to avoid unnecessary medicines. "My anxiety is getting unbearable," he confessed, "in fearing a thousand ills may befall thee." Judge George Badger was often riding the circuit, but he found time to warn his pregnant wife to avoid stumbling and to keep him constantly apprised of her condition, and to forbid her to bend "her knees in prayer" at church services. Dr. Treadwell, absent during his wife's illness in one pregnancy, instructed Mattie on the dangers of opium overdose (he seems to be one of the few southern physicians who recognized its dangers), urged her to evacuate her bowels, and closed his lengthy instructions with "God restore you, my good wife." Obviously, from the amount of advice he provided, Dr. Treadwell felt almost as responsible as God for improving his wife's health.[54]

Other husbands were dotingly attentive at home. Each week, Charles Jones spelled out the progress of his wife's condition. He dutifully reported to his parents that his dear Ruth was "grievously burdened with the primal sorrow of her sex." Early in Ruth's pregnancy, his greatest concern was that her condition coincided with her first exposure to the malarial fevers of a Savannah summer. Mrs. Lacy, who was very ill during one pregnancy, boasted that her husband was the "best nurse I ever saw." Selina Lenoir proudly described her son-in-law

54. John Charles Peters, *A Treatise on the Diseases of Married Females: Disorders of Pregnancy, Parturition, and Lactation* (New York, 1854), 23; Henry Lawrence to Fanny Brashear Lawrence, June 3, 7, 22, 1845, all in Brashear Family Papers, Southern Historical Collection; Mary Polk Badger to George Badger, April 12, 1827, in Polk, Badger, and McGehee Papers, Southern Historical Collection; E. W. Treadwell to Mattie Treadwell, 1859, in E. W. Treadwell Collection.

as "one of the best of husbands and . . . one of the best of nurses" during her daughter's sickly nine months. Undoubtedly these were treasured words from a mother-in-law. Other husbands assumed responsibility for locating a physician when a pregnant wife became ill.[55]

Male relatives were equally anxious. The Reverend Charles Jones urged his daughter Mary not to overexert herself in her expectant state. He suggested that she not attend "four services on the Sabbath (including your Sunday school) when you feel badly," probably the ultimate concession by a devout Presbyterian minister. Ashley DeRosset, whose own wife was approaching confinement, empathized with his pregnant sister:

> You are often in my thoughts, dear sister, especially when I see our poor child here, burdened, anxious, wearied and waiting, and having like you sufficient course for wishing the day of trial past in knowing that she herself may possibly be left in the way of flesh, or obliged to see another home before most persons would think a removal prudent. We feel assured that our heavenly Father will do all things well, and therefore do not indulge in much carefulness about a future beyond our control. . . I feel great anxiety to hear of the favorable issue we have been looking for so long.

Although his words may now seem morbid, probably an antebellum woman found them comforting.[56] It is apparent that love and devotion motivated the sympathy and concern of many men.

The psychological state of antebellum southern women during pregnancy added to their difficulties. Almost universally they spent months in worried anticipation of their confinement. The possibility that either the mother or the child would die was very real. Interestingly, the concerns of middle- and upper-class women focused more on their own lives than on the fetus. The apparent self-interest does not evince an indifference to the unborn child but reflects the view of society at the time, which placed a higher value on the life of the mother than on that of the fetus. When doctors had to choose between saving the mother and saving the unborn child, they invariably chose to save the mother. A Maryland doctor noted that physicians had a "positive duty" to use any means in behalf of the mother, "disregarding

55. Myers, *Children of Pride,* 486, 494; Sally Lacy to Margaret Graham, July 21, 1817, in Graham Family Papers; Selina Lenoir to Betsy Lenoir, November 8, 1841, in Lenoir Family Papers.

56. Myers, *Children of Pride,* 368; Ashley DeRosset to Mary Jane DeRosset Curtis, January 10, 1838, in Moses Ashley Curtis Papers, Southern Historical Collection.

every consequence that may result to the child." Since women experienced pain, complications, and potential ill health during pregnancy, it was natural they should think more about themselves. Though most southern women behaved in the unborn child's best interest—at least according to their own perceptions and the medical ideas of the time—they may not have accepted fully the doctors' concept of fetal viability. Infant death was quite common, and women may have prepared themselves psychologically for the worst, regarding each infant as a temporary gift from God. Perhaps they felt the fetus was in God's hands until they assumed responsibility for its care. Or as an emotional defense, southern women may not have wished to consider at all the possibility that their baby might die. Whatever the reasons, women's fears focused heavily on their own lives until the infant was born.[57]

Doctors tried to offset women's worries and discouraged morbid thoughts. They urged women to be cheerful and to substitute happiness for fear. Like Buchan, they hoped that pregnancy would be a time of "pleasure." They believed that depression and negative thoughts could have an impact upon the woman's mind and health and perhaps could mark the child's character. Yet despite the admonitions, southern women approached childbirth with apprehension, for they were well aware of the grim possibilities. Young girls entered adulthood knowing the risks associated with childbearing. One pious Louisiana girl declared, "I think it would be wrong for me to marry, my health or more properly my constitution is too feeble to sustain the burden which a wife and mother must bear." The fact that several of her brothers and sisters died as infants may have affected her outlook, though within a few years she found the courage she needed. Sensitive young girls witnessed agonizing confinements that must have made a deep impression. After observing one delivery, a young lady wrote her mother, "It appeared to me if suffering could make one die, she should have sunk under it, for certain am I that all the suffering I have ever experienced or witnessed of every description, hers far exceeds." Tales of women dying in childbirth were circulated among friends and family, even among women who were expectant. Southern physicians, with some accuracy, believed that women fueled one another's fears. The Louisiana State Medical Society criticized "injudicious female friends" who often mentioned the "terrible suffering and great peril of giving birth to a child."

57. John B. Beck, "Observations on Ergot," *Western Journal of Medicine and Surgery,* n.s., II (1844), 65.

The resulting fears, it concluded, diminished a woman's vitality during labor.[58]

Often, however, women needed no friendly warnings, for their own experiences entitled them to apprehension enough. Multiparous women seem to have had the greatest fears, for the seasoned veteran knew what lay ahead. After several confinements, Mrs. Gwynn despaired, "This business of having children is an awful thing." Mrs. Howe noted in a letter to her aunt, "I have at times many fears (many more than I had before)." Other women acknowledged death as a distinct possibility. Frances Bumpas, a minister's wife, confided to her journal, "I often think of the approaching critical period—its sufferings and its dangers. May I be prepared for the event, whatever it may be. What if death should come!" Not even her religious background could dispel her fears for the task that lay ahead.[59]

58. Buchan, *Advice to Mothers,* 10–11; Sarah Lois Wadley Diary, October 1, 1840 (Southern Historical Collection); unidentified girl to her mother, describing labor of Margaret Cameron Mordecai, May 16, 1854, in Thomas Ruffin Collection, Manuscript Department, William R. Perkins Library; Hort, "Report of the Committee," 576.

59. Mary Ann Gwynn to Sally, December 31, 1843, in Lenoir Family Papers; Julia Howe to Selina Lenoir, May 7, 1841, in Lenoir Family Papers; Frances Bumpas Journal, February 6, 1844 (Southern Historical Collection).

3 To Alleviate Her Anxieties

ASSISTANCE DURING LABOR

The biblical phrase "In sorrow thou shalt bring forth children" un-doubtedly struck a chord with many antebellum mothers, who had no effective pain-killers and little knowledge to prepare them for the phys-ical and emotional suffering they would endure in childbirth. Whether female midwives or relatives or male doctors assisted during delivery, parturition could prove distressing and painful. No attendant could truly alleviate the suffering.

But childbirth also had a positive side. Bearing a child provided antebellum women with important personal rewards. The parturient woman became the focus of attention as female relatives, friends, and at least one medical assistant gathered to help her through parturition and to care for her immediate needs. Family and friends involved them-selves in decisions concerning her confinement, and thus created a sense of female and kin bonding. Childbirth occasionally united black and white women, dissolving for a moment racial barriers. The confronta-tion with death and suffering enhanced the importance of religion by strengthening the dedication of women to their religious beliefs. Soci-ety glorified the achievement of bearing a healthy child.

Despite the frequency and even ritualism of confinements, they could never be approached with detachment. Preparations for every birth required planning and involved the participation of nuclear and extended family members as well as friends. Where to have the baby, who would be present, and who would officiate were all questions that required answers and, fortunately for historians, substantial letter writ-ing as well.

Nearly all middle- and upper-class southern women delivered their babies in their own or someone else's home. Urban centers such as New Orleans and Charleston boasted at least one municipal hospital, but this was a charitable as well as a teaching institution, serving immigrants, blacks, and the poor. Privileged women were unwilling to bear their children in an institutional environment, far from support groups and familiar surroundings. Antebellum hospitals could offer a woman no better care—and often far less sanitary conditions—than she received in a domestic setting.

Many southern mothers remained in their own homes for their confinements. Comfortable surroundings and the presence of husband, family, and friends provided the greatest emotional comfort. Since a pregnant woman's health was often precarious and travel conditions could prove difficult and distances considerable, remaining at home had a practical advantage. But careful preparations were essential. For instance, Mary Henderson, of Salisbury, North Carolina, spent several weeks creating a special birthing chamber in the family dining room. Anticipating an extended stay downstairs, she had her bed and bureau moved into the room. Mary also invited several female relatives to assist her. In another instance, Rebecca Holcombe, of Mississippi, turned her husband's medical office into her birthing room, forcing her bemused husband to work among diapers, bottle nipples, and baby clothes.[1]

Frequently southern women chose their parents' home for their confinement, particularly for a firstborn. Care and support from an attentive, experienced mother could prove invaluable. For some women, the opportunity to use a familiar physician or seasoned midwife or to have childhood friends in attendance was the motive. Fanny Brashear Lawrence traveled from Louisiana to her parents' home in Lexington, Kentucky, months before the due date of her first confinement. Rebecca Cameron delivered her first baby in her parents' North Carolina plantation home. Her recovery period was so pleasant that she remained several weeks after the baby's birth, ignoring pleas from her lonely husband. Rebecca repeatedly reminded him that travel might impair her own and the newborn's health. Perhaps she also enjoyed sharing maternal concerns with her mother and basking in the special care she received from doting parents. Adelaide Baker, of Little Rock, Arkansas, was so determined to be with her parents that she traveled to her Connecticut home during her last trimester of pregnancy. Adelaide had already prepared her front chamber in Little Rock as a delivery room, but loneliness or nostalgia for her family home apparently over-

1. Mary Henderson Diary, July, August, 1855 (Southern Historical Collection, L. R. Wilson Library, University of North Carolina at Chapel Hill); William Henry Holcombe Diary, February 21, 1855 (Southern Historical Collection).

came her. The presence of several educated Little Rock doctors was not enough to persuade her to remain.[2]

In some instances, strong parental pressure made expectant women accede to family wishes and come home. Whether they and their husbands were happy about this is hard to know. Probably attitudes varied by individual. In one interesting case, Thomas Ruffin, a justice of the supreme court of North Carolina, wrote a long letter to his wealthy son-in-law, Paul Cameron, seeking his cooperation in encouraging his wife, Anne, to return to the Ruffin home for her first confinement. The entreaty apparently created a good deal of disquiet, and Anne intimated her preference for remaining with her husband. That was unacceptable to her parents. "She may rest assured that our thoughts are almost as much engrossed by her perils as yours and hers can be," wrote Anne's concerned father. "It has been our consolation that in the approaching crisis of our beloved child she would be under the immediate observation of her dear and devoted Mother in whose affections and attentions she has that confidence which greatly tends to alleviate the anxieties of that momentous hour." Apparently, Mrs. Ruffin's feeble health precluded her leaving home to be with her daughter. The most effective argument Ruffin could offer was the threat that Anne might go through her confinement without her mother altogether: "If Anne has entertained thoughts of remaining at home, she should immediately change her plan and come up to us shortly. We do not suppose that she proposes to dispense with her Mother's assistance entirely but that she requires it as indispensable." He finally ended his lengthy argument. "Our opinions therefore and our affections incite us to forwarn our child to make haste to us, and with us await the course of nature and the will of God." Obviously he viewed the case as closed, for he concluded, "Our carriage will be at her service, whenever commanded."[3]

Here a woman's father and her husband apparently discussed her case with little consideration for her own wishes. Maybe Anne's father felt it easier to deal with another man, maybe he was thoughtfully sparing his pregnant daughter additional worry, or maybe he felt men rather than women should make such decisions. Ruffin clearly had his

2. Fanny Brashear Lawrence to Henry Brashear, June, 1845, in Brashear Family Papers, Southern Historical Collection; Rebecca Cameron, August 27, September 2, 9, 1806, all in Cameron Family Papers, Southern Historical Collection; Edwin Baker to his parents, June 23, 1842, Adelaide Raphel Baker to Edwin G. Baker, September 4, 1842, both in Edwin Baker Letters, Southern Historical Collection.

3. Thomas Ruffin to Paul Cameron, April 8, 1844, in Cameron Family Papers.

daughter's best interest at heart and thought that he had the right to determine where she would have her baby. Anne eventually acceded to her father's wishes, whether willingly or not. Since she had at least three more of her children in her parents' home, the suggestion is that the experience was more agreeable than she expected or that her father's will prevailed. Perhaps this was a power struggle between parents and husband to determine Anne's principal loyalty. Paul may have resented his father-in-law's intrusiveness and control. On the other hand, he may have breathed a sigh of relief, knowing that his wife's confinement was in someone else's hands. Certainly family pressure proved difficult to ignore. That in this case two men handled an issue of childbirth perhaps symbolizes a southern woman's lack of power within the family, but it surely demonstrates family members' involvement and concern in planning a woman's confinement.

Anne ended by receiving the sort of care a southern woman most valued during labor. Whenever circumstances allowed, a woman's principal support came from her own mother. Southern mothers regarded parturient care of daughters as a natural duty, and most assumed this responsibility. Antebellum mothers and daughters appeared to have a particularly close relationship that generational differences rarely strained. Family letters reveal deep intimacy and shared feelings. As Carroll Smith-Rosenberg has noted in her study of nineteenth-century female relationships, daughters grew up tracing their mothers' patterns. That fostered harmonious relationships across two generations. In addition, mothers were experienced and could empathize with the pain and difficulties of labor. Southern women made every effort to have their mothers present, either by traveling home or by inducing them to come. Pressing responsibilities at home, poor health, illness of another family member, or difficult traveling conditions were almost the only reasons for a mother's being absent from her daughter's confinement.[4]

Anxiety resulted when a daughter could not depend on her mother. Ruffin obviously knew the importance of his wife's presence during his daughter's confinement—critical not only to his daughter Anne but also to his wife, who wished to be present. An expectant woman often sent urgent requests to her mother, long before the due date. A mother's reluctance could arouse feelings of abandonment and hurt. Laura Nor-

<hr>

4. Carroll Smith-Rosenberg, "The Female World of Love and Ritual: Relations Between Women in Nineteenth-Century America," in Michael Gordon (ed.), *The American Family in Social-Historical Perspective* (2nd ed.; New York, 1978), 334–58.

wood, of Hillsboro, North Carolina, believed that only her mother's affectionate care would sustain her through the ordeal, but she had difficulty in persuading her mother to come for her several confinements. "I cannot tell you, my dear mother," she wrote, "what a comfort it would be to me if you could be here at the time of my approaching event." Her husband, Joseph, either felt more concern than Laura or thought her appeal far too gentle. "I wish very earnestly you would be with us at a certain time," he added in a postscript to Laura's letter. "It would be a great relief to my mind." Playing upon Mrs. Lenoir's natural apprehension, he added, "I think you would also escape much uneasiness and suspense." Unfortunately, her mother could not come, but Laura did not let that inhibit similar entreaties during another pregnancy. Once again she sent "strong reasons and arguments" to persuade her mother to come, remarking, "If you would only write and say you are coming, . . . I think it would completely drive the blues away from me." Mrs. Lenoir still did not bend. The reasons for her virtually unbroken chain of refusals to help Laura are unknown, but personal problems probably underlay her decision. Laura's demanding father seems to have suffered poor health, and perhaps he objected to his wife's absence. But the mother's unwillingness increased Laura's apprehension about her delivery.[5]

Southern mothers were welcome in the birthing chamber; husbands apparently were not. A recent study based on medical advice books maintains that a husband's presence became more acceptable by the mid–nineteenth century. Nonetheless, prescriptive literature, most of it written in the North, often reflected wishful thinking and rarely accounted for regional differences.[6] And not all advisers supported a husband's presence. Some physicians argued that another man in the room could prove distracting. Dr. Joseph Warrington stated that the only acceptable man was one "of good moral force, competent to comfort, encourage and aid in sustaining his wife through the conflict of parturition, and to calm and compose her in the excitement or ecstasy to which she is often subject upon delivery." He showed little doubt that few men could meet such standards. More important but seldom admitted by doctors was their reluctance to share authority

5. Laura and Joseph Norwood to Selina Lenoir, February 19, 1837, May 20, 1842, both in Lenoir Family Papers, Southern Historical Collection.

6. Jill J. Suitor, "Husbands' Participation in Childbirth: A Nineteenth-Century Phenomenon," *Journal of Family History,* VI (1981), 278–93.

with another male. Female relatives and friends were acceptable because they knew their place. A husband could prove more threatening. "The husband, whether present or absent," Warrington candidly noted, "must regard the physician and nurse as substitutes, or attorneys to whom is deputed the entire control of the affairs of the chamber."[7]

In the few detailed accounts of confinements written by women, husbands are rarely mentioned as being among the people present. So long as other assistants were there, females apparently placed little value on a husband's participation. Childbirth was an event reserved for a skilled practitioner and empathic females. Mary Anderson, of Virginia, typified these sentiments. She wrote her nephew, Duncan Cameron, reassuring him about his wife's condition before one delivery and noting that Rebecca "is in such good hands in those of her Mother that whether you are absent or present, you ought not to worry." Thomas Chaplin, Jr., of South Carolina, wrote that he "remained in the hall very quietly reading the newspaper" while his wife suffered through another confinement. Husbands were better off staying out of the delivery room, for women could handle the matter. In some cases, a squeamish or fainthearted male may have preferred this detached role.[8]

Only unusual circumstances brought the husband into the birthing chamber. A doctor might serve at the accouchement of his own wife. If the midwife or physician did not arrive in time, a husband might be solicited to assist. During an emergency delivery of a premature infant, Ella Clanton Thomas, of Georgia, sent for her mother, a physician, and a midwife, but the infant would not wait for skilled attendants. Ella had to rely on family slaves and her husband. Describing the event later, Ella wrote, "Jule, Mr. Thomas, and Tamah were all that were with me." She found little to compliment. "Neither of them knew anything, Mr. Thomas was already fully frightened." Despite the burden of her husband's fears, Ella directed the three apparent novices to a successful result. Her reaction is particularly interesting since her husband had attended medical school. Evidently, Ella felt he was more skilled at growing cotton than delivering babies.[9]

In a more distressing case, Ebenezer Pettigrew, of North Carolina,

7. Joseph Warrington, *The Obstetric Catechism, Containing Two Thousand Three Hundred and Forty-Seven Questions and Answers on Obstetrics Proper* (Philadelphia, 1853), 171.

8. Mary Anderson to Duncan Cameron, January 6, 1804, in Cameron Family Papers; Theodore Rosengarten, *Tombee: Portrait of a Cotton Planter* (New York, 1986), 369.

9. Ella Clanton Thomas Diary, April 6, 1855 (Manuscript Department, William R. Perkins Library, Duke University).

witnessed a portion of his wife's labor. Ebenezer was called into the birthing room when the attending midwife could not extract the placenta. "After the second unsuccessful attempt, I desired the midwife to desist," Ebenezer wrote. "In these two efforts, my dear Nancy suffered exceedingly and frequently exclaimed, 'O I shall die, send for the doctor.' " Ebenezer tried to help his wife, but there was little he could do apart from summoning a physician. The doctor arrived too late, for the poor woman had died in her husband's arms. Probably because Nancy Pettigrew's situation had become life threatening, Ebenezer's presence seemed natural and necessary.[10]

What seems more common was the expectation that husbands would be nearby, like Thomas Chaplin with his newspaper, even if not actually in the chamber. Parturient women expressed disappointment when their husbands were absent and missed the entire birth. Since southern women approached each confinement as easily their last moment on earth, to know that the husband was nearby was reassuring. After a successful delivery, the new mother wished to share her success and the joy of a healthy newborn. Julia Howe, of Alabama, who had no friends or relatives living close to her, glowingly related her affectionate feelings toward her husband. "I believe if I had not had such kind and judicious nursing, I should not have got well so soon," she wrote. "What a blessing it is, my dear Aunt, in this greatest trial of our suffering sex, to have an anxious and tender husband to watch over us. I am sure if anything can endear that name to us it is his sympathy at such a time." L. F. H. Colcock, of Charleston, South Carolina, wrote a friend, "What a privilege to have loved ones near even if not with us. To have your husband, but as you've never had the trial of being without him at such a time, you hardly know how to appreciate it." Apparently she had felt the absence of her own spouse during at least one confinement. Other women feared that they might die before a husband returned home. Southern husbands often played a key role in viewing the infant and announcing its birth.[11]

Female attendants were important in the birthing room, sometimes even substituting for the absent mother of the woman giving birth. The

10. Ebenezer Pettigrew, June 30, 1830, relating death of Ann (Nancy) Shephard Pettigrew, in Pettigrew Papers, Southern Historical Collection. This is one of the most detailed and poignant descriptions of a southern woman's death in childbirth.

11. Julia Pickens Howe to Selina Lenoir, March 31, 1837, in Lenoir Family Papers; L. F. H. Colcock to Octavia Wyche Otey, March 8, 1858, in Wyche-Otey Collection, Southern Historical Collection.

female rituals surrounding childbirth provided a unique opportunity for women to bond together. According to the historian Nancy Cott, a number of rituals throughout women's lives enhanced their consciousness of being female and may have helped them define and maintain a sphere separate from men. Much female bonding occurred during adolescence, through shared experiences and friendships based in church and school. But the rituals of childbirth proved the most universal and important instruments for bonding married women. At least until the Civil War, the parturient southern woman depended on female friends and relatives to assist her.[12]

An unmarried sister was an important attendant, since she often had few demands on her time and could be particularly sympathetic and helpful. Caroline Plunkett, of Wilmington, North Carolina, invited her spinster sister, Ellen, to assist her during parturition. Though Ellen lived in Petersburg, Virginia, and had spent a portion of the previous year nursing another sibling, she willingly made the long journey. Probably she welcomed both the chance to be useful and the change from her normal quiet. Unfortunately, Caroline's baby arrived before Ellen, but the sister jumped to assume the role of chief nurse. Some sisters took charge of maternal and domestic duties as well. The sister of Frances Bumpas arrived nine days before Frances' confinement, and she not only helped with the delivery but also took over the new mother's teaching duties.[13]

When mothers and sisters were not sufficient support or were not available, expectant women called upon other relatives, friends, and neighbors, often creating a large network of attendants. The number present in the birthing chamber varied by individual circumstance. Sally Graham Lacy, of Missouri, felt that four helpers were too few. "Mrs. Neale, Eliza, and a woman of Mrs. Tucker's and the Doctor was all that was with me," she complained to her mother. Since Sally had recently moved to Missouri, there was a special poignancy to her being without her mother and family members. Mary Hering Middleton noted that her daughter-in-law Sally, who was to remain in Charleston for her infant's birth, would have family members in attendance as well

12. Smith-Rosenberg, "The Female World," 334–58; Nancy Cott, *The Bonds of Womanhood: "Woman's Sphere" in New England, 1780–1835* (New Haven, 1977).

13. Ellen Mordecai to Sam Mordecai, January, 1822, M. Lazarus to Solomon Mordecai, February 6, 1822, both in Jacob Mordecai Papers, Manuscript Department, William R. Perkins Library; Frances Bumpas Journal, March, 1844 (Southern Historical Collection).

as "Susan and Mrs. Pringle to be with her frequently and perhaps Mrs. W. P. who has given birth to her twelfth child." It must have been reassuring that an experienced mother would be included among Sally's attendants. Virginia Shelton expressed gratitude toward newly formed friends, writing her aunt after one successful confinement, "I cannot but feel that I am greatly blessed, in being able to pass through severe trials with so much support." No other event in a married woman's life encouraged such close bonding with other women.[14]

In addition to the wish for emotional sustenance, practical considerations counseled the presence of several friends, neighbors, and domestic servants. Medical complications often prolonged parturition, and women spelled one another during extended labor. The need for female support continued long after delivery. Tradition dictated that new mothers remained in bed at least two weeks, and doctors concurred, in view of their understanding of childbirth as a pathological condition. Reality often imposed extended nursing as well, for new mothers might suffer infections or prolonged illnesses. Henry Watson, of Alabama, wrote to his mother back in Connecticut, explaining why so many friends and neighbors had gathered during and after one confinement. "In accordance with our custom here, they were calling every day, even on Sunday, some came in," he observed. "We have no women in this country who make it a business to nurse as they do with you, but have to depend upon friends and relations or negroes." Southern women formed unusually close bonds during such periods and perhaps came to depend upon one another more than women did in settled regions of the country.[15]

For southern women living in rural areas, female attendants were not always available. Mary Polk Badger sympathized with her sister-in-law, who lived in an isolated region: "Poor sister Mary, I feel very much

14. Sally Graham Lacy to Mrs. Margaret Graham, July 14, 1821, in Graham Family Papers, Manuscript Department, William R. Perkins Library; Mary Hering Middleton to her daughter Eliza, February 6, 1841, in Hering-Middleton Collection, South Carolina Historical Society Library; Virginia Campbell Shelton to Mrs. William Campbell, February 10, 1852, February 10, 1857, both in Campbell Family Letters, Manuscript Department, William R. Perkins Library.

15. This two-week period was counseled by most medical and maternal advisers, including Charles Delucena Meigs (*Obstetrics: The Science and the Art* [3rd ed.; Philadelphia, 1856], 347), Warrington (*The Obstetric Catechism,* 176), and John C. Gunn (*Gunn's Domestic Medicine; or, Poor Man's Friend* [Madisonville, Tenn., 1834], 370). See also Henry Watson to Mrs. Watson, May 26, 1848, in Henry Watson, Jr., Papers, Manuscript Department, William R. Perkins Library.

for her—in that almost wild country, without any intimate friend—about to be confined—and lost her eldest son." Julia Howe anticipated her own confinement without the female support she desired. Her husband had moved the family to the Deep South, leaving Julia far from family and friends. From her home on the Alabama frontier, Julia wrote to her cousin Laura that she was pregnant. Laura did her best to offer consolation. "How much do I feel for you, dear Julia," she wrote from North Carolina, "the prospect of being so far from all near relatives at such a time, but I trust that providence will provide kind friends for you and that you will not feel want of those you left." Unfortunately providence failed her, and Julia's situation was no better two years later, during her next pregnancy. "I feel anxious and unusually low-spirited at times," she confessed, "but this perhaps is natural as I shall be far from all my friends except my own dear husband." Undoubtedly Julia's pregnancy heightened her reaction to the situation. Nevertheless, loneliness made her approaching confinement even more intimidating.[16]

Jane Woodruff's case was particularly touching but not unparalleled. Jane's pregnancy was difficult, but her loneliness in childbirth was far more devastating. Jane's labor pains began while her husband was in St. Augustine, Florida, trying to locate a doctor. The baby would not wait for a hired assistant, and Jane had to rely on an "old negro woman out of the field." Jane was unfamiliar with the slave woman, not knowing even her name. A woman who had never before faced childbirth without her mother was virtually alone. Years later, Jane wrote of the desperate hours leading to the newborn's death and of her sense of isolation: "I was the only one awake to listen to the dying moans of my child which were becoming more and more faint; at last they ceased altogether." Jane saw to it that she never endured such an ordeal again. She returned to either St. Augustine or her family's home in Charleston for her subsequent confinements.[17]

Beginning in the 1820s and continuing until the Civil War, families migrated heavily to the Southwest to acquire cheap land and, potentially, riches in the cotton boom. According to the historian James Oakes, planters were obsessed with economic success and with enlarging their holdings of land and slaves. Transience was normal for many

16. Mary Polk Badger to George Badger, October 21, 1825, in Polk, Badger, and McGehee Papers, Southern Historical Collection; Laura Norwood to Julia Howe, March, 1843, in Chiliab Smith Howe Papers, Southern Historical Collection; Julia Howe to Selina Lenoir, January 4, 1845, in Lenoir Family Papers.

17. Jane Woodruff Diary, 1824 (Clarkson Family Papers, Special Collections, J. Murray Atkins Library, University of North Carolina at Charlotte).

antebellum southern families. But what men regarded as a golden opportunity women often found lonely and difficult. Typically, one Alabama woman grieved to her sister, "I can't describe to you my feelings here in this strange country without a house or home, so far separated from my dear friends." Like women in the westward movement of the late 1840s and 1850s, southern women experienced loneliness and hardship in leaving friends and family behind. Many fretted over the scarcity of neighbors and over having to walk several miles to church. Although some eventually adjusted to their isolation, childbirth was a reminder of the need for female companionship. Many women found themselves facing delivery without their principal support group. These had to find assistance within the immediate family or from a slave or a professional, or they had to handle the situation on their own.[18]

Few letters by white women mention the active participation of slaves during parturition except as midwives. Yet domestic servants undoubtedly assisted in the birthing chamber. White women rarely expressed apprehension toward a black woman's presence and sometimes praised the help they received. Ella Clanton Thomas, who was particularly empathic toward her female slaves, noted after one birth, "Aunt Tinsey's presence inspired me with a great deal of confidence." The participation of slaves at childbirth in a capacity other than that of servant was probably inversely proportional to the number in, and reflected the composition of, the group of white females present; in all likelihood it did not reveal racial attitudes. Middle- and upper-class women's letters rarely note a slave's presence. That may be because none was present, because the slave's status made it inappropriate to mention her in a letter, or because the presence of black women was exceedingly common.[19]

18. For a description of the mobility of the southern planter, see James Oakes, *The Ruling Race: A History of American Slaveholders* (New York, 1982), 76–79, 87–88. For information on women in the westward movement, see Johnny Faragher and Christine Stansell, "Women and Their Families on the Overland Trail to California and Oregon, 1842–1867," *Feminist Studies*, II (1975), 150–66; Julie Roy Jeffrey, *Frontier Women: The Trans-Mississippi West, 1840–1880* (New York, 1979); and Lillian Schlissel, *Women's Diaries of the Westward Journey* (New York, 1982). Sarah Fountain to Hannah Coker, December 27, 1835, Carlowville, Alabama, in Fletcher Green (ed.), *The Lides Go South . . . and West: The Record of a Planter Migration in 1835* (Columbia, S.C., 1952), 9.

19. There is surprisingly little mention of slave participation during white women's confinements. Consulted for this study was George P. Rawick's *The American Slave: A Composite Autobiography* (41 vols. and index; Westport, Conn., 1972–81), including supp. 1st ser., I (Alabama), III–IV (Georgia, Parts 1, 2), VI–IX (Mississippi), X (Arkansas), XI (North and South Carolina), and 2nd ser., II–VII (Texas). Ella Clanton Thomas Diary, November 17, 1858.

Of growing importance during the antebellum period was the choice of medical assistant, where circumstances permitted options. The right attendant might ensure the life of both mother and child and could inspire confidence. Privileged southern women, as part of a trend that began in the urban Northeast, gradually turned to male accoucheurs instead of female midwives. But the change occurred slowly in the South, and southern male doctors probably presided at fewer than half the births of middle- and upper-class women in the years immediately before the Civil War. Table I (see Appendix One), which is based on the letters and journals consulted for this study, records the choices of attendant, by type, that a small sample of southern women made. In this sample, doctors by the late antebellum period were still being used in under half the deliveries.

Whether urban women were more likely than plantation mistresses to depend on doctors is unclear. Urban-rural differences do not fall into a tidy pattern. First of all, many southern women did not bear their children in their own home. Second, although many doctors gravitated toward towns, many others were drawn to rural areas by the hope of making a fortune in cotton. Table II shows that in the South in 1850 the ratio of total population (both black and white) to the number of doctors was *lowest* in rural states like Arkansas and Texas. Thus, urban populations did not always have readier access to medical professionals. In some rural areas, doctors were almost a surfeit. Theodore Rosengarten has noted that the wealthy sea island of St. Helena, South Carolina, boasted a doctor for every eight planters. Here parturient women probably had their choice of attendant. (Yet Thomas Chaplin's wife, Mary, used a midwife—perhaps because her husband was perpetually in debt and wished to cut costs or because she preferred an all-female assemblage.) Nor were doctors necessarily plentiful in southern cities. A study by Suzanne Lebsock shows that both midwives and doctors had a lively business in Petersburg, Virginia. That may indicate a shortage of doctors or an abundance of midwives. In 1829, the ratio of residents to doctors in the frontier town of Little Rock, Arkansas, was only 55 : 1. Seven years later, after the community had grown, the ratio was 78 : 1. On the other hand, an older, better-established city, Atlanta, had only nine physicians for its three thousand white residents in 1850, or a ratio of 333 : 1. Professionals were often attracted to areas like Arkansas, where land was cheap and the future looked bright.[20]

20. Rosengarten, *Tombee*, 156. Little Rock statistics; Suzanne Lebsock, *The Free Women of Petersburg: Status and Culture in a Southern Town, 1784–1860* (New York, 1984),

Antebellum advice books give the impression that doctors had the edge over midwives. But prescriptive literature can present a distorted view of reality. Perhaps physicians were more popular in the urban Northeast, but medical accounts, women's diaries, and personal correspondence present a less clear-cut situation in the South. First of all, despite physicians' vitriol against midwives, personal accounts reveal that southern male practitioners frequently cooperated with them during the birthing process or became involved when natural efforts failed. Physicians' cases in the medical journals of the period commonly note the presence of a midwife. In many instances, families first employed a midwife, but when delivery was difficult, or labor protracted, or the woman's or infant's life endangered, the family or the midwife sent for a physician. The male doctor then assumed responsibility but often relied on female attendants or the midwife to assist him. In reality, the midwife was not the ignorant bumpkin so ridiculed in medical dissertations and journals, and it was not unusual for both attendants to be present.

In one way, midwives gained from the ascendancy of doctors. True, many midwives experienced a loss of status and even of earnings. Prevented from seeking training in medical colleges and identified in the public mind with unscientific methods, they in many quarters no longer inspired trust. But doctors afforded midwives a way to withdraw gracefully from difficult situations. One black midwife spoke of the advantages she saw in the change. Her record was now perfect. "Ain't never lost a case," she wrote. "It's cause I used my haid. When I'd go in, I'd take a look at de woman, and if it was beyond me, I'd say 'Dis is a doctor case. Dis ain't no case for a midwife. You git a doctor.'" Smart midwives could now leave to male practitioners difficult cases and those in which failure was likely.[21]

How involved the parturient woman was in any decision to bring in a male accoucheur to assist an attending midwife probably depended on the woman's physical condition and on what influence she could exert. There are instances where women demanded and received the assistance of a male doctor. Probably the impossibility of locating a physician was the most common reason for denying a woman's request.

170; are from John T. Fulton to his father, David Fulton, 1829, in Marion Stark Craig (ed.), *An Anthology of Arkansas Medicine* (Little Rock, Ark., 1975), 9. Atlanta statistics are from "Federal Census of Atlanta, 1850," *Atlanta Historical Bulletin*, VII (1942), 16–68.

21. Dorothy Sterling, *We Are Your Sisters: Black Women in the Nineteenth Century* (New York, 1984), 17. See also Diana S. Perry, "The Early Midwives of Missouri," *Journal of Nurse-Midwifery*, XXVIII (1983), 16; Lebsock, *The Free Women of Petersburg*, 171.

Second, although midwives undoubtedly missed their wealthier clients, a large enough number of babies were being born in the antebellum South to keep both doctors and midwives busy. In some southern cities, the influx of European immigrants in the 1840s and 1850s improved the standing of midwives. Some European women arrived with training in the field, and immigrant women who were accustomed to using female attendants became their patients. Midwifery was a strong competitor until early in the twentieth century.

Slave and free black women played an important role as midwives in the Old South. A former Virginia slave, Mildred Graves, who allowed that she was "what you call a midwife," left an account of one frightening case. A Judge Leake arrived one midnight, desperately seeking Mildred Graves's services of her owner. His wife was in critical condition. "When I got dare she had two doctors from Richmond, but dey won't doin' nothin' fer her," she reported. She attempted to intercede, but the physicians rebuffed her efforts as "witch doctor's or hoodoo stuff" and wanted another professional opinion. Mrs. Leake, in anguish, finally called for Mildred, who for the next seven hours served as midwife. "I did ev'ything I knowed an' some things I didn' know." The newborn weighed only five pounds, but Mildred was able to "fix him up." Mildred received the begrudging praise of the attending doctors and must have achieved a special intimacy with the baby's mother. It would be useful to know how many slave women became midwives, what percentage filled this female occupation, and how often white women relied on slaves' assistance, but such statistics are unavailable.[22]

Race was of small import to middle- and upper-class women when they needed a midwife. Diaries and letters reveal little distress at using a black slave during confinement. White women were grateful to anyone who could ease their pain and render assistance. Some women, like Mrs. Leake, actually preferred a reliable attendant like Mildred. For slave women, the occupation could bring status, independent income, and even some personal latitude within the constraints of slavery. Slaves often benefited psychologically as well, for black midwives could gain a greater sense of confidence and self-worth. Victoria McMillen, a former Louisiana bondswoman, remarked, "In slavery times, my grandma was almost as free as she was in freedom because of her work [as midwife]." White women whose lives and whose infants' lives de-

22. Charles L. Perdue, Jr., Thomas E. Barden, and Robert K. Phillips (eds.), *Weevils in the Wheat: Interviews with Virginia Ex-Slaves* (Charlottesville, Va., 1976), 84.

pended on the ministrations and skill of slaves must have developed a closer relationship with their black servants.[23]

But during the antebellum period, privileged southern women with access to male doctors began to rely on them more often. Many came to prefer the services of a male accoucheur. Some southern women eased their mind by arranging for a male attendant weeks in advance of their due date. The idea was to plan ahead and hope circumstances allowed the preferred attendant to be present. Mrs. Henderson worried, for her doctor had a prior commitment and was unwilling to guarantee his availability. In the end, she had to use a midwife. Though she expressed no dissatisfaction, her disappointment was evident.[24]

Some women were pleasantly surprised by their doctors' skills. Despite the use of heroic remedies and the chance of sepsis, the majority of births were natural. An educated doctor or an experienced midwife could handle most births with ease. In the main, male attendants did little more than their female competitors. Antebellum women expected to suffer during parturition. Pain seemed inevitable, and death was always a possibility, whoever happened to be present. When antebellum doctors employed remedies that now seem unsound or even harmful, southern women may have perceived the physicians' medical efforts as beneficial. Sally Graham Lacy, of Missouri, had traditionally used female attendants, yet when the midwife hired by her husband failed to arrive as expected during one confinement, the family turned to a local physician. Sally's husband noted, "We were obliged to depend on the Doctor and have no reason in the world to regret the circumstance." Sally reacted even more positively. "I have great confidence in Dr. Means," she wrote her mother. "I consider it a great blessing to be so near a Doctor." In 1832, Selina Lenoir wrote of her confinement, "I think I may compare myself to an old Boat which the doctors finding much shattered . . . but without jesting, I think Dr. Jones was of a great deal of service to me, his attention was unremitted and his care of me not to be forgotten." Selina obviously appreciated the care she received from an attentive male physician. Clients frequently showed respect for their doctor's education and solid credentials. Rarely did southern women express their positive sentiments toward a midwife, perhaps because her presence seemed routine and not deserving of comment. Mention of midwives' services usually focused

23. Rawick, *The American Slave*, 1st ser., X (Arkansas), 33.
24. Mary Henderson Diary, July 17, 1855.

on complaints about the bill. A male doctor, on the other hand, gave grounds for boasting.[25]

In practice, the debate over the choice of attendant often proved academic. Pregnant women and doctors rarely predicted due dates accurately. They often based their calculations on false—or misunderstood—assumptions. Babies, then and now, seldom arrived when anticipated, and the unexpected onset of labor could send a family scurrying for whatever medical assistant it could find. Even the best-laid plans had to give way to an importunate infant. The person close at hand was often a slave woman, a neighbor, a husband, or a friend.

The variety in the accoucheurs on whom one woman might depend over the years is evident in the life of Mary Bethell, of Rockingham, North Carolina. For her first baby, born in 1841, a Dr. Cain assisted Mary and bled her profusely. Sucky, the local midwife, helped with the second child. Mrs. Oliver, a white midwife, remained with Mary the entire week before the delivery of the third child. In 1846, another white midwife, Mrs. Ratliff, helped Mary. Three years later, Harriet, one of the domestic servants, was Mary's chief assistant. In 1851, Dr. D'Jarnette appeared for Mary's confinement. Four years later, when Mrs. McKinney, a white midwife, failed to appear, Harriet again officiated. And for the last baby, Mrs. McKinney arrived in time to help. For the births of her children, Mary used two male physicians, a black midwife, a black slave, and three white midwives. In no instance did she lose an infant during confinement. Why she and her family chose the attendants they did is unknown, and what satisfaction she received from the help is also unstated.[26]

The rejection by middle- and upper-class women of female medical assistants in favor of male accoucheurs may seem odd, in that it belies the importance of women's central role in the birthing process. And a significant number of privileged women did prefer to keep parturition an exclusively female event and to regard men as an intrusion. But male accoucheurs were more and more in demand, for practical reasons. The medical profession was growing, and we have seen that doctors had become readily available in some areas. Physicians actively advertised their services as trained accoucheurs and emphasized their education and skills, urging southern women to place labor in their competent

25. William Lacy to Margaret Graham, July 14, 1821, in Graham Family Papers; Selina Lenoir to Selina Louise Lenoir, winter, 1832, in Lenoir Family Papers.
26. Mary Bethell Diary, 1841–1860 (Southern Historical Collection).

hands. Once doctors established their right to practice obstetrics and women accepted the idea of males in the delivery room, it was only a matter of time until men took over.

The acceptance of male doctors at childbirth qualifies the popular belief in the Victorian modesty of the southern woman. Men celebrated southern women for upholding morals and embodying all that was pure and good in southern society. What greater threat to a white woman—beyond the possibility of miscegenation—than to have a male doctor attend labor and offer gynecological treatment? In advice literature, doctors who performed vaginal examinations typically knelt next to layers of petticoats, reaching beneath them with eyes averted to perform their examination solely by touch. Advice books insisted that as a precaution against a doctor's lustful urges during delivery, a female relative or friend be present. Yet southern women, at least in their personal writings, rarely objected to a male doctor's presence. One woman noted after her physician visited, "I allowed him to explore me as much as my timidity would allow." But such comments from women are rare. It is possible, of course, that women were too embarrassed by this intimacy to discuss it in their personal writings.[27]

On the other hand, men were frequently vocal in opposing male involvement in the birthing room. Judge George Badger, often riding the circuit, openly disapproved of his wife's doctor. His uneasiness finally got the better of him, and he wrote urging her to avoid the physician's "further intrusions." Isaac Avery, a North Carolina planter, imputed his own feelings to women. "I know that female delicacy is apt to be shocked at having a physician with them on such occasions," he observed when his sister employed a male doctor to attend her delivery. Southern doctors constantly warned their colleagues of women's "natural modesty" and supposed it the reason many preferred midwives. Yet southern women were gradually accepting male doctors at the same time that society was defining them by their Victorian modesty.[28]

For the explanation of women's desire to use male doctors, one must look beyond the obvious in advice books. Women rarely read medical journals, and hence the arguments there promoting doctors' skills had

27. Lizzie Lenoir to Sallie Lenoir, August 7, 1851, in Lenoir Family Papers.

28. George Badger to Mary Polk Badger, April 17, 1827, in Polk, Badger, and McGehee Papers; Isaac Avery to Thomas Lenoir, March 14, 1823, in Lenoir Family Papers; L. P. Yandell [Y], "Bad Midwifery," *Western Journal of Medicine and Surgery,* 3rd ser., VIII (1851), 182.

little bearing on their decision. Rather, male practitioners gave women something of value that midwives could not provide, especially status. Southern women were impressed by a male physician's position and professional training. Sophia Watson, of Alabama, writing of a friend's confinement, said, "Dr. Webb was her physician and she imagines that she has been managed better than usual. You know he spent a year in Europe—and is expected of course to do better than our every day Doctors." Sophia and her friend obviously held the man's credentials in high esteem. Doctors often enhanced their patients' awe by maintaining an aura of mystery about their medical approach. Physicians urged their colleagues not to reveal professional secrets to their patients or to midwives who might be present.[29]

During the antebellum years, institutional training and a scientific approach to the nation's problems became increasingly important to middle- and upper-class society. A male accoucheur with a degree in hand brought status and professional training into the birthing room. The medical profession laid special claim to authority by associating doctors' remedies with what it claimed to be irrefutable facts and scientific answers. Increasingly, these added to the status as well as the mystery surrounding the profession. In addition, anything male had an implicit air of legitimacy about it, a perception that female midwives had difficulty in overcoming. This was particularly so in the antebellum South, where from birth women had been taught to praise and value masculine skills. By gender alone, physicians had greater authority and status than midwives.[30]

Also important was the fact that women had always regarded pregnancy, parturition, and the postnatal recovery as difficult and unhealthy. The medical profession concurred heartily, by conceiving childbirth as an illness. For southern women, who suffered numerous health problems in achieving motherhood, the perception of the doctors fitted their own notions of childbirth. It placed women in the limelight they desired but rarely achieved except within their maternal and domestic sphere. An entire profession was now eager to attend to their illnesses and improve their situation. Doctors' interest in obstetrics, the development of new instruments and techniques, and extensive writings on the sub-

29. Sophia Watson to her mother, April 12, 1852, in Henry Watson, Jr., Papers; Ann Oakley, *Women Confined: Towards a Sociology of Childbirth* (New York, 1980), 11.
30. Paul Starr, *The Social Transformation of American Medicine* (New York, 1982), 44, 50; Judy Litoff, *American Midwives, 1860 to the Present* (Westport, Conn., 1978), 3.

ject focused attention on an experience that had been taken for granted. Even if the remedies attempted by doctors were occasionally unsound and experimental, the profession was plainly trying its best to improve women's condition and, in the process, expending a great deal of energy and enthusiasm.

Significant, too, were doctors' efforts to adopt a more warmly sensitive approach. In order to secure a place in the birthing chamber, antebellum doctors had to assume some of the very characteristics that were deemed feminine. Women in labor needed and desired tenderness and understanding, particularly as they entrusted their bodies and the fate of their unborn babies to a male doctor. Antebellum physicians gradually adopted what we now refer to as a "bedside manner," believing women would more likely accept male attention if it resembled the care they had traditionally received from midwives and female attendants. Warrington was well aware of this need and urged his colleagues to keep the expectant mother calm and optimistic. He noted that it was a doctor's responsibility to "offer candidly all reasonable prospects of a happy and safe delivery." S. C. Webster, an eager southern medical student, observed that a physician's first duty was to charm female patients by his faith, skill, and confidence. A South Carolina student, William Babcock, maintained that a physician's charm was just as important as his professional abilities. He believed that obstetric duties "call not only for great professional skill but also for a display of that gentlemanly decorum and those soothing attentions, so grateful to the suffering patient." If male doctors were to supplant midwives and eventually even the female support system, it was essential to provide an empathic posture and establish a personal, but professional, relationship with the patient. "The physician who clearly understands these duties, and who at the same time displays the courtesy and feeling which should characterize the true gentleman, will gain the good-will and gratitude of the weaker sex," Babcock noted. Southern women undoubtedly found a sensitive, understanding male very appealing.[31]

If women generally expressed positive reactions to their male doctors, they also left their female support systems intact, and few antebellum doctors were imperious enough to challenge the important

31. Warrington, *The Obstetric Catechism,* 149; S. C. Webster, "A Thesis on Obstetrical Instruments" (1858), in Waring Historical Library Annex, Medical University of South Carolina, Charleston; William Babcock, "Management of Natural Labour" (1852), in Waring Historical Library, Medical University of South Carolina, Charleston.

tradition of the feminine presence in the birthing chamber. In fact, some physicians urged their colleagues to accommodate the patient's customs rather than force her to adjust to the physician's needs. "Be in the sick room as little as possible," urged Babcock, "and afford her opportunities of enjoying unrestrained conversation with her friends." Babcock suggested also that his colleagues keep their instruments out of sight to avoid alarming the parturient woman. Dr. Alva Curtis, a botanist, advised that the physician remain outside the birthing room until his services were needed. As intruders into the process, doctors still felt a certain diffidence.[32]

Religion played an important role for the woman during childbirth. Church membership gave southern women an acceptable way to channel their energy and talents outside the home. On a more personal level, a belief in God imparted to women the emotional strength that is especially needed during childbirth. Everyone involved in a woman's confinement recognized that God was responsible for the outcome.[33]

The prayers and blessings of people close to the expectant woman asked that she might be spared intense pain and, more important, survive her ordeal. Adelle Allston's aunt wrote her niece days before her confinement, urging her to "Pray the Lord, to Put his Everlasting Arm to strengthen and support You and quickly to relieve you from your Sorrow and Misery." Ann Rutherford received similar encouragement from an aunt who begged her to "put your trust in God and have no fear of the result." Southern women approached each confinement hoping that God could sustain them. Lucilla McCorkle, of Alabama, whose religious intensity bred constant self-scrutiny, professed to feel little anxiety because she relied on God. Prior to one delivery she noted in her journal, "No forebodings for the crisis before me. I feel that I am in the hands of a merciful friend." Her attitude may seem unusually morbid, or simply wistful. Yet most southern women knew similar feelings during at least one, and usually all, of their confinements.[34]

32. Babcock, "Management of Natural Labour"; Alva Curtis, *Lecture on Midwifery and the Forms of Disease Peculiar to Women and Children* (2nd ed.; Columbus, Ohio, 1841), 38.

33. For a discussion of religion and southern women, see Donald G. Mathews, *Religion in the Old South* (Chicago, 1977); Anne C. Loveland, *Southern Evangelicals and the Social Order, 1800–1860* (Baton Rouge, 1980); and Jean E. Friedman, *The Enclosed Garden: Women and Community in the Evangelical South, 1830–1900* (Chapel Hill, N.C., 1985).

34. Elizabeth F. Blythe to Adelle Allston, December 31, 1834, in Allston Family Papers, South Carolina Historical Society Library, Charleston; W. W. Roy to Ann Rutherfoord, July, 1857, in John Rutherford Collection, Manuscript Department, William R.

If the delivery proved successful, southern women believed that God's intervention had been decisive. Even when labor was difficult or painful, they did not reproach God but accorded him credit for sparing their lives. Certainly it would have seemed foolhardy to ignore God's power and benevolence so long as other confinements were to follow. Mrs. Bethell evaluated each of her seven successful deliveries with a fair degree of feminine perspective and celebrated God's blessings. After the birth of her third child, she wrote, "The Lord was with me at the birth of the child and gave me a safe and speedy delivery, thanks and praise to his holy name, he is my best friend, he has been with me in many trials." Isabel Fraser, of Beaufort, South Carolina, recalled, "The Lord has been very merciful to me. My travail, though severe and of longer duration than ever before experienced, I have been safely carried through it." Mrs. Bumpas was similarly joyful and felt that God deserved praise for his part in her relatively easy delivery. "Through the mercy and kindness of the Lord," she noted, "my life has been prolonged, my sufferings comparatively light, and my health soon restored and I am blessed with a little daughter." Notwithstanding her illness for four days preceding the delivery, God received full credit for the happy outcome.[35]

During another confinement, Mrs. Bethell had a speedy, three-hour delivery, but for ten days afterward, she was extremely sick with chills, fever, stomach pains, and cough. Feeling that she had only herself to blame, she confessed, "I felt like I did not have enough religion." Often a woman attributed a painful delivery to her own inadequacy or her failure properly to express belief in God. On the whole, women gave more credit to God than to their attendants. For all that doctors touted their education and their scientific understanding of the birthing process, the greater number of southern mothers did not see it that way. They may have preferred male doctors as attendants, but it was through the strength of their religion and God's beneficent nature that they had survived.[36]

Male family members seemed to share this conviction. In 1846, Ruffin wrote his son-in-law describing Anne's experiences during la-

Perkins Library; Lucilla Gamble McCorkle Diary, December, 1847 (Southern Historical Collection).

35. Mary Bethell Diary, 1844, p. 7; Isabel Fraser to her mother-in-law in a footnote, July 24, 1824, in Mary De Saussure Fraser Collection, Manuscript Department, William R. Perkins Library; Frances Bumpas Journal, May 14, 1844.

36. Mary Bethell Diary, January 25, 1855.

bor. "It was a period of suffering and apprehension on the part of our dear daughter, and of much anxiety among her friends around her," he related, "but . . . God in our time mercifully granted her a safe deliverance." A man seemingly preoccupied with power, he was willing all the same to credit the Deity with Anne's success. Similarly, Thomas Mann Randolph, of Virginia, expressed his "sincere thanks to God that my daughter has passed over the critical and dangerous period in safety." God was always present in the birthing room and was roundly praised for a success. When the outcome proved unhappy, Southerners could draw on their belief that death would bring a far better future for mother or child. John Wilson wrote in his medical dissertation that this idea served doctors well. If medical treatment failed, he observed, "how good it is to know that death is but a transit from Earth to Heaven—but a happy Eternity." Death could be consoling if one believed that a far better world was to follow. Religion could mitigate women's fears and provide strength during a tentative and painful experience.[37]

37. Thomas Ruffin to Duncan Cameron, April 18, 1846, in Cameron Family Papers; Thomas Mann Randolph to his son-in-law Francis Asbury Dickins, March 17, 1844, in Francis A. Dickins Papers, Southern Historical Collection; John Wilson, "Pregnancy as a Complication of Disease," Dissertation for the Medical College of South Carolina (1843), in Waring Historical Library Annex.

4 *In Sorrow Does She Bring Forth*

MEDICAL CONCERNS OF CHILDBIRTH

Behold amidst the youthful bloom of life
The tender mother, the beloved wife
To death's unalterable call attends
And dies lamented by her numerous friends.
Her infant child had just received its breath
When to the parent mother sinks in death
Survivors, all this solemn lesson read
Prepare this life to rest among the dead.

This epitaph in a southern cemetery poignantly brings out what child-birth often meant for antebellum southern mothers.[1] Although the inscription was written at the close of the eighteenth century, it reflects the reality that surrounded childbirth throughout the antebellum years: the possibility of death for the parturient woman. More often, poor health or debilitation followed delivery and altered the way mothers led their lives. In the latter part of the twentieth century, with its obstetrical care and its medical control of sepsis, convulsions, and hemorrhaging, as well as its procedures for complicated births, it is easy to forget that childbirth in the antebellum period entailed much suffering and a high mortality rate.

During the first half of the nineteenth century, doctors focused upon alleviating women's sufferings. Whether they employed heroic thera-pies, water cures, or botanic medicines, they launched a major cam-paign to prove themselves indispensable in the birthing room. Their procedures, often impeding nature, may have promoted morbidity and mortality.[2] Despite the physicians' claims to superior knowledge and

1. Ann M. Gin tombstone, dated 1797, in Hopewell Presbyterian Church Cemetery, Mecklenburg County, North Carolina.
2. See Wyndham Bolling Blanton, *Medicine in Virginia in the Nineteenth Century* (Richmond, 1931); Judith A. Chaney, "Birthing in Early America," *Journal of Nurse-*

skills, their medical efforts rarely improved a woman's overall physical condition, and whatever benefits occurred were probably due to luck or a sound constitution.

Doctors were prone to overestimating their capabilities, owing to their limited knowledge of diseases and of the process of labor. Often inexperienced, poorly trained, and overanxious, they might interfere prematurely or administer harmful drugs. Infecting the patient was always a possibility, because hands and instruments frequently went unwashed and street clothes were worn by the physician attending delivery. In the South, bloodletting continued. It was employed in emergency situations, as a means to lessen pain, and occasionally, even to handle routine deliveries. The remedies doctors attempted in childbirth could be as heroic as any others of the antebellum period, and physicians too often lost the patients they were trying hardest to save. The surprise is the number of southern women who survived their ordeal and continued to bear children.

In spite of the central role that childbirth played in southern women's lives, few women chronicled their confinements. Their silence is understandable, because, probably, most wished to forget the experience, put pain and suffering behind, and move ahead to the joys and demands of caring for the newborn. Babies required full-time nurturing, and maternal responsibilities left mothers little time or energy for writing. Ella Clanton Thomas, like other southern women whose diary entries and letters became sporadic during the busy years of child rearing, commented that "housekeeping and married life are not compatible with keeping journals."[3] Other mothers were too ill or exhausted after labor to write. Anyway, to dwell on the details of childbirth may have been embarrassing to feminine sensibilities. Consequently, there are only scattered personal comments, which leave incomplete impressions. But even so, the few accounts to be found in letters, diaries, and doctors' records offer evidence enough of the sorrowful and painful aspects of the experience.

Midwifery, XXV (1980), 5–13; Joseph Kett, *The Formation of the American Medical Profession: The Role of Institutions, 1780–1860* (New Haven, 1968; Westport, Conn., 1980); Catherine M. Scholten, *Childbearing in American Society, 1650–1850* (New York, 1985); and Edward Shorter, "Maternal Sentiment and Death in Childbirth: A New Agenda for Psycho-Medical History," in Patricia Branca (ed.), *The Medicine Show: Patients, Physicians, and Perplexities of the Health Revolution in Modern Society* (New York, 1977), 67–88.

3. Ella Clanton Thomas Diary, November 14, 1858 (Manuscript Department, William R. Perkins Library, Duke University).

Census information demonstrates that childbirth was associated with high maternal mortality in the antebellum period. Difficulties in parturition proved to be a major cause of death during women's most vital years, and maternal mortality rates of women between twenty and forty years old were invariably high. What is more, the South experienced a higher maternal mortality rate than the northeastern region of the country did (see Table III in Appendix One). The 1850 federal census was the only statistical effort during the antebellum period to separate mortality figures by race and cause of death. Childbearing for all antebellum women was risky. But as the census figures reveal, at least one out of twenty-five white women in the South who died in 1850 died in childbirth, twice the maternal mortality rate in the New England and Middle Atlantic states.

There are a number of possible explanations of why southern women were more likely to die as a result of childbirth. The South was an unhealthy place for all residents. The historians Anita Rutman, Darrett Rutman, and Daniel Blake Smith have shown in their studies of the colonial Chesapeake that the region was from its initial settlement unhealthy for white settlers. As early as the seventeenth century, New England residents lived on average approximately twenty years longer than people of the Chesapeake. By the antebellum period, malaria, dysentery, and a host of fevers were endemic in the South, for the region's milder winters had less effect in killing disease-carrying organisms. Settlement patterns and new strains of malaria probably worsened the situation by the nineteenth century. Furthermore, antebellum southern women bore more children than women living in the Northeast. They thus put their lives at risk more often. Whether the southern medical profession was inferior to the northern is not clear—particularly since many southern doctors had trained in the North. But the continuing commitment of southern doctors to heroics may have contributed something to the region's mortality rates.[4]

4. Darrett B. Rutman and Anita H. Rutman, "Of Agues and Fevers: Malaria in the Early Chesapeake," *William and Mary Quarterly*, XXXIII (1976), 31–60. For a discussion of southern climate and related health problems, see Kenneth Kiple and Virginia Himmelsteib King, *Another Dimension to the Black Diaspora: Diet, Disease, and Racism* (New York, 1981); Richard H. Shryock, "Medical Practices in the Old South," in *Medicine in America: Historical Essays* (Baltimore, 1966), 56; Daniel Blake Smith, "Mortality and Family in the Colonial Chesapeake," *Journal of Interdisciplinary History*, III (1978), 403–27; and Lois Green Carr and Lorena S. Walsh, "The Planter's Wife: The Experience of White Women in Seventeenth-Century Maryland," *William and Mary Quarterly*, XXXIV (1977),

Southerners clearly realized the chanciness of childbirth. Few had access to census information, but almost all were aware of the impressionistic evidence or had firsthand knowledge of the risk. Tombstones throughout the region corroborated the general perception. In one well-preserved North Carolina cemetery, epitaphs on simple slate stones preserve the memories of mothers and often of their children:

> Sacred to the memory of
> Mary Adaline Patterson
> who departed this life
> on the 9th of May 1825
> aged 20 years 6 months 10 days
> also her infant
> who lies by her side

> In memory of Elizabeth A. Tagbet
> who died December 16 1846
> aged 40 years 2 months 20 days
> and an infant babe aged 5 days

How these mothers and unnamed infants died is not told. Perhaps the Tagbet and Patterson infants succumbed for lack of maternal nourishment; perhaps the Patterson child was stillborn. Their mothers, like so many others, may have suffered from infection, hemorrhage, prolonged labor, placenta previa, or convulsions.

In other cases, only an infant's adjacent tombstone reveals the cause of a woman's death. One stone bears the inscription,

> M. E. Parks
> consort of G. D. Parks
> died January 3 1853
> aged 24 years 8 months 12 days,

and next to that a stone, much smaller, reads,

> William
> born January 3
> died April 12.

Elsewhere a slate carries the words,

542–71. For an interesting discussion on the uniqueness of the southern climate, see A. Cash Koeniger, "Climate and Southern Distinctiveness," *Journal of Southern History*, LIV (1988), 21–44.

> Sacred to the memory of Susanna Stitt
> consort of N. M. Stitt
> departed December 29 1845
> in the 36th year of her age,

and beside it a stone commemorates young Susanna, fondly named for her dead mother, who died in August, 1846, when only eight months old.[5]

Obituaries in newspapers also disclosed the frequency of maternal death, though rarely did death notices record specific causes. In the Hillsboro (North Carolina) *Recorder,* a notice stated that Mrs. Harriet Bruce, mother of six, perished after bearing a baby three weeks earlier. The *Arkansas Gazette* carried an obituary of Mrs. Ichabod Dunn, who lost her newborn and then died the following day. The Charleston *Gazette* noted that a nineteen-year-old woman, Mary Dale, died "and left her first child of about two hours and an affectionate husband to lament their loss." In each case, it is no far-fetched surmise that the difficulties of childbirth caused the death.[6]

In personal correspondence, Southerners unhesitantly shared news of friends and relatives who died as a result of their confinements. In letters, as in journal entries chronicling local news, one of the most recurrent themes is the death of a woman in childbirth. Catherine Holmes, of Wilmington, North Carolina, curtly described a friend's demise: "For two hours after her birth she was very well and the next morning at 7 o'clock she was a corps[e]." Walter Lenoir learned that an acquaintance, Lu Derrick, "died on the 9th of February leaving an infant son only a week old," and he sadly added, "Less than a year since, she was a joyous bride." In a single journal entry, Thomas Chaplin, of South Carolina, noted the deaths of three women in childbirth. One of the most telling, but not atypical, comments came from Eliza Clitherall, who recorded her own daughter's death in childbirth. "On the 30th my blessed Gena was confin'd of a little boy—on the 2nd of Dec'r her chastin'd spirit took its flight," she wrote. "Another sad call to our family to 'Prepare'—this is the third member of our family who has in the past few months died in childbirth." Remarks such as these

5. Tombstones in Providence Presbyterian Church Cemetery, Mecklenburg County, North Carolina.

6. Hillsboro (N.C.) *Recorder,* October 30, 1842, p. 3; James Logan Morgan (comp.), *Marriages, Deaths, and Other Notices in the Arkansas Gazette, 1819–1825* (Newport, Ark., 1971), 6; *South Carolina Historical and Genealogical Magazine,* XXVIII (January, 1927), 48.

sprinkle the pages of southern correspondence and diaries. Parturition was a cause of maternal death well acknowledged in cemeteries, newspapers, census figures, and letters.[7]

The ever-present thought of death and the fear of suffering affected women's composure regarding childbirth. Foreboding and uneasiness in some cases made for a more painful and dangerous confinement. Recent studies confirm that tension during the last trimester of pregnancy can lead to a higher incidence of labor complications, including hemorrhaging, preeclampsia, prolonged labor, and a poor fetal state.[8] Antebellum southern women had no regular prenatal care or childbirth education courses to prepare themselves physically and psychologically for labor. Family members and friends soothed, sympathized, and offered helpful advice. But by talking at length of their sufferings and of the risk of death, women fueled much apprehension.

Notwithstanding the joys of having a newborn and the importance that motherhood conferred upon women, their reactions to childbirth were rarely positive. Immediately after labor, when a mother might have been expected to bask in the good fortune of being alive and having a healthy child, enthusiasm was rare. Jane Petigru, of South Carolina, noted that a friend "had an excellent time, and has one of the largest boys I ever saw." But she added, almost apologetically, "She is not looking so well now." In 1811, the Reverend William Turner of North Carolina described the confinement of his wife Nancy as an "easy time"

7. Catherine Holmes to Elizabeth Holmes Blanks, June 1, 1837, in Elizabeth Holmes Blanks Letters, Manuscript Department, William R. Perkins Library; Walter Lenoir's sister to him, March 1, 1859, in Lenoir Family Papers, Southern Historical Collection, L. R. Wilson Library, University of North Carolina at Chapel Hill; Theodore Rosengarten, *Tombee: Portrait of a Cotton Planter* (New York, 1986), 569; Eliza Clitherall Autobiography and Diary, December 5, 1851 (Southern Historical Collection).

8. For information on stress and its complications, see Alex J. Crandon, "Maternal Anxiety and Obstetric Complications," *Journal of Psychosomatic Research*, XXIII (1979), 109–11; Neils C. Beck, "The Prediction of Pregnancy Outcome: Maternal Preparation, Anxiety, and Attitudinal Sets," *Journal of Psychosomatic Research*, XXIV (1980), 343–53; Lawrence Klusman, "Reduction of Pain in Childbirth by the Alleviation of Anxiety During Pregnancy," *Journal of Consulting and Clinical Psychology*, XLIII (1975), 162–65; B. Areskog, "Experience of Delivery in Women with and Without Antenatal Fear of Childbirth," *Gynecologic and Obstetric Investigation*, XVI (1983), 1–12; Ellen A. Farber, "The Relationship of Prenatal Maternal Anxiety to Life," *Early Human Development*, V (1981), 267–77; Ronald Melzack, "Labour Is Still Painful After Prepared Childbirth Training," *Canadian Medical Association Journal*, CXXV (1981), 357–63; and Mireille Laget, "Childbirth in Seventeenth- and Eighteenth-Century France: Obstetrical Practices and Collective Attitudes," in Robert Forster and E. Orest Ranum (eds.), *Medicine and Society in France: Selections from the Annales—Economies, Sociétés, Civilisations* (6 vols.; Baltimore, 1975–80), VI, 137–76.

but added that "she was taken with fainting fits, but by the timely arrival of my family physician, she is now quite well and in good spirits." Anne Cameron concluded that childbirth had in one case finally proved beneficial. "Your Cousin Phebe's health is better since the birth of her tenth child," she wrote to a relative in 1838, "than it has been for a great many years." This was indeed a telling comment about a woman who had endured years of suffering and finally achieved good health. Since these assessments were by observers rather than participants, they were probably rosier than the reality. Women expected to suffer during parturition, and it was unusual to endure a confinement with relative ease. Far more typical were women who experienced and recorded their difficulties. Southern women who had been ill during pregnancy might find their problems compounded during delivery. A physical ailment, a lingering illness, malaria, or improper medical attention could magnify their difficulties.[9]

Relatives of Mary Ann Gwynn described her as an "invalid" who had experienced "a great many back setts" with "distressing pains and nervous affections" during and after labor. Her family remained convinced that an overdose of mercury prescribed by her physician during pregnancy caused her distressing confinement. Mary Ann's two sisters, Laura and Sarah, who attended the unfortunate woman for six months, were "nearly broken down by long and intense watching." One commented on the situation several weeks after Mary Ann's delivery. "I hope her present situation is owing only to her being so very weak before the birth of the child," Laura Norwood wrote. After three months of attentive nursing, Mary Ann and her baby finally returned home. Even then, Mary Ann felt anything but confident about her health, and she confessed, "I never know what it is to feel well an hour. . . . I still manage to keep up all day pretty much but when night comes I am tired almost to death and sometimes so stupid that I feel as if I had no sense at all." She eventually recovered a semblance of her former self and gave birth to another infant a year and a half later. Mary Ann had entered her confinement afflicted by illness and overmedication, and she suffered long afterward.[10]

9. Jane Petigru to Adelle Allston, April 30, 1834, in Allston Family Papers, South Carolina Historical Society Library, Charleston; Rev. William Turner to Mrs. Phebe Caruthers, February 17, 1811, in Graham Family Papers, Manuscript Department, William R. Perkins Library; Anne Cameron to Margaret Cameron, March 6, 1838, in Cameron Family Papers, Southern Historical Collection.

10. Selina Lenoir to Betsy Lenoir, November 8, 1841 (first and second quotations); Polly Summey to Selina Lenoir, December 5, 1841, Laura Lenoir Norwood to Selina

Julia Pickens Howe related a dramatic case of a woman whose ill health in pregnancy had a profound effect on her confinement and led to her death. Julia's pregnant sister, Ann Eliza Jewell, and her husband suffered from diarrhea so severe that attending physicians realized they could do nothing to help. The doctors recommended a trip to a healing spring as the couple's only hope. The visit to the spring, however, achieved nothing. On the Jewells' journey home, labor pains forced a stop in La Grange, Georgia, where Ann Eliza bore her child prematurely. Jewell, despite his own poor health, left his wife to her recovery and returned to their plantation to attend to domestic matters. "My dear sister had been declining gradually from the time of her confinement," Julia related, "and was then so weak she could scarcely turn herself in bed." Aware that she was dying and desiring the comfort of her husband and friends, Ann Eliza set out for home with her newborn "if it was but to take one look farewell and then die." When their boat docked in St. Louis, a physician on board ordered Ann Eliza to be moved to a private home. Julia rushed to her sister's bedside, only to watch her kiss her baby farewell and expire. Ann Eliza's husband never saw his wife again, for he died on his journey to retrieve her. Childbirth proved too much for a body weakened by prolonged illness.[11]

Other women experienced healthier pregnancies, but labor brought suffering anyway. Many southern mothers described their confinements as "dreadful" or painful "beyond my expectations." Problems could continue long after delivery even for a woman who had an untroubled pregnancy. Sarah McCulloch wrote to her friend Rebecca Cameron three months after her confinement. "One well day is more than I have had since her birth but I am satisfied at having recovered so far which is more than was ever expected," she noted. "For a fortnight after and three days before her birth each day was thought to be my last but by the assistance of that all merciful God whose name you so often call, I hope I shall soon be perfectly well but never expect to wear that appearance of health which was once my happy lot for never was there a constitution more injured than mine." Sarah's stream-of-consciousness writing may lend additional credence to her difficulties. She remained convinced that her confinement destroyed her health. Some women,

Lenoir, February 6, 1842, Mary Ann Gwynn to Selina Lenoir, April 25, 1842, all in Lenoir Family Papers.

11. Julia Pickens Howe to her uncle Thomas Lenoir, October 25, 1844, in Lenoir Family Papers.

like Mary Chaplin, of South Carolina, never recovered their health but remained partial invalids after bearing a child. Mary had to leave her domestic duties in her sister's care and was never able to fill her maternal role.[12]

Frightening medical problems—such as convulsions or hemorrhages during or shortly after delivery—caused family and physicians enormous concern. Few personal accounts of these medical problems exist, perhaps because hardly any of the affected women lived to tell their own tale. Puerperal convulsions usually resulted in the death of the mother, and often of the fetus. Mary Fraser wrote her mother from Lansford, South Carolina, of "one of the most melancholy and solemn events" she had witnessed, the death of a friend, Mrs. Jones, who went into premature labor after several weeks' illness. "On Friday morn she went into strong convulsions. We staid with her until Sunday evening. . . . There was no hope for her, the child had come into the world." Mrs. Jones had several more fits, and by Wednesday, "we found her with death in every feature." The poor woman held hands with both her husband and Mary "until she become insensible"; she died that night "without a struggle or a groan." Doctors, uncertain how to stop convulsions, resorted to dramatic medical interventions. One Tennessee physician thought he had discovered a successful procedure. In a case of puerperal convulsions, he opened orifices in the woman's arms and temporal arteries and bled "until the convulsions ceased or as long as the blood would flow." He urged his colleagues to drain no less than sixty ounces of blood and, in order to speed the process along, to pierce the jugular vein. Doctors who followed his instructions mentioned occasional success.[13]

Hemorrhaging was also a threat immediately prior to delivery or

12. Sarah McCulloch to Rebecca Cameron, August 24, 1809, in Cameron Family Papers; Rosengarten, *Tombee,* 168–72.

13. Mary Fraser to her mother, Mary, October 12, 1833, in Mary De Saussure Fraser Collection, Manuscript Department, William R. Perkins Library; William P. Hort, "Report of the Committee on Midwifery and the Diseases of Children," *New Orleans Medical and Surgical Journal,* II (1845), 513. The Tennessee doctor was George Thompson, of Jefferson ("Cases of Puerperal Convulsions," *Western Journal of Medicine and Surgery,* 3rd ser., VIII [1851], 340–43); a physician who followed his advice was Benjamin C. Drury ("A Case of Puerperal Convulsions Relieved by Bloodletting," *Western Journal of Medicine and Surgery,* 3rd ser., IX [1852], 15–16). See also "Hypertensive Disorders in Pregnancy," in Jack Pritchard, Paul C. MacDonald, and Norman F. Grant, *Williams Obstetrics* (17th ed.; Norwalk, Conn., 1985), 525–56. For nineteenth-century cases during childbirth, see Richard H. Thomas, "Cases in Midwifery," *North American Archives of Medical and Sur-*

during the third stage of labor, when the placenta was expelled. It also could occur postpartum, owing to lacerations of the birth canal by obstetrical instruments, retention of pieces of the placenta, or inadequate contraction of the uterus. Mary Ann Gwynn, who was fortunate to suffer only a mild case, remarked after the birth of her second baby that she sat up briefly "but was afterwards threatened with hemorrhage." The doctor recommended horizontal rest. She bled again the following day but recovered within two weeks. Nancy Pettigrew gave birth to a baby girl, but when her placenta would not dislodge, she suffered severe hemorrhaging. The midwife, Mrs. Brickhouse, tried to detach her placenta manually, causing the poor woman to scream repeatedly, "O, Mrs. Brickhouse, you will kill me." The midwife eventually ceased her efforts and ran from the room crying and praying, in such distress that she fainted. Nancy bled violently for six more hours before she died in her husband's arms.[14]

Antebellum southern doctors resorted to dramatic expedients in these cases of "flooding." Several physicians suggested applying cold water or ice to the abdomen or vagina. Dr. Thomas Ewell, of Virginia, recommended that the accoucheur place cold rags on a woman's stomach and in the "birth place." Cold water could be forced into the womb with a syringe or poured "unhesitatingly" upon the woman's abdomen. Several medical advisers suggested that in resistant cases, the doctor might insert a bag of snow or ice into the womb. The idea had practical merit: if snow or ice was available, it would constrict the blood vessels. But it might also be dirty, increasing the risk of sepsis. William Potts Dewees, ever faithful in his advocacy of bloodletting, felt that bleeding a hemorrhaging woman was best. He believed it to benefit the patient by "unloading the vessels; and more especially, in diminishing the velocity of the blood within them." It would be hard to argue with his conclusion. Other physicians felt that bleeding would cause a

gical Science, II (April, 1835), 22; Z. P. Landrum, "Fatal Case of Puerperal Convulsions," *Southern Medical and Surgical Journal,* X (1854), 162; Samuel Bard, *A Compendium of the Theory and Practice of Midwifery* (New York, 1807), 147; and Joseph Eve, "Cases of Convulsions and Other Nervous Affections," *Southern Medical and Surgical Journal,* III (1847), 513.

14. James Gwynn to Sarah Lenoir, January 28, 1844, in Lenoir Family Papers; Ebenezer Pettigrew Account, June 30, 1830, in Pettigrew Papers, Southern Historical Collection.

woman to become unconscious and in that way would hasten clotting of her blood.[15]

Another problem for a number of parturient southern women was the abnormally large size of the babies they bore. Cephalopelvic disproportion can intensify and prolong labor, increase the chance of stretching and tearing the cervix, and augment the risk of sepsis and maternal and fetal death. Doctors know today that particularly heavy babies are more common when women develop a form of diabetes during pregnancy. The fetus absorbs blood sugar from the mother, creating its own fat and growing larger than normal. The number of times large infants are mentioned in letters and other records is striking. Perhaps their size was unusual, generating a sense of paternal pride and therefore eliciting written comment more often than normal births. Fathers frequently wrote of a heavy newborn, and doctors' account books include notations of "large" babies. Descriptions of difficult deliveries many times accompanied the claims of remarkable size. Paul Cameron, of North Carolina, expressed delight with his son, a "buster" of prodigious size at twelve pounds, but he also added that his wife's labor was "long and protracted." He gave an account. "From 12 last night to 7 this morning she suffered as much as ordinarily falls to the lot of poor woman. She became much excited and alarmed." He added that Anne suffered "much from the after pains; the Doctor is attempting to put her under the influence of opium." Paul, too, was exhausted by the experience and confessed, "It is no little relief to me that it is over." Frederick Fraser, of Beaufort, South Carolina, boasted that his wife, Isabel, delivered "as big a Boy as you ever saw" but added that she had a "severe time." Isabel, who was only too glad to be alive, added a postscript to the letter, describing her confinement as "severe and of longer duration than ever before experienced." One can guess the suffering of other southern women, who noted babies ranging from ten to over thirteen pounds.[16]

---

15. Thomas Ewell, *Letters to Ladies, Detailing Important Information, Concerning Themselves and Infants* (Philadelphia, 1817), 125; William Potts Dewees, *A Compendious System of Midwifery* (Philadelphia, 1828), 377; Professor Bedford, "Uterine Hemorrhage," *New Orleans Medical and Surgical Journal,* I (1844), 91; *Southern Medical and Surgical Journal,* XIII (1857), 170; N. U. Smith, "Puerperal Hemorrhage," Dissertation 399 (1858), in Vanderbilt University Medical Center Library.

16. Information from Pritchard, MacDonald, and Grant, *Williams Obstetrics,* 598–

Internal damage to reproductive organs could produce long-term negative effects. Fallen wombs were common, a part of the aftermath of frequent and complicated deliveries and improper medical attention. Laura Norwood's condition deteriorated after her child was born, with fevers, chills, headaches, and severe pain her initial complaints. More than two weeks after delivery, her anxious husband, Joseph, wrote his mother-in-law, "representing Laura's case as being so serious, that her friends here and the Doctor thought it advisable that you should come down immediately to see her." The older woman, who had been unable to attend her daughter's confinement, still did not appear, and three weeks later Laura finally described her problem: "I am suffering from that most weakening complaint of a falling down of the womb which was probably brought on by those violent pains." She added that she could neither sit nor walk and that she had to use a daily injection of oak bark and alum to loosen her bowels. The doctor planned to strengthen her with daily dousings of cold water and suggested that she wear a "plaster of Burgandy pitch" on the small of her back. Two months after the baby's birth, Laura remarked that she still had not ventured downstairs, and her high fever and headaches continued. "I was bled pretty freely and took a dose of calomel . . . leaving me a good deal weakened," she remarked. Four months after delivery, Laura noticed some improvement but added, "I feel weak and good-for-nothing though I am never to say sick." Like other women who suffered fallen wombs, Laura resorted to bed rest and probably wore a pessary to hold her uterus in place. Although her disability impaired her effectiveness domestically, it did not keep her from bearing additional children.[17]

604; and Dr. William MacDonald, an obstetrician and gynecologist in Charlotte, North Carolina (interview). Paul Cameron to Duncan Cameron, November 23, 1850, in Cameron Family Papers; Frederick Fraser to Mrs. Fraser, July 23, 1840, in Mary De Saussure Fraser Collection. For other examples of large babies, see Virginia Campbell Shelton to William Campbell, May 13, 1856, in Campbell Family Letters, Manuscript Department, William R. Perkins Library; Mary Davenport to William Davenport, August 18, 1820, Israel Pickens to William Lenoir, January 29, 1820, both in Lenoir Family Papers.

17. Joseph Norwood to Selina Lenoir, April 9, 1837, Laura Norwood to Selina Lenoir, May 11, 1837, end of May, 1837, all in Lenoir Family Papers. Pessaries, which were the common solution for a fallen womb, could cause infection. For nineteenth-century information on fallen wombs, see Alfred G. Hall, *Womanhood: Causes of Its Premature Decline* (2nd ed.; Rochester, N.Y., 1845); Daniel H. Whitney, *The Family Physician and Guide to Health in Three Parts* (New York, 1833); and Hort, "Report of the Committee," 514. See also Sarah Stage, *Female Complaints: Lydia Pinkham and the Business of Women's Medicine* (New York, 1979), and Richard W. Wertz and Dorothy C. Wertz, *Lying In: A History of Childbirth in America* (New York, 1977), 110.

Malaria was another danger for southern women during and after childbirth. For the most part, it did its harm by causing debilitation and a susceptibility to other diseases. Yet in at least one case, a southern woman held malaria directly responsible for a friend's death during her confinement. Mary Fraser, of Charleston, noted that a townswoman, Mrs. Gaillard, was struck by the "fever which strangers die of." The Gaillards, following a common strategy, had tried to avoid the disease by leaving the lowlands during the hot season. But as a result, the immunities they had acquired were attenuated, and thus, "from not having it in her power to spend the summer in town," Mrs. Gaillard contracted a severe case of the disease when she returned to Charleston late in her pregnancy. She "expir'd the moment after she gave birth to her infant, which is alive." Southerners recognized that the discomforts of a hot, humid summer were often preferable to the risk of losing their seasoning, and Mrs. Gaillard was especially vulnerable because of the immunosuppression of the final trimester. Whether malaria, such as the most deadly form, *Plasmodium falciparum,* was really the cause of her death is uncertain. Doctors today are still unsure what impact malaria has on the parturient woman. But in several instances, women contracted "fever and ague" during the postnatal recovery period and complained of poor health for weeks. The symptoms of malaria at the least increased the discomforts of labor, produced a susceptibility to other diseases, and lengthened the mother's recovery period.[18]

Prolonged, often unnamed ailments and a weakened physical condition were a normal sequel to parturition. Several months might pass before a woman regained her health and energy and emerged from bed. Jean Syme, of Virginia, had a baby in early January but wrote four months later, "My strength returns so slowly that I sometimes feel I shall never be strong again." Her doctor finally recommended a trip to the coast to hasten her recovery. After one birth, Anne Cameron had difficulty regaining good health. Three weeks after confinement, her husband observed that "Anne can sit up part of the day—complains of very great debility and frequently of pain." Six weeks later he was still afraid to leave her alone. Such remarks were not unusual, and they underscore how the difficulties of labor could continue long after the birth of an infant. Fortunate women survived their ordeal, endured the

18. H. M. Gilles *et al.,* "Malaria, Anemia, and Pregnancy," *Annals of Tropical Medicine and Parasitology,* LXIII (1969), 245–63; Mrs. T. Fraser to Mary Fraser, Monday the 8th, 1800, in Mary De Saussure Fraser Collection.

pain, and recovered within a few weeks' time. But many others were permanently injured, never regaining any semblance of physical vigor after they bore their first child.[19]

In addition to physical suffering, postpartum depression occasionally figured in the experience of southern mothers. The discussion of this in personal correspondence is infrequent. Perhaps nineteenth-century mothers had been raised to a high standard of stoicism. They were certainly inured to tragedy, sorrow, and personal difficulties. They may have had low expectations and may not have believed that personal fulfillment would follow the birth of a baby. Anyway, a heavy load of responsibilities left almost no time for the healthy mother to repine. Ill health, rather than the disappointment of heightened expectations after parturition, seems to have lain behind most of the mental suffering of women in the nineteenth century. Still, one introspective southern woman described her postpartum depression in considerable detail. After one confinement, Laura Norwood wrote to her cousin, "This miserable state of mind began to creep up on me very soon after the birth of my last child, and was no doubt occasioned by the anxiety, loss of sleep, and fatigue I endured for several months." Laura saw her "state of wretchedness" as the toll exacted by labor and the demands of raising a newborn. After another child was born, she complained of being weak, nervous, and "good for nothing," and she blamed her condition on lack of sleep and overwhelming domestic responsibilities. While considering a trip to the beach to comply with her physician's prescription of a change of scenery, Laura wrote her mother," "I got through a similar trial twice before in my life. . . . I mean this state of mental suffering, this unaccountable depression which at times seems to deprive me of all interest in life and yet I have no real affliction except the painful sense of my own situation." Laura knew that it was her "duty to do everything in [her] power to restore [her] health and spirits" but confessed, "I fear it will be long enough before I feel like myself again." She admitted that mental suffering seemed far worse than physical ailments. "Tell my dear Annie that sickness and real afflictions are blessings compared with what I feel, for they admit of so many consolations but for this there seems to be none save the hope that in time it may be removed." A few months later, Laura found herself pregnant again,

19. Jean Syme to Rebecca Cameron, May 11, 1811, Paul Cameron to M. B. Cameron, April 21, May 16, 1853, all in Cameron Family Papers.

with "sick stomach" and "miserable torpid feelings." The physical problems of pregnancy supplanted her emotional inanition.[20]

Doctors and midwives tried to alleviate women's sufferings and reduce the high maternal mortality rate through active involvement. On the whole, midwives were less apt to take active measures than physicians were, and doctors encouraged them to limit their efforts. But they might take action if they felt they could save the mother's or infant's life. From experience, they learned to turn a baby externally—in a procedure called version—when the fetus was upside down or its head was twisted. They tried to dislodge an adherent placenta by gently pulling on the cord or inserting a hand. Some midwives administered ergot or herbal remedies such as blackberry-root tea or a mixture of black gunpowder and water to encourage contractions. If labor seemed to lag, they might try to stretch the cervix manually. Most had techniques for rousing unresponsive newborns. Yet most midwives hoped that nature would prove kind. They relied upon a woman's natural strength and good health, their own experience and knowledge, and God's will, to ensure a successful delivery.[21]

No hard numbers prove that active intervention decreased maternal morbidity and mortality; the impression is that doctors did not yet deserve the confidence placed in them. The women and infants saved by instruments and heroic therapies were probably more than offset by those who died from the dramatic techniques and from infection. In the antebellum South, the ambitious approach of the physicians was no safer, no less painful, and no more sensible than the ways of the midwives. Parturient women who used midwives may even have had a better survival rate, because attendants who did not examine their patients and who shrank from intrusions upon the natural process were less likely to expose women to infection. It is important to remember, however, that sometimes southern doctors were called in only to assist

20. Laura Norwood to Julia Pickens Howe, March, 1843, in Chiliab Smith Howe Papers, Southern Historical Collection; Laura Norwood to Selina Lenoir, April 24, June 13, 1844, both in Lenoir Family Papers.

21. Catherine Scholten, "'On the Importance of the Obstetrick Art': Changing Customs of Childbirth in America, 1760–1825," *William and Mary Quarterly*, XXXIV (1977), 426–45; Irving S. Cutter and Henry R. Viets, *A Short History of Midwifery* (Philadelphia, 1964); Harold Speert, *Obstetrics and Gynecology in America* (Baltimore, 1980); William Ray Arney, *Power and the Profession of Obstetrics* (Chicago, 1982); John Whitridge Williams, *A Sketch of the History of Obstetrics in the United States up to 1860* (N.p., 1903).

with a dangerous situation and that in such instances the woman's chances of survival were already poor.

A few surveys showed that slave women had a lower maternal mortality rate than white women. Statistics from Kentucky recorded sixty-six maternal deaths in 1855, eleven involving black women, and fifty-five white. According to a Tennessee doctor's survey, white women were in labor twice as long as slave women, and in one medical journal it was stated that stillbirths occurred five times as frequently among white women as among slaves. Perhaps statistical reporting for slave women was particularly negligent, but the startling difference deserves attention. Some people of the time thought that the stronger constitution that slave women had acquired through years of hard labor was the explanation. Perhaps, too, slave women were more likely to have midwives or friends attending them in labor, thereby sparing themselves heroic therapies. Or it may just be that because slave women were less prone to malaria, they entered their confinements healthier. Besides that, slave infants, being on average smaller than white babies, were easier to deliver.[22]

Lower-class farm wives seldom depended on doctors, because of the expense or because of distance. Their attendants in the birthing chamber were as a rule midwives or female friends and relatives who clung to the natural process. By lessening the exposure to infection, yeoman farm wives may have had healthier pregnancies, more successful deliveries, and a higher survival rate than more privileged women had. Moreover, as the historian Frank Owsley has observed, yeoman families often settled at the higher elevations, following isothermic patterns of migration. They consequently escaped malaria's worst brunt. Plantation families, on the other hand, sought a fortune in cotton, rice, or sugar in the rich bottomlands, where malaria was endemic. It is possible, therefore, that higher class was associated with poorer maternal health. Yeoman wives, provided that their diet was adequate, may have had healthier pregnancies and confinements.[23]

22. The author observed that this was "quite an undue proportion of whites" ("Vital Statistics of Kentucky," *Western Journal of Medicine and Surgery*, 3rd ser., III [1855], 288). W. A. Brown ("Midwifery in a Country Practice," *Nashville Journal of Medicine and Surgery*, VII [1854], 460) noted that white women were in labor an average of eight and three-quarters hours and black women an average of four. For a discussion on the size of slave newborns, see Richard H. Steckel, "Birth Weights and Infant Mortality Among American Slaves," *Explorations in Economic History*, XXIII (1986), 173–98.

23. See Frank L. Owsley, *Plain Folk of the Old South* (Baton Rouge, 1949), and Sally

In medical texts and journals of the antebellum period, there were few mentions of antisepsis. Probably sepsis was the single largest cause of maternal death, for few doctors took the precaution of cleaning either their instruments or their hands. Some physicians followed the recommendation of oiling their hands and trimming their fingernails, but not until Louis Pasteur and Joseph Lister, after the Civil War, was there a wide recognition of the virtue of cleanliness.

The proper atmosphere in the birthing chamber interested doctors more. In 1817, Thomas Ewell suggested that the room be airy and cheerful. Dewees, on the other hand, believed a dark room preferable, as a "most scrupulous regard to delicacy." Three decades later, perhaps in an effort to unite his quarreling colleagues, Dr. Joseph Warrington, of Philadelphia, urged doctors to examine their patients in a darkened chamber but to arrange for a spacious, well-ventilated room for labor. Several physicians encouraged women to walk or sit until the baby's birth was imminent. But Dewees, who promoted full professional involvement, called such freedom of movement a "preposterous custom." He wanted women in a horizontal position as soon as contractions began. Dewees found perambulation a contradiction of medical science and far too similar to the approach of midwives.[24]

It was customary for doctors to tell women to lie on their left side during labor. Knees were to be drawn close to the abdomen and perhaps separated by a pillow. Feet were to rest on a bedpost, with the doctor beside the bed. On all this, there was virtually universal—and an altogether rare—agreement in the medical profession. Occasionally, however, a physician had second thoughts. Dr. C. A. Hentz, of Florida, made special note of his success in delivering a baby while the husband held his laboring wife erect. That he mentioned this detail in his cryptic medical records probably suggests that he found it unusual.[25]

The horizontal position for childbirth was far different from what tradition counseled. For centuries, parturient women in widely diver-

McMillen, "Obstetrics in Antebellum Arkansas: Women and Doctors in a New State" (Unpublished paper for the History of Medicine Associates, University of Arkansas for Medical Sciences Library, 1987).

24. Thomas Ewell, *Letters to Ladies*, 151; Dewees, *A Compendious System of Midwifery*, 185; Joseph Warrington, *The Obstetric Catechism: Containing Two Thousand Three Hundred and Forty-Seven Questions and Answers on Obstetrics Proper* (Philadelphia, 1853), 144; Dewees, *A Compendious System of Midwifery*, 185.

25. Charles A. Hentz, Obstetrical Records, Case 22, Mrs. F. L. Hansford, 1853 (Hentz Family Papers, Southern Historical Collection).

gent cultures had stood, kneeled, sat on a chair or birthing stool, or found other methods of ensuring an erect posture. Lying on the side may in fact have impeded delivery by defying natural gravitation. Midwives believed that walking encouraged contractions. Once a woman's labor became intense, she crouched, was held, or sat on someone's lap. But practicality, tradition, and sensitivity to women's needs were not primary in the doctors' recommendation. Foremost was the desire to establish science in the birthing chamber and to dictate new methods that set medicine apart from nature. In addition, putting the woman in bed made it easier to associate childbirth with typical pathologies. The sick are often in bed. Physicians explained that the horizontal position made it easier to use instruments, since forceps could not be inserted into the womb when a woman stood up or crouched on a stool. That few southern practitioners used forceps was irrelevant.[26]

All attendants, whether doctors or midwives, wanted parturient women to empty their bowels and bladders before delivery. If necessary, a drug such as calomel was used for clearing the bowels, and a catheter for the bladder. Some doctors encouraged their colleagues to examine the patient to determine her "readiness." Yet the examination was to be handled discreetly, according to advisers, preferably in the presence of others in a darkened room. Touch could establish the dilation of the cervix. Physicians warned their colleagues not to overdo such an examination, for fear of drying out a woman's "private parts." Should that occur, a mild ointment, hog's lard, or oil might be applied to moisten them. By the 1850s, some doctors suggested the use of the speculum for determining whether the woman was ready to deliver, but few southern practitioners seemed to use one.[27]

During the antebellum period, medical texts and advice books became increasingly scientific in their appearance and included more information. By midcentury, many volumes came with detailed drawings and descriptions of the female reproductive organs, of alterations

26. Yuen Chou Liu, "Position During Labor and Delivery: History and Perspective," *Journal of Nurse-Midwifery,* XXIV (May–June, 1979), 23.

27. For nineteenth-century information on the preparation for delivery, see William Babcock, "Management of Natural Labour" (1852), in Waring Historical Library Annex, Medical University of South Carolina, Charleston; John C. Gunn, *Gunn's Domestic Medicine; or, Poor Man's Friend, Shewing the Diseases of Men, Women, and Children* (2nd ed.; Madisonville, Tenn., 1834), 366–68; Thomas Ewell, *Letters to Ladies,* 151–57; and Charles Delucena Meigs, *Obstetrics: The Science and the Art* (1st ed.; Philadelphia, 1849), 286–89, 300–26.

in fetal growth, of complicated deliveries, and of new instruments. Doctors defined the three stages of labor carefully and spelled out the possible complications in each. They examined postnatal problems and dealt with illnesses and fevers more thoroughly, listing symptoms and possible cures. Statistics and numbers became more important. The items that attending physicians were expected to bring to the delivery room grew both in number and complexity. Early in the century, doctors and midwives were told to bring scissors, catheter, linen, thread, mild soap, and lard. A doctor was to add forceps. In 1858, S. C. Webster, a student at the Medical College of South Carolina, suggested that the "saddle bag of the accoucheur" contain delivery, crochet, and abortion forceps, vectis, sharp and blunt hooks, fillet, Smellie, scissors, sound, perforator, extractor, repoussoir, symphsis, knife, blistories, and craniotomy hook.[28]

Influenced by the initial enthusiasm of northern physicians, the majority of southern doctors remained convinced that heroic remedies were indicated in complicated deliveries, despite their poor record of success. Allopaths regarded bloodletting as the best method to lessen the severe pain of contractions. As early as 1804, Peter Miller pronounced bloodletting the "best remedy we can employ" in lessening the pain of parturition. He reported that he extracted forty-eight ounces of blood from a woman in prolonged labor, and concluded, "A large quantity of blood may be drawn without injury to the patient." Only two years later, Dewees took up the cry and became the most outspoken advocate of extensive bleeding. Basing his conclusions upon the numerous confinements he had attended, Dewees stated unequivocally that bleeding was innocent and useful during labor. "I have never known it fail in being serviceable," he stated confidently, "or ever saw it any degree do harm." His successor as a childbirth expert, Dr. Charles Delucena Meigs, was a bit more cautious. He gently criticized Dewees for his boldness in venesection and urged his colleagues to moderation. Yet in cases of hemorrhaging, convulsions, or apoplexy, Meigs declared, "The lancet should be used in a most fearless manner."[29]

28. S. C. Webster, "A Thesis on Obstetrical Instruments" (1858), in Waring Historical Library; Alva Curtis, *Lectures on Midwifery and the Forms of Disease Peculiar to Women and Children* (2nd ed.; Columbus, Ohio, 1841), 48. For the importance of statistics and data in the South, see James H. Cassedy, *American Medicine and Statistical Thinking, 1800–1860* (Cambridge, Mass., 1984), 104–17.

29. Peter Miller, *An Essay on the Means of Lessening the Pains of Parturition* (Philadelphia, 1804), 29, 31; William Potts Dewees, *An Essay on the Means of Lessening Pain, and*

Southern medical journals included accounts of cases in which doctors employed bloodletting as a matter of course. Yet the approach was often experimental, although sometimes carried out cavalierly, and luck more than medical skill was frequently what kept the parturient woman alive. Doctors were wont not to measure the amount of blood lost by a patient but watched for individual reactions to determine when to stop drawing. Leeches were sometimes put alongside the vagina to draw blood slowly, especially when infection seemed a possibility. Occasionally the creatures worked their way inside the canal and caused the woman excruciating pain. A Virginia doctor who in 1855 reviewed Meigs's latest book on childbed fevers gratefully acknowledged that the book's distinguishing feature was "the professor's earnest advocacy of the use of the lancet in these inflammations." The reviewer continued, "How refreshing it is to hear the clarion tones of the professor as in the work before us, he calls us to the rescue of this noble instrument." Another southern physician, Dr. John Hume Simons, advocated bleeding and leeching the private parts of any woman whose womb was inflamed after childbirth. However crude and insensitive antebellum cures now appear, they usually created a strong reaction and, in some cases, at least did little harm. Up through the Civil War, the majority of southern doctors reposed confidence in bleeding for complicated deliveries and the relief of pain.[30]

Southern women varied in their reactions to this. In 1841, Mary Bethell related that her doctor bled her during labor, and she found this beneficial. "I had no pain at all," she reported. Mrs. Norwood wrote that poor health and fever after her confinement necessitated drastic remedies. "I was bled pretty freely and took a dose of calomel," she said, "leaving me a good deal weakened." Not all women welcomed heroic methods, despite a growing confidence in male accoucheurs and scientific remedies. Mary Fraser described a friend who "positively refused to be bled and would not listen to her husband or the doctor's entreaties." The poor woman went into convulsions and died a few hours after giving birth to a daughter, "without a struggle or a groan." Since the woman probably suffered from puerperal convulsions, it is

---

Facilitating Certain Cases of Difficult Parturition (Philadelphia, 1806), 81; Charles Delucena Meigs, *Obstetrics*, 324.

30. Review of Charles Delucena Meigs's *On the Nature, Signs, and Treatment of Childbed Fevers,* in *Virginia Medical and Surgical Journal,* IV (1855), 75; John Hume Simons, *The Planter's Guide and Family Book of Medicine* (Charleston, S.C., 1848), 124.

doubtful that bleeding could have prevented her demise. Nevertheless, her friends held her accountable for her death since she had refused treatment. Generally, comments on bleeding during confinement are rare in diaries and letters, particularly considering its frequent mention in southern medical journals. Perhaps bleeding was so common that it went without saying. Moreover, women who needed to be bled were probably the least likely to describe their confinements, owing to their debility. Some may not have survived. The reticence of women about bleeding was similar to their silence about childbirth overall.[31]

Nineteenth-century physicians seemed especially apprehensive of potential damage to the perineum. Nearly all medical texts cautioned doctors to avoid injuries and tears to this area, and William Babcock warned that "very serious and distressing accidents may be the result" if doctors were careless. One suggestion was that physicians try to retard contractions and the presentation of the infant's head to allow for slow expansion of the perineum. The advice was to keep one hand on the perineum to avoid injury, and the other in readiness for cradling the infant's head. Still, tears were common. Lacerations could extend into the rectum or the area of the urethra and cause permanent damage or extreme discomfort. Some women found it painful to walk, and others suffered infections, endured foul discharges, or were unable to exercise bladder control. A few were doomed to a life of seclusion. In 1849, Dr. J. Marion Sims, of Alabama, developed, and tested on slave women, a surgical procedure to cure vesicovaginal fistula. By the mid-1850s, a number of progressive American and European doctors had heralded Sims's technique as a solution to an age-old problem, but it did not become a standard surgical procedure until after the Civil War.[32]

Medical texts also recommended close attention during the third stage of labor, when the placenta was expelled. Dr. John Gunn, of

31. Mary Bethell Diary, April, 1841 (Southern Historical Collection); Laura Norwood to Selina Lenoir, end of May, 1837, in Lenoir Family Papers; Mary Fraser to her mother, Mary, October 12, 1833, in Mary De Saussure Fraser Collection.

32. Babcock, "Management of Natural Labour." For additional information on doctors' concerns about tearing the perineum, see Curtis, *Lectures on Midwifery*, 52; Gunn, *Gunn's Domestic Medicine*, 367; Simons, *The Planter's Guide*, 200; and Samuel Bard, *A Compendium of the Theory and Practice of Midwifery* (New York, 1807), 121. Dr. James Marion Sims (1813–1883) was born in Lancaster County, South Carolina, was educated at the Medical College of South Carolina and Jefferson Medical College, and moved to Alabama to practice medicine. He developed his surgical cure by experimenting on slave women with the use of a speculum.

Tennessee, warned that this was the "period in which so many women are injured *for life* by ignorance and imprudent haste." If the placenta did not emerge naturally, doctors could tug on the cord or try to dislodge it by inserting a hand inside the womb and gently loosening it from the uterine wall. The overriding fears were the premature expulsion of the placenta, which could lead to hemorrhage, and its failure to dislodge.[33]

Physicians received instruction on the steps to take immediately after a birth. Nearly always, the advice was to clean the newborn with lard, egg yolk, or soap and water. After tying and severing the umbilical cord, the doctor was to pass the cord through a piece of linen rag, wrap it, and secure it with a bandage. Soap and water and a syringe filled with warm water and milk could serve to wash a mother's "privates." If her perineum was torn or sore, a solution of vinegar, salt, and water was to be applied several times a day. Soft cloths could absorb the lochial discharge. All allopathic physicians suggested that a wide bandage be wrapped around the woman's abdomen—"as tightly as the patient can bear with comfort," according to Dewees. The idea, presumably, was to help control relaxed abdominal muscles and to strengthen the womb. Medical consensus judged daily bowel evacuations critically important in helping to avoid additional injury and illness.[34]

Doctors, at least in the urban Northeast, often used instruments to hasten delivery and to manage dangerous situations. They especially recognized the usefulness of forceps during difficult or prolonged labor. The instrument, which was restricted to male practitioners, could re-move a fetus in breech position or midpelvic arrest and could assist in delivering a particularly large infant. Forceps, known to the Egyptians and Greeks of ancient times, had been reinvented in the late sixteenth century by the Chamberlens, an English family, but had been held secret by them. Knowledge of the instrument did not begin to spread until more than one hundred years later. By the late antebellum period, elaborate descriptions and clear pictures of the various types of forceps, as well as of other instruments, filled the pages of obstetrical texts.

Medical books mentioned forceps frequently, but these volumes were northern or European in origin and reflected urban practices. It would appear that the majority of southern practitioners did not use the instrument. Some may have been fearful of the consequences. Others may not have wished to purchase what they felt ill trained to use even if

33. Gunn, *Gunn's Domestic Medicine*, 368.
34. Dewees, *A Compendious System of Midwifery*, 193.

they were convinced of its value. In one recorded case, a Tennessee doctor who encountered a difficult delivery requested the services of another physician who owned a pair of forceps.[35]

The personal writings of southern women make no reference to the use of forceps. The silence may reflect reticence, embarrassment, or just the fact that the instruments were rarely used. For physicians, however, the appearance of staying abreast of science and medical innovation was important, whether or not it was true to actual practice. Describing the new instruments in texts and journal articles put a professional and scientific luster on doctors' reputations and further separated them from midwives.

A wholehearted endorsement of the use of instruments was rare, though. Conservative doctors recognized that improper use could bring permanent injury to mother and child. The Louisiana State Medical Society's report affirmed that instruments should be avoided if possible. Thomas Ewell counseled accoucheurs to employ forceps only when labor was prolonged. Webster, in his dissertation, recommended forceps only when the head of the fetus was impacted. He outlined the functions of other instruments as well. Crochet hooks, he thought, should be reserved for extracting a dead fetus, and abortion forceps for removing a dead fetus or retained placenta in a final effort to save the mother. He advised a blunt hook for bringing down an unborn infant's arm or leg and a sharp hook for cutting up the child's head when it was too big to pass through the pelvic opening. In extracting the fetus piecemeal to save the mother, doctors showed little hesitancy in using instruments.[36]

Dr. John Watson, head of obstetrics at the medical department of the University of Nashville, was appalled that few physicians knew how to use forceps. Southern practitioners commonly fell back on drugs such

35. Edward Shorter (*A History of Women's Bodies* [New York, 1982], 85) states that forceps were not widely used before the end of the nineteenth century. Judy Litoff (*American Midwives, 1860 to the Present* [Westport, Conn., 1978], 8) argues that the development of forceps was the most important event leading to the displacement of midwives by male doctors. The Tennessee physician was Dr. Crutcher, of McMinnville. See "Right Occipito Iliac Position and Protracted Labor," *Nashville Journal of Medicine and Surgery,* XV (1858), 279.

36. Hort, "Report of the Committee," 532; Thomas Ewell, *Letters to Ladies,* 192; Webster, "A Thesis on Obstetrical Instruments." See also John Travis, "An Obstetrical Case, and Craniotomy Performed," *Nashville Journal of Medicine and Surgery,* III (1852), 349; and W. P. Moore, "Obstetric Medicine," *Tennessee State Medical Proceedings* (1858), 34–38.

as ergot, he observed, rather than trying to advance obstetrical surgery. "Practitioners of medicine, with few exceptions indeed, have not prepared themselves for the skillful use of obstetric instruments," he complained. He deplored the impression that "instrumental delivery is generally associated with the certain death of the child and often with that of the mother."[37]

Few southern doctors heeded Watson. Dr. W. P. Moore, of Mitchellsville, Tennessee, expressed the typical attitude when he asked, "How often has a young healthy woman been rendered an invalid for life by unnecessary application of the forceps injuriously applied?" In 1854, a Georgian, Dr. W. A. Brown, voiced his frustration with the way medical journals emphasized urban professionals and their use of instruments. He noted that urban women often gave birth in hospitals and were commonly beset by the problems associated with unhealthy city living. Criticizing the dependence on instruments, he maintained that rural southern women faced few problems that required forceps and that "it is very seldom necessary to resort to them in country practice."[38]

Southern physicians were unhesitant, however, in their use of medications during and after delivery. Both personal and medical accounts note the use of drugs. Many allopaths considered a drug that created the greatest reaction—whether purgative or narcotic—the most effective. They might administer laudanum or opium to make a woman drowsy and inert during labor. But a few accoucheurs believed that certain drugs could impede the infant's birth, and they refused to administer them; their position was that women needed all their strength during delivery. Some medications could alter the force of contractions. Ergot, a derivative of rye, had long been a favorite of European doctors and midwives to hasten delivery, and it became popular in the United States by the early part of the nineteenth century. Nonetheless, conservative doctors urged its administration only as a last resort, for it produced unnatural contractions that could lead to abortion or fetal death. John Watson feared that his colleagues used the drug far too often. Morphine

37. John M. Watson, "A Treatise on Obstetric Surgery," *Nashville Journal of Medicine and Surgery,* XII (1857), 92–111. This article provides valuable information on obstetric surgery in the South.

38. W. P. Moore, "Tennessee Medical Society," *Savannah Journal of Medicine,* I (1858), 203; W. A. Brown, "Midwifery in a Country Practice," *Nashville Journal of Medicine and Surgery,* VII (1854), 458–60.

and opium, standard for postnatal pain, were often used for labor pains as well.[39]

When, in the 1840s, ether and chloroform came into use in surgery and dentistry, debate raged over their use in childbirth. Both anesthetics were employed successfully in childbirth and surgery in the United States by the late 1840s. Queen Victoria dramatized the safe and effective use of chloroform in 1853 and again in 1857, proving to the world that a live baby could be delivered painlessly. Despite the enthusiasm of the British royal family, the South was slow to give in. Southern physicians, more than their northern colleagues, remained unconvinced, or at least cautious.[40]

The most vocal critic of chloroform was Meigs, who managed through his eminence to keep Philadelphia's doctors from adopting any anesthetic for labor. His fame ruled, despite a wide recognition that his opinions were at times old-fashioned and intractable. Sounding as if he had personally experienced the pains of parturition, Meigs intoned, "I have always regarded a labor pain as a most desireable, salutary and conservative manifestation of life-force. I have found that women, provided they were sustained by cheering counsel and promises and carefully freed from the distressing element of terror, could in general be made to endure, without great complaint, those labor pains." It is doubtful that Meigs consulted women in order to arrive at his breezy declaration that labor pains were desirable. Plainly, he placed the needs of the physician before the comfort of female patients. A woman's sensations during childbirth, he observed, "afford us our best guide for the introduction of instruments." Critics of Meigs answered that a good doctor understands female anatomy well enough not to need his patients' reactions as a guide. But undaunted, Meigs persisted in his conviction: "I sincerely regret the introduction of anaesthetics into Midwifery." Other opponents, including clergymen, argued that anesthesia defied the biblical dictate "In sorrow thou shalt bring forth children." Many believed that people most love what they acquire through the greatest pain. According to that reasoning, the intense pains of child-

39. Watson, "A Treatise on Obstetric Surgery," 96; R. B. Sayers, "Ergot," Dissertation 398 (1858), in Vanderbilt University Medical Center Library; John B. Beck, "Observations on Ergot," *Western Journal of Medicine and Surgery,* I (1840), 53.

40. J. Emanuel Josey, "Anaesthetics," Dissertation 394 (1858), Felix Grundy, "Anaesthesia," Dissertation 53 (1853), W. M. Neal, "Chloroform," Dissertation 54 (1853), all in Vanderbilt University Medical Center Library. Chloroform was first used for obstetrics in 1848.

birth enhanced a mother's love for her offspring. Without pain, the maternal attachment, forged by trauma and suffering, might fail.[41]

On the other hand, Walter Channing, a professor of obstetrics at Harvard Medical School, was zealous in his advocacy of ether to eliminate pain during parturition, and he developed his case in *A Treatise on Etherization,* in 1848. In the South, Dr. Henry Miller, a prominent specialist in obstetrics at Louisville Medical College, urged the adoption of anesthesia for childbirth. His own experience with chloroform on women in labor convinced him that physicians had the capacity to "assuage every pain of parturition." In 1858, William Babcock suggested that doctors carry chloroform in their medical bags, "since its valuable properties have been so fairly tested." The Louisiana State Medical Society gave its cautious approval to chloroform as a means to lessen labor pains.[42]

Yet in the personal correspondence and diaries examined for this study, no southern woman mentions an anesthetic. If any woman or her relatives or friends had benefited from its use, the good news would doubtless have spread quickly. Despite the support that anesthesia received from several prominent physicians in the South, the majority of the doctors there did not use ether or chloroform routinely before the Civil War. Many physicians avoided anesthetics out of prudence, others out of fear, and some, like Meigs, simply because they were entrenched in their ways. The antebellum southern women who most benefited were probably the handful of immigrant and free black women who were more apt to deliver babies in hospitals served by medical students.

Ironically, the use of anesthesia would have been the surest way for doctors to solidify the authority of medical science in the birthing room. Only a few southern physicians recognized that the ending of pain was a service they alone were trained to perform. A prescient southern physician insisted that it was a doctor's duty not only to attend

41. Charles Delucena Meigs, *Obstetrics,* 373; Review of Charles Delucena Meigs's *Obstetrics: The Science and the Art,* in *Western Journal of Medicine and Surgery,* 3rd ser., IV (1849), 51; "Editorials and Synopsis of Monthly Intelligence, Medical Items," *Nashville Journal of Medicine and Surgery,* IX (1856), 547; Theodore Cianfrani, *Short History of Obstetrics and Gynecology* (Springfield, Ill., 1960), 274.

42. Walter Channing, *A Treatise on Etherization in Childbirth* (Boston, 1848); Channing, *Six Cases of Inhalation of Ether in Labor* (Boston, 1847); Review of Henry Miller's *Report of the Obstetric Committee on Anesthesia in Midwifery, and the Speculum Uteri,* in *Nashville Journal of Medicine and Surgery,* IV (1853), 183; Babcock, "Management of Natural Labour"; Hort, "Report of the Committee," 569.

parturient women but also to mitigate their pain. "To allay the pain and anguish is the duty of the obstetrician," declared Henry Miller. Women did not enjoy the suffering they endured in childbirth, and all would have been less fearful of delivery if the process had been less stressful and painful. Maternal attachment might even have strengthened without suffering, for with less painful deliveries, women would have been better able to cope with their frequent confinements and with infant care. Not until after the Civil War would pain-killers find their way into most southern birthing rooms.[43]

Puerperal fever, the most feared of the epidemic illnesses associated with childbirth, was rare among middle- and upper-class southern women. The disease was caused by the introduction of bacteria into the birth canal, usually by the unclean hands and instruments of the attendant. In 1843, Oliver Wendell Holmes noticed that it frequently occurred in hospitals and almshouses where physicians assisted with several confinements in succession. Doctors for the most part refused to admit their complicity, however, and blamed the spread of the fever on miasmic conditions, damp air, the delicate feminine frame, and of course, the incompetence of midwives. Because southern women gave birth at home, they had some protection from epidemics. Doctors and midwives who delivered only a few babies each month were highly unlikely to spread infection from one woman to the next. In one instance, though, a Tennessee woman wrote that she "had a violent and very dangerous attack of puerperal fever." She noted that "it was by far the severest spell of sickness [she] ever had" and that it forced her to remain in bed for several weeks. Ruth Berrien Jones, of Savannah, who used a male attendant, apparently died of the infection in 1860. Despite the small number of cases, southern medical journals frequently carried articles on the subject. But physicians noted with relief that the disease occurred most often among urban and European women.[44]

Doctors agreed that women should spend several days recumbent

43. Henry Miller, "Anaesthesia in Surgery," *Western Journal of Medicine and Surgery,* XI (1853), 237; J. N. Graham, "Chloroformization in Midwifery," *Nashville Journal of Medicine and Surgery,* X (1856), 184.

44. Oliver Wendell Holmes, "The Contagiousness of Puerperal Fever," in *Medical Essays, 1842–1882* (Boston, 1897), 103–72. This essay first appeared in the *New England Quarterly Journal of Medicine and Surgery* in 1843 and caused an immediate outcry from doctors, including Meigs. V. A. Callum to Fannie Campbell, January 29, 1852, in Campbell Family Letters; Robert Manson Myers (ed.), *Children of Pride: A True Story of Georgia and the Civil War* (New Haven, 1972), 701–16.

after giving birth. Bed rest—usually lasting from four to eight days—was essential. Meigs sternly admonished that "to rise before the fifth day is to go forth to seek disease." Women who ignored his advice and arose prematurely had to shoulder the blame for postnatal problems. One southern doctor who performed a cesarean operation ascribed the death of the patient not to his unfamiliarity with the procedure but to her getting out of bed before he had given permission. Physicians also directed that mothers wait from three to four weeks before venturing outside. Everything reinforced the idea that childbirth was an illness and that parturient women should be treated as partial invalids. Many indulged women adhered to the schedule the doctors recommended, perhaps out of obedience and tradition, perhaps out of thirst for a little pampering. Probably more women adhered to it out of necessity, lacking the strength and good health to do otherwise.[45]

Fanny Lawrence, of Louisiana, seemed committed to remaining indoors for a full month. "As my month is not quite up yet I shall not venture out until it is," she remarked obediently. Mary Henderson, of Salisbury, North Carolina, commented that she had her first carriage ride twenty-three days after her baby was born. Henry Watson, who found his wife's health good, mentioned that she remained in "her bed and her room in all about five weeks but did admirably." There were always exceptions. A South Carolina woman, Isabel Fraser, ignored the restrictions imposed after a very difficult labor. She was soon up and about, even cutting out patterns for sewing. Overactivity, however, forced her back to bed. Three weeks later her husband reported that Isabel's health had improved and that she "would renew her family labors on Monday. She has been receiving her cake and wine visitors." During these quiet weeks of recovery, southern women in reasonably good health welcomed friends and neighbors paying respects to newborn and mother. One can imagine the gossip and delighted chatter that occurred. Perhaps after delivery and among intimate female company, women felt freest to share details of their difficulties in labor.[46]

45. Charles Delucena Meigs, *Females and Their Diseases: A Series of Letters to His Class* (Philadelphia, 1848), 315. Babcock ("Management of Natural Labour") recommended that women remain in bed from eight to ten days, Warrington (*The Obstetric Catechism*, 176) suggested four to five days in bed but that women not walk for two weeks, and Thomas Ewell (*Letters to Ladies*, 125) believed that five to six days of horizontal rest and at least another week in the room would be sufficient. Doctors now believe that it is important for women to walk as soon as possible after labor.

46. Fanny Brashear Lawrence to Henry Lawrence, January, 1830, in Brashear Family

One of the best ways to improve the health of southern women and to lower their high maternal mortality rate would have been to reduce the number of children they bore. Southern men customarily showed concern over a wife's illnesses and pains, and over the problems connected with pregnancy and childbirth, but they were loath to carry their worry so far as a campaign to limit family size. Typical of many southern husbands was E. Cameron, of Franklin, Kentucky, who wrote to a relative, "I have myself enjoyed a good share of health ever since I have been in the county, but I cannot say so of the rest of my family. My wife scarcely ever enjoys a well hour yet we increase in number though not in wealth. We have a Duncan, a John who promises to be a scollar, a William, Eliza Ann and a boy about three months old." It is likely that Mrs. Cameron's poor health was exacerbated—if not caused—by her many confinements and the demands that child rearing placed upon her. Whether her husband saw a tie between his wife's frequent confinements and her debilitated condition seems doubtful. Mary Chaplin, of St. Helena Island, South Carolina, spent most of her years as an invalid after the birth of her fourth child, yet she bore three additional children before she died at the age of twenty-nine. Men may have assumed that pain and poor health were women's lot. Doctors, in agreement with society, assumed that women's happiness was "centered around the hope of giving birth to children." They paid little mind to the effect constant childbearing had on female health. Large families were something to celebrate in the antebellum South, not something to limit.[47]

How actively women sought to control their own fertility is a question that has generated a fair amount of discussion among historians. Women were not as delighted by their numerous confinements and offspring as their husbands appear to have been. But the large size of many middle- and upper-class antebellum southern families suggests that birth-control efforts in the region must have been limited and unsuccessful if not nonexistent. Abstinence was the most reliable method but not one that many husbands—or perhaps wives—would

Papers, Southern Historical Collection; Mary Henderson Diary, September 22, 1855 (Southern Historical Collection); Henry Watson, Jr., to his mother, December 21, 1846, in Henry Watson, Jr., Papers, Manuscript Department, William R. Perkins Library; Frederick Fraser to his mother, August 13, 1840, in Mary De Saussure Fraser Collection.

47. E. Cameron to Duncan Cameron, July 24, 1813, in Cameron Family Papers; Rosengarten, *Tombee*, 168–72; W. B. Mills, "The Signs of Pregnancy," Dissertation 270 (1857), in Vanderbilt University Medical Center Library.

have accepted. Abortion has always been available but has not always been condoned. It was not unknown in the South. In one incident, a doctor attended a patient who had suffered the bungled ministrations of an old woman. When southern women turned to abortion or birth control, they were unlikely to discuss the matter even in the privacy of a journal.[48]

In one set of correspondence, two sisters did cautiously approach the subject. Elizabeth Haywood, who served as a surrogate mother to her younger sister, Rebecca, made what seems a veiled comment about her unmarried sibling's pregnancy and abortion. The older sister wrote, "You know there are many Gossips in our town, the accident which has befallen you has leaked out from some of them." She added, "Should you ever be similarly circumstanced, attend to the premonitory symptoms, be bled immediately, and by all means have the best medical advice; many women have lost their lives by being too careless at such times." Elizabeth had good cause for concern beyond the impropriety of the situation: "Call to your recollection the great and protracted sufferings of our lamented mother, her ill health was owing in a great measure to becoming a mother early in life." An abortion in this instance was better than premature death. More typical for her naïveté was Mrs. Norwood, who never seemed to consider birth control a possibility. With a note of surprise, she wrote, "I often feel startled at the thought of the size which my own family is attaining so rapidly." Birth control not only remained a private matter but the possibilities were very limited. Most southern women found it unacceptable for personal or religious reasons.[49]

Despite the rigors of childbirth, babies continued to appear and the majority of southern mothers survived their ordeal. Husbands often spread the happy news. Only a short while after his wife's delivery, Henry Bedinger could foresee his daughter's future. He proudly reported to the family that little Virginia was not only "fat and lusty" but "destined doubtless to be the smasher of many hearts." The occasion of gaining an heir overwhelmed R. M. Price, and he confessed to his sister-in-law that "it was an event which caused my heart to overflow with

48. On birth control, see Norman Himes, *Medical History of Contraception* (1936; rpr. New York, 1970); James C. Mohr, *Abortion in America: The Origins and Evolution of National Policy, 1800–1900* (New York, 1978); and the next chapter.

49. Elizabeth Haywood to Rebecca Haywood, February 28, 1835, in Haywood Family Collection, Southern Historical Collection; Laura Norwood to Julia Pickens Howe, March, 1843, in Chiliab Smith Howe Papers.

tears of gratitude to our great Preserver." In 1835, Leonidas Polk announced his new son: "He is of course the finest boy that ever was born, given already strong indications of both eminence and usefulness."[50]

Some fathers reacted with greater restraint. J. Syme, whose wife had refused him permission even to see their new infant, noted his son's arrival with despair. "There is another little Pilgrim ushered into this troublesome world," he wrote. Albert Hall, who conveniently managed to be away during the birth of his first child and did not return home for two weeks afterward, learned of the infant's arrival from a relative and wrote his wife Rebecca with seemingly few regrets. "I hope my absence has not the appearance of neglect," he penned. Rebecca was already disenchanted with her husband and tried not to know of his wanderings. Fortunately she now had a baby daughter to fill her loneliness. William Lenoir's reaction has to count as jaded. "As it will probably be the last," he wrote, "I have thought of calling it after its mother. It is not uglyer than several of the rest of the children were." But John Johnston, of Abingdon, Virginia, articulated the ecstasy he felt as a new father. "The birth of a first-born is in a family what the discovery of a continent is in a world," he exclaimed.[51]

One might expect southern parents in a patriarchal society to have preferred boys, but that was not always so. Preferences depended on the sex of the other children in the family as well as on individual yearnings. A Virginia woman reported that "the whole House felt disappointed it was not a daughter, she says she does not half like the cold welcome her son received." Thirty years later, a new generation noted that the mother was "perfectly satisfied that the newly arrived is a girl—and is sorry for the disappointment of its other relatives." Perhaps fathers favored boys, but in such large families it was almost inevitable that everyone was eventually satisfied. Mothers did not necessarily wish for daughters, though one woman felt happy about a baby girl: "How much less trouble they give than boys." On the other hand, Ann Elliott,

50. Henry Bedinger to his sister Susan, January 22, 1842, in Bedinger-Dandridge Letters, Manuscript Department, William R. Perkins Library; R. M. Price to Betsy Blanks, January 5, 1839, in Elizabeth Holmes Blanks Letters; and Leonidas Polk to his brother, March 2, 1835, in Leonidas Polk Collection, Southern Historical Collection.

51. J. M. Syme to Duncan Cameron, January 8, 1844, in Cameron Family Papers; Albert Hall to Rebecca Haywood Hall, January 30, 1836, in Haywood Family Collection; William Lenoir to his father, January 9, 1819, in Lenoir Family Papers; John Warfield Johnston to Captain Rees Bowen, February 20, 1836, in John Warfield Johnston Collection, Manuscript Department, William R. Perkins Library.

of South Carolina, could not restrain her disappointment over the "prospect of having old maids in the family instead of bustling sons." One wise mother declared that "an equal number of each is preferable." And women who had lost other infants or had had several miscarriages could not afford to be choosy. A Georgia woman, Martha Screven, wrote of a friend that "it was not her wish to have a son, but as she has been so unfortunate that she will not complain for fear that this may be taken from us." Women knew that they were blessed by any healthy child whatever its sex and that they had no warrant for regret or wishful thinking. Mothers were also grateful that their confinement was over and that they and their baby had survived.[52]

Childbirth for antebellum southern mothers was painful and life threatening. Southern women spent twenty-five to thirty years risking their lives and exposing their bodies to illness and injury. Yet bearing healthy infants and raising children proved to be the premier role of antebellum women. Those who survived delivery and retained a semblance of good health were now ready to embark upon their most important and sacred duty as mothers.

52. Jean Syme to Rebecca Cameron, June 1, 1805, MMLB to Mildred, May 9, 1844, both in Cameron Family Papers; William Elliott to his mother-in-law, Ann Smith, August 7, 1829, in Elliott-Gonzales Letters, Southern Historical Collection; Lizzie Lenoir to Selina Lenoir, March, 1850, in Lenoir Family Papers; Martha Proctor to her brother-in-law James Screven, January 18, 1820, in Arnold-Screven Letters, Southern Historical Collection.

5 So Sweet an Office

MATERNAL BREAST-FEEDING

"It will be a trial for me to wean him," wrote Rebecca Allen Turner of her eighteen-month-old son. "How am I to relinquish so sweet an office—that of giving nourishment to my darling? Are these foolish tears that dim my eyes when I think of the times, when he will no longer nestle in my bosom through the silent watches of the night?"[1] Rebecca's sentimental remarks are true to the commitment middle- and upper-class southern women made to breast-feeding and the joy that healthy mothers found in the task. Maternal nurturing was an accepted rite of motherhood and critically important to the infant in an age of dramatic medical procedures and poor sanitation.

Long-established myths and misperceptions have prevented an accurate appreciation of how uniformly southern mothers accepted their traditional maternal responsibility. Because of the presumed easy availability of black wet nurses, it is sometimes imagined that plantation women typically delegated breast-feeding to slaves. A romantic vision of the antebellum mistress—slightly debilitated, crinoline clothed, eternally beautiful, and untouched by any burden that could be taken on by slaves—adds to this misunderstanding.

Reminiscences of southern white childhood written after the Civil War often tell of white babies suckling at the breasts of black mammies.[2] Yet a careful examination of personal letters and journals reveals that a large proportion of middle- and upper-class southern women

1. Rebecca Allen Turner, Little Jesse's Diary, August 29, 1857 (Manuscript Department, William R. Perkins Library, Duke University).

2. Arthur Wallace Calhoun (*A Social History of the American Family from Colonial Times to the Present* [3 vols.; Cleveland, 1945], II, 285) concludes that southern white babies commonly had black nurses and that an early exposure to slaves might explain the southern gentleman's alleged predilection for a black mistress. W. E. B. Du Bois (*The Gift of Black Folk: The Negroes in the Making of America* [Boston, 1924], 65) claims unequivocally that white children "were nursed at the breast of black women." John W.

breast-fed their infants, out of concern for the children's health and development as well as in recognition of their own duties as mothers.

Physicians and medical advisers were unanimous in proclaiming a mother's duty to breast-feed her baby. A major theme in maternal advice books and medical guides was that breast-feeding was an integral part of a mother's commitment to child rearing. Lydia Child and Lydia Sigourney, popular authors who promoted female domesticity, extolled the joys of infant care. As if she personally had discovered a new occupation for women, Mrs. Sigourney implored mothers to create a "season of quietness" during lactation, forgoing, the suggestion was, their accustomed gay social lives for the tranquil rewards of infant care. The author of another guide, *The Maternal Physician,* gave no quarter in entreating each mother to "undergo everything short of death or lasting disease . . . to suckle her child." Dr. William Potts Dewees' thirteenth rule for mothers was to breast-feed their newborn. He noted that only a small minority of women were selfish enough to ignore their babies' needs, and only a handful of men selfish enough to place the shapeliness of their wives above the happiness of their children. Dewees supposed maternal breast-feeding superior to all other ways of providing infant nourishment: it benefited the mother by relieving her of milk abscesses, headaches, nervousness, and even sore eyes, it was better for the baby's health and moral well-being, and it was preferable to a wet nurse's possibly indifferent care. He wanted women to rejoice in the task as God-given and as a "duty rendered sacred both by nature and by reason." John Eberle, an Ohio physician, called breast-feeding a woman's "sacred office" and declared that "the mother's breasts constitute the

---

Blassingame's judgment (*The Slave Community: Plantation Life in the Antebellum South* [New York, 1972], 167) is that the plantation mammy's role, presumably including that of the wet nurse, was "inestimable" in influencing white behavior. Eugene Genovese (*Roll, Jordan, Roll: The World the Slaves Made* [New York, 1974], 355–57) also emphasizes the mammy's critical role as domestic servant. But both Carl Degler (*At Odds: Women and the Family in America from the Revolution to the Present* [New York, 1980], 79) and Claire Elizabeth Fox ("Pregnancy, Childbirth, and Early Infancy in Anglo-American Culture, 1675–1830" [Ph.D. dissertation, University of Pennsylvania, 1966], 228) suggest that by the 1830s, mothers nationwide usually breast-fed their own infants. Guion Griffis Johnson (*Ante-Bellum North Carolina* [Chapel Hill, N.C., 1937], 252), after thoughtful analysis, suggests that only when a mother's health problems or an insufficient milk supply prevented breastfeeding did North Carolina women use wet nurses. Catherine Clinton (*The Plantation Mistress: Women's World in the Old South* [New York, 1982], 190–92) states that in the eighteenth century, most southern mistresses breast-fed their own babies, but by the nineteenth century, wet nurses were much more common.

only genuine fountain from which this delicious and congenial nutriment is to be drawn."[3]

Southern physicians waxed just as eloquent over the benefits of maternal feeding. A southern doctor writing for the *Charleston Medical Journal and Review* stated that "with his mother's milk, the young child drinketh education." And another adviser, innocently imagining that he had sufficient understanding to comment, wrote, "There is no period in a woman's life in which she has so great enjoyment, such perfect health, as when she is nursing the off-spring of her own blood." This southern writer lamented the "fashion of transferring the duties of mother to the wet nurse."[4]

The most significant advantage doctors saw in maternal breast-feeding lay in the healthfulness of mother's milk. Although wet nurses might provide milk as nutritious as the mother's, physicians often regarded substitute feeders warily. There was no guarantee that the wet nurse was healthy, clean, and attentive to the baby's needs. Doctors cautioned mothers that a nurse's milk might be unwholesome, that she could resort to clandestine bottle-feedings, that she might administer drugs to quiet a screaming infant, and that syphilis or another pernicious disease could be transferred from nurse to suckling babe. A few doctors believed that breast milk communicated the characteristics of the lactating woman and that wet nurses thus posed still another risk. Whether physicians had proof that wet nurses were inadequate or whether their reactions were dramatized to influence the indecisive mother, the advice they gave mothers was another side of their pursuit of professionalism. Here too doctors sought to establish themselves as experts on an activity mothers had been performing for millennia. Some doctors may simply have been echoing the warnings of British and French physicians, who had more cause for concern, for wet nurses

3. Lydia Sigourney, *Letters to Mothers* (New York, 1848), 9 (see also Lydia Child, *The Mother's Book* [Boston, 1833]); *The Maternal Physician: A Treatise on the Physical and Medical Treatment of Children* (9th ed.; Philadelphia, 1847), 44; William Potts Dewees, *A Treatise on the Physical and Medical Treatment of Children* (Philadelphia, 1847), 44; John Eberle, *A Treatise on the Diseases and Physical Education of Children* (Cincinnati, 1833), 26.

4. Review of Fleetwood Churchill's *On the Diseases of Infants and Children* and D. Francis Condie's *A Practical Treatise on the Diseases of Children*, in *Charleston Medical Journal and Review*, V (1850), 198; Review of Joel Shew's *Midwifery and the Diseases of Women and Children: Their Diseases and Management*, in *New Orleans Medical and Surgical Journal*, IX (1853), 652.

had been quite popular among well-to-do European families during the eighteenth century.[5]

Antebellum doctors understood that mothers who were ill or who lacked sufficient nourishment could not breast-feed their babies. When a substitute was essential, they urged women to take great care in selecting a wet nurse. The checklist included the proper moral and physical bearing of the nurse as well as the correct consistency and color of her milk, to be tested in a wine glass or, better yet, under a microscope. The habits of the wet nurse were to be temperate, and mothers were to be on guard against wet nurses with a predilection for alcohol. The age of the nurse's own baby was to be considered, for doctors believed that a mother's milk altered as the infant matured. Dewees cautioned against red-haired nurses, for his experience confirmed that that hair color indicated an unstable personality.[6]

Wet nurses were regarded skeptically, but hand-feeding or bottle-feeding was esteemed even less desirable. It was apparent that breast-fed babies were healthier than bottle-fed infants. It was also evident that

5. Eberle, *A Treatise on Diseases and Physical Education*, 27. Jay Mechling ("Advice to Historians on Advice to Mothers," *Journal of Social History*, IX [1975], 44–63) points out the need to consider whether advice manuals reflected current practices or desired behavior. In addition, before using the guides as sources, one must ask whether parents learned anything from them. Mechling feels parenting is a behavior learned primarily from imitation and instruction. He states, "At best, childrearing manuals reflect but do not change childrearing behavior." Yet the wide availability of the volumes in libraries today and the fact that a book by Dewees might run to ten editions give some indication of the number of copies sold in antebellum America. Even though it is true that mothers learned primarily from tradition and the advice shared among friends, family, and neighbors, one should not derogate the manuals' influence, for it is possible that a respected physician like Dewees or Meigs could have had as great an impact on nineteenth-century parenting as Benjamin Spock has had on twentieth-century. It is interesting to note that many of the books were carbon copies of the advice of the experts and that new editions rarely altered earlier suggestions. Does this mean that few new ideas invigorated the medical profession, or does it mean that publishers controlled the later editions, reprinting without revising? In any case, though advice books provide fascinating reading, they do not necessarily reflect maternal ideas and practice nor even the thinking of the majority of physicians. For information on the European custom of sending infants to rural wet nurses, see Lawrence Stone, *The Family, Sex, and Marriage in England, 1500–1800* (New York, 1980), 428–32; and George D. Sussman, *Selling Mother's Milk: The Wet-Nursing Business in France, 1715–1914* (Urbana, Ill., 1982).

6. Charles Delucena Meigs, *Observations on Certain of the Diseases of Young Children* (Philadelphia, 1850), 219; William Buchan, *Advice to Mothers, on the Subject of Their Own Health, and of the Means of Promoting the Health, Strength, and Beauty of Their Offspring* (Boston, 1809), in *The Physician and Child-Rearing: Two Guides, 1809–1894* (New York, 1972), 50–51; Dewees, *A Treatise on the Treatment of Children*, 99.

when babies were weaned from breast milk to other liquids, they often became ill. Nineteenth-century doctors did not know that breast milk carries certain antibodies that help the infant fight disease and that animal milk lacks those antibodies. They were also unaware of bacteria and its presence in foods. Statistics circulated by an English physician revealed that, in the early nineteenth century in London, seven out of eight hand-fed infants died. Americans were reluctant to admit that their numbers were as dismal, but it was obvious that bottle-feeding often conduced to ill health. In an era of questionable sanitation—without pasteurization, refrigeration, or an understanding of bacteria—any food was a potential health hazard. Few southern families could cool their food properly, and during long, hot summers, keeping food and milk fresh was difficult. Yet doctors acknowledged that under certain circumstances mothers had to resort to hand-feeding. When that was necessary, they recommended clean bottles and a substitute closely resembling the maternal product. Ass's milk received the highest commendation. One practical female writer suggested that the ass be brought to the front door and milked six times daily to ensure freshness. A mixture of cow's milk, water, and brown sugar—or cow's milk mixed with bread, and called pap—was the most common replacement for breast milk in the antebellum South.[7]

Infant death remained alarmingly common through the antebellum period. One of the most frightening causes of illness and mortality was cholera infantum. The federal census of 1860 reported the disease to be five and a half times as great in the South as in the North. The disease, commonly referred to as summer diarrhea, is a severe intestinal disorder, particularly common from late spring through early autumn. Symptoms include severe diarrhea, vomiting, headaches, dehydration, and debilitation. Youngsters between the ages of six months and two years were the most susceptible, and personal comments attest to the endemic presence of the disease in the Old South. Jean Syme wrote of her rural Virginia county, "This place is already getting sickly for infants, as many as six died in the course of this week, with bowel com-

7. Samuel J. Fomon, *Infant Nutrition* (2nd ed.; Philadelphia, 1974), 1; Mrs. J. Bakewell, *The Mother's Practical Guide in the Physical, Intellectual, and Moral Training of Her Children* (3rd American ed., New York, 1846), 32. For nursing practices, see also Thomas E. Cone, *Two Hundred Years of Feeding Infants in America* (Columbus, Ohio, 1976), and Randolph Trumbach, *The Rise of the Egalitarian Family: Aristocratic Kinship and Domestic Relations in Eighteenth-Century England* (New York, 1978).

plaints." Jane Woodruff, of Charleston, lost four of her young children to the "bowel complaint." Rebecca Haywood Hall reported from her plantation home that her infant Betsy "has been sick with dysentery ever since I last wrote." In October, 1846, and again in June, 1847, Eliza Jane DeRosset, of Wilmington, North Carolina, wrote that her baby suffered "violent dysentery." Physicians' children were not immune. Phoebe Elliott, of Beaufort, South Carolina, remarked that the young children of three of their local physicians had all been sick with dysentery. Although doctors often spoke as if the disease was peculiar to urban areas, comments like these indicate that it was prevalent throughout the South.[8]

If the number of journal articles on a subject indicates the level of medical concern, cholera infantum caused antebellum physicians a good deal of worry. The endemic and virulent nature of the disease was part of the problem. Doctors tried, without success, to pinpoint the disease's causes and discover effective remedies. So poorly understood was the illness that the federal census of 1850 included it under "teething" as a cause of death, for that broad heading encompassed all disturbances of the digestive tract. The true causes of cholera infantum were many, though the most common one, undoubtedly, was spoiled food and milk, particularly during the time when a child was being weaned. Since that period coincided with an increased mobility of the child, exposure to unfamiliar and unhealthful bacteria both indoors and out could also induce the diarrheal illness.[9]

8. *U.S. Federal Census, Statistics of the United States (Including Mortality, Property, &c.) in 1860* (Washington, D.C., 1866), 246. On cholera infantum, there are numerous nineteenth-century studies available, including information in the standard medical advice books as well as specific articles and monographs. See, for example, N. Potter, "Observations on Cholera Infantum," *Baltimore Medical and Surgical Journal and Review,* I (1833), 104–25; A. Griggs, "Cholera Infantum," *Atlanta Medical and Surgical Journal,* V (1860), 589–95; J. M. Dill, "Observations Principally on the Acute Form of Cholera Infantum," *Carolina Medical Journal,* I (1825), 31–49; and Moses L. Knapp, *Essay on Cholera Infantum* (Cincinnati, 1855). Jean Syme to Rebecca Cameron, May 11, 1811, in Cameron Family Papers, Southern Historical Collection, L. R. Wilson Library, University of North Carolina at Chapel Hill; Jane Harris Woodruff Diary, 21 (Clarkson Family Papers, Special Collections, J. Murrey Atkins Library, University of North Carolina at Charlotte); Rebecca Haywood Hall to Elizabeth Haywood, June 17, 1839, in Haywood Family Collection, Southern Historical Collection; Eliza Jane DeRossett to Kate De-Rossett, October 12, 1846, in DeRossett Family Papers, Southern Historical Collection; Phoebe Elliott to her son William Elliott, August 3, 1836, in Elliott-Gonzales Letters, Southern Historical Collection.

9. I wish to thank Dr. K. David Patterson, of the University of North Carolina at Charlotte, for contributing background information on cholera infantum.

The difficulty physicians had in determining the causes of cholera infantum tempted them to speculation. J. H. Buchanan, a student at the Medical College of South Carolina, had trouble pruning his long list of principal causes. In his thesis of 1841 discussing the disease, he included improper food, dentition, worms, contaminated air, the milk of pregnant women, unhealthy nurses, and dirty skin among possible causes. Dr. Samuel Dickson, a professor at the same institution, added high atmospheric temperatures and malaria to the list. Dr. John Gunn suggested that sudden temperature changes encouraged cholera infantum; J. M. Dill blamed the disease on summer fruit, excessive food, and "some fish." A physician in Murfreesboro, Tennessee, who attributed most diseases to miasmic conditions, declared that cholera infantum was due to a "high thermoelectrical condition" in the atmosphere. Occasionally, close observation brought a doctor near to the truth. Dickson noted that "the attempt to wean a child while teething, and the substitution of paps and other kinds of improper food for its natural and healthy aliment—breast milk—often prove fatal, by exciting a diarrhea." Another doctor observed in the *New Orleans Medical and Surgical Journal* that when a child passed from an agreeable diet of breast milk to one less suited to its system, illness often followed.[10]

Physicians prescribed as many cures for cholera infantum as they found causes, and most of their remedies were heroic. The best one, according to the Murfreesboro doctor, was a dose of rhubarb and magnesia, and if that failed, a purging with calomel. Dickson suggested a purging with calomel, rhubarb, or castor oil, and a leeching behind the ears. Gunn suggested blistering the stomach as a last resort, which he declared "scarcely fails." By midcentury, physicians appeared no closer to an effective management of cholera infantum than they had been in 1800. With multiple causes ascribed and questionable cures recommended, there is little wonder that cholera infantum continued to be a major health problem. But on the eve of the Civil War, southern doctors became aware that the illness was less prevalent in some regions. Its

10. J. H. Buchanan, "Cholera Infantum" (1841), in Waring Historical Library, Medical University of South Carolina, Charleston; Samuel Henry Dickson, *Elements of Medicine: A Compendious View of Pathology and Therapeutics; or, The History and Treatment of Disease* (Philadelphia, 1855), 533; John C. Gunn, *Gunn's Domestic Medicine; or, Poor Man's Friend* (2nd ed.; Madisonville, Tenn., 1834), 403; Dill, "Observations," 35; William T. Baskette (president of the Medical Society of Rutherford County, Tennessee), "Cholera Infantum," *Southern Journal of the Medical and Physical Sciences*, I (1853), 82–84; Dickson, *Elements of Medicine*, 534; *New Orleans Medical and Surgical Journal*, VII (1850), 379.

decline, observed first in urban areas, seemed conjoined to improved public health measures, particularly better drinking water. Dr. L. P. Yandell, of Louisville, stated that Nashville had fewer reported cases by the late 1850s. "Since the erection of water works there, the children of that city have suffered much less with bowel complaints, and the improvement is attributed to the substitution of river for limestone water," he remarked. The elimination of limestone had less to do with the disease's reduction than the elimination of pollution did, but the step was positive, whatever the reasoning. Unfortunately, few southern cities duplicated Nashville's efforts before the Civil War.[11]

The best way for southern women to protect their baby's health was to provide proper nourishment—ideally, maternal milk. An examination of personal journals and letters shows that the majority of middle- and upper-class southern women breast-fed their babies whenever possible (see Table IV in Appendix One). A count of every mother's comment on infant feeding in the manuscripts consulted for this study suggests that more than 85 percent of all southern mothers breast-fed their babies. Approximately 20 percent used a wet nurse, while 10 percent had to hand-feed their newborn. The fact that two or more methods of feeding were often necessary explains why the percentages add up to more than 100. The relatively high status of the women's husbands—planters, clergymen, lawyers, and merchants—means that these families could have afforded a wet nurse. One must remember, too, that women who had problems breast-feeding were usually the most articulate about infant nourishment, and thus the data are, if anything, skewed in favor of alternative methods. The strong preference of southern mothers to breast-feed their infants was influenced by tradition, feminine pride, health concerns, and a desire to accept responsibility for their babies' well-being. From the moment of birth, most southern infants received from their mother not only love and attention but also healthful nourishment.

Probably the most powerful motive southern women had for breast-feeding was tradition. Women had always nursed their babies, and most would never have considered doing otherwise. In fact, because southern mothers considered breast-feeding the norm, they rarely felt impelled to write on the subject. Often the only comment

11. Baskette, "Cholera Infantum," 88; Dickson, *Elements of Medicine*, 535; Gunn, *Gunn's Domestic Medicine*, 404; L. P. Yandell, "On Cholera Infantum," *Western Journal of Medicine and Surgery*, 3rd ser., XII (1853), 93.

one finds after reading dozens of letters on infant rearing will be a cryptic reference or the brief comment "Weaned baby from breast." Mothers were far more eager to expend ink on descriptions of infant antics and health.

Yet there is more than silence revealing women's reactions to infant nurturing. Just as both doctors and women assumed that most women could bear children, so they also assumed that most mothers could breast-feed their babies. Feminine pride was tied up with nursing, and when a woman fell short, she often felt guilty or inadequate. In 1854, Kate DeRosset Meares had to supplement her limited milk supply. She wrote her mother that she had accepted a slave's offer to help feed her infant son, but she clearly felt reservations: "If I was certain that it was right, I would be delighted to have him well filled twice a day." Laura Norwood, of Hillsboro, North Carolina, regretted her inability to breast-feed and wished that she could be a "good" mother. A very devoted mother who was able to nourish all her own children, Margaret Mordecai Devereux expressed sorrow that her sister could not breast-feed her first child. "Your last letter, my dearest sister," she wrote, "saying that you are unable to nurse your baby has made us all very unhappy."[12]

It was not unusual for men to take pride in a wife's ability to feed the newborn or even for them to tout her capacity. In 1801, Daniel Anderson proudly remarked to his brother-in-law that their infant "has not had one hour's sickness," because his wife Mary "has aplenty for him."[13]

Second, mothers had a motive for breast-feeding their newborn because, like Rebecca Allen Turner, they found the experience rewarding. A mother's commitment to her child involved personal nurturing. Special moments with the suckling infant fortified the bond between mother and child. Pregnancy was regarded as a "time of trouble" and was often debilitating. Parturition was extremely painful and could be life threatening. But the presence of a helpless, healthy infant was a joy and caused memory of the earlier trials to fade. Mothers could forget

12. Kate DeRossett Meares to Eliza Jane DeRossett, July 23, 1854, in DeRossett Family Papers; Laura Norwood to Selina Lenoir, April 9, 1837, June 9, 1837, both in Lenoir Family Papers, Southern Historical Collection; Margaret Devereux to Ellen Mordecai, January 11, 1851, in Jacob Mordecai Papers, Manuscript Department, William R. Perkins Library.

13. Daniel Anderson to Duncan Cameron, August 21, 1801, in Cameron Family Papers.

the suffering they had undergone, as the blessed newborn lay at their breast. Eugenia Phillips empathized with her daughter after the arrival of a child. "Thank God all is over and I picture your happiness, gazing on the little dough lump in your arms," she wrote. "There is no happiness equal to what you are now enjoying." Virginia Caroline Clay, of Alabama, echoed the feelings of many southern mothers: "Since the birth of my sweet babe it seems that my maternal instinct is so strong hope can never die again."[14]

Precious moments with the infant were often some of the happiest a southern mother knew or, at least, wrote about. Mrs. Hall, who deteriorated mentally and physically during her brief, unhappy marriage, found breast-feeding rewarding. In a blissful moment following the birth of her first child, Rebecca emoted to her absent husband, "Oh! Would that you were here to see her at the breast suckling as she was on Sunday last when I received your letter." Mary Ann Gwynn, of Hillsboro, North Carolina, whose poor health necessitated the hand-feeding of her first infant, was delighted to breast-feed her second child. "I have plenty of milk for her," she wrote her sister, "and I count it a great blessing and privilege to be able to suckle my babe." It was assumed that infants preferred their mother's breast. Selina Lenoir, of North Carolina, believed her granddaughter's taste buds explained why her daughter was breast-feeding after a year. "Her little ladyship has such a nice and delicate taste," she decided, "she did not relish the nurse they hired for her and shewd symptoms of disgust, whenever she took nourishment from her."[15]

An indication of maternal attachment was the difficulty many mothers had in weaning their infants. Only sixteen mothers of those whose diaries and letters figure in this study give enough information for us to know their infants' ages at weaning. In this small sample, breast-feeding ceased at between six and twenty-two months of age, with a mean age of thirteen and a half months. Women tried to avoid making the change during the hot summer months when cholera infantum was epidemic. Physicians recommended weaning at between six and twelve months of

14. Mrs. Phillips to her daughter, 1862, in Phillips and Myers Family Papers, Southern Historical Collection; Virginia Caroline Clay to Mr. T. T. Tunstall, January 25, 1857, in Clement Claiborne Clay Letters, Manuscript Department, William R. Perkins Library.

15. Rebecca Haywood Hall to Albert Hall, February 24, 1836, in Haywood Family Collection; Mary Ann Gwynn to Sarah, March 11, 1844, in Lenoir Family Papers; Selina Lenoir to Julia Howe, April 12, 1845, in Chiliab Smith Howe Papers, Southern Historical Collection.

age. But it appears that women nursed as long as they desired, until nursing was uncomfortable, or as long as they felt it beneficial to the child.

Whether breast-feeding was to end when the child was six months old or not "till he gets his teeth," weaning was traumatic. Some southern mothers shunned the infant, sent it away for several days, or covered their nipples with bitter-tasting salve. When Frances Bumpas, of Raleigh, had to stop feeding her daughter after six months, she noted sadly that it was "grievous to wean her." Poor health forced Caroline Laurens to wean her daughter early. Missing her special moments alone with the infant, Caroline was "almost tempted to wake her and give her the breast one night." She fought temptation by avoiding the baby at mealtimes, when her resolve was most vulnerable. An extreme degree of maternal devotion was demonstrated by Mrs. L. E. Lenoir, of Boone County, North Carolina, who seems to have carried her nurturing beyond the limits of propriety. "My dear father and mother will be ready to scold me," she confessed to her sister, "when they have heard I have not yet weaned a boy that is large enough to talk of horse-racing, can make a fire, and feed calves." Even if the youngster was terribly precocious, his weaning had been delayed too long.[16]

A number of women breast-fed despite pain or physical problems. Many mothers suffered illnesses while lactating yet did not seek an assistant nor rely on bottle-feeding. Despite a severe case of malaria, Eliza Clitherall's daughter, Frances, continued to nurse her baby. Rebecca Holcombe, who had an abscess on one breast and an incapacitating illness that kept her housebound for six months, fed her baby as frequently as possible. Mary Jeffreys Bethell broke out with measles the day she gave birth, had a relapse a month later in which she suffered chills, fever, cough, and stomach pains, yet managed to feed her infant until her milk ran dry. Suffering fever and ague, Ann Beasley breast-fed her son; she was able to report, "Our dear little Charles sucks and grows finely." Both Lydia Turrentine, of North Carolina, and Ruth Jones, of Georgia, nursed their babies on their deathbeds.[17]

16. Frances Bumpas Journal, September 13, 1845 (Southern Historical Collection); Caroline Laurens Diary, April 18, 1827 (Southern Historical Collection); Mrs. L. E. Lenoir to Martha Boucheville, in Lenoir Family Papers.

17. Eliza Clitherall Autobiography and Diary, VIII, 1832–51 (Southern Historical Collection); William Henry Holcombe Diary, February–April, 1855 (Southern Historical Collection); Mary Bethell Diary, January 25, 1855, p. 22 (Southern Historical Collection);

Perhaps southern mothers also favored breast-feeding because they understood that lactation could impede conception. But if they did understand it, the results were not especially striking, judging by the size of southern families. Current studies indicate that breast-feeding can help space births about two years apart, with variations in the time depending on the frequency of nursing and the infant's dependence on maternal milk as its major source of nourishment.[18] Lactation usually prolongs amenorrhea; moreover, a nursing infant sometimes slept with its mother, perhaps limiting coitus as well. Though most southern women found motherhood satisfying, many must have agreed with Ella Clanton Thomas, who remarked during her third pregnancy in as many years of marriage, "I would dislike to think I would never have other children but then I would willingly have a considerable lapse of time between them." The *Charleston Medical Journal and Review* and other southern medical journals carried an article by Robert Barnes, a nineteenth-century physician, assessing the effectiveness of lactation as a method of contraception. On the basis of surveying one hundred English women, Barnes concluded that "mammary activity" retarded uterine action. He discovered that mothers who breast-fed their infants had a lower rate of conception. Despite the appearance of this article in well-respected southern journals, birth control was seldom discussed in medical advice books. Physicians must have been aware of the relationship between nursing and the inhibition of fertility, though whether they privately spread word of it is unknown. Since southern fathers preferred large families, there is no evidence that they encouraged birth control of any sort. Southern women, however, may have quietly shared the knowledge that breast-feeding delayed the return of menstruation, but they seldom, if ever, discussed such matters in their letters or journals.[19]

Ann Beasley to John Beasley, June 10, 1805, in Sarah M. Lemmon (ed.), *The Pettigrew Papers*, Vol. I, *1685–1818* (Raleigh, N.C., 1971), 374; L. P. Rothwell to Dorothy Parish, December 7, 1847, in Parish Family Papers, Southern Historical Collection; Robert Manson Myers, *Children of Pride: A True Story of Georgia and the Civil War* (New Haven, 1972), 705, 715.

18. Robert G. Potter, "Application of Field Studies to Research on the Physiology of Human Reproduction," *Journal of Chronic Diseases*, XVIII (1965), 1125; R. V. Short, "Breast Feeding," *Scientific American*, CCL (April, 1984), 35–42.

19. Ella Clanton Thomas Diary, June 11, 1856, p. 143 (Manuscript Department, William R. Perkins Library); *Charleston Medical Journal and Review*, IX (1853), 250, and noted in *Nashville Journal of Medicine and Surgery*, VI (1854), 152.

From a practical point of view, breast-feeding may sometimes have been practiced simply because southern women felt it easiest for themselves and healthiest for the infant. They found bottle-feeding a nuisance and, like physicians, observed that it could be detrimental to the baby's health. In an age of primitive sanitation, there was little assurance that a bottle—of glass, metal, or bone, and covered with a cow's teat or piece of linen—would be clean. Preparing a proper substitute for breast milk and ensuring its freshness were often difficult. The weary mother had no premixed formula or refrigerated bottle for midnight feedings. Fanny Lawrence, of Louisiana, who had little milk of her own, first used a wet nurse and then hand-feeding. She related that she found bottles a nuisance and that one night she "took him down stairs and before they could get his milk ready he made such a fuss that Aunt took him." Mrs. Gwynn knew firsthand the contrast between bottle- and breast-feeding. "When I think of the trouble we had to raise my little Sally with the bottle," she wrote, "I feel like I could never be thankful enough for being so blest with this one." Her sister Laura complained of the extra work involved in bottle-feeding. "My time has been very much occupied with the children," she said, "as always must be the case with a fed child." Not only were bottle-feedings inconvenient and the contents often unhealthful, but they could also keep women from doing what they wanted. Laura wished to show off her two-month-old daughter but decided against the long stagecoach ride to her mother's home. She declined the invitation because her baby was "obliged to be fed frequently through the day and I could not stop to get milk for her if I were in the stage—she could not depend on me for support, for I have not milk enough to keep a kitten from starving." From a mother's perspective, breast-feeding was not only the most satisfying and salubrious but also the least restrictive way of feeding the newborn.[20]

Since bottle-feeding had few supporters, the usual option for mothers who could not breast-feed was a wet nurse. Yet finding a suitable nurse was often tricky, even in an area of the country with a large slave population. The nurse probably had to be feeding her own infant, with enough milk to sustain two babies, or to have just lost a child she had been breast-feeding. Yet sometimes locating a satisfactory wet nurse

20. Fanny Brashear Lawrence to Henry Lawrence, September 4, 1845, in Brashear Family Papers, Southern Historical Collection; Mary Ann Gwynn to Sarah Lenoir, March 11, 1844, Laura Norwood to Selina Lenoir, April 24, 1844, May, 1837, all in Lenoir Family Papers.

was relatively easy, or at least letters and diaries make it seem so. Ella Clanton Thomas lost her first child, had a spontaneous abortion, had a miscarriage, and then lost another infant when it was seven months old. Ella foresaw more sorrow when she discovered that she did not have enough milk to keep her newborn healthy. But her wise mother offered a solution. "Ma concluded I had better have a wet nurse as I did not give nourishment enough," Ella wrote. "One of the women at the plantation had just lost a baby a week old, and Pa kindly offered us the use of her." After the birth of her next child, Ella made a similar arrangement. The Charles Jones family, of Liberty County, Georgia, temporarily adopted an infant granddaughter after its mother died of puerperal fever. From their more than one hundred slaves on three large plantations, the Joneses apparently had little difficulty in choosing an altogether satisfactory black woman to nurse the baby. Samuel Pickens, who was distraught over his wife's death after childbirth, found some relief in his sister's concern for the infant. "My sister Dorothy took it home as soon as she thought it could be safely removed," he wrote his mother, "and she fortunately had a woman who had a child about one month old. . . . The woman who suckles the child was a field hand." It is doubtful that any of these families took the precaution of examining the nurse's milk under a microscope. When an infant was crying for a nipple, most families probably accepted whomever they could find. Whether slave women resented feeding a white baby, particularly if their own had just died, or whether their maternal instincts prevailed is only to be guessed.[21]

But other correspondence reveals that it could be hard to find a wet nurse. In some cases, mothers who because of poor health or inclination would have preferred to cede nursing to others could not, because no one was there to take their place. Most plantation families probably relied on word of mouth among friends and neighbors to find a slave woman. In cities like Charleston, finding a nursing woman could involve an active campaign. Newspaper advertisements attest to the effort expended. As the population increased, the city's papers carried a greater number of calls for nurses. Some advertisements stated the obvious, but others laid down specific requirements:

21. Ella Clanton Thomas Diary, December 26, 1858; Myers, *Children of Pride*, 715–20; Samuel Pickens to Selina Lenoir, April 26, 1836, in Lenoir Family Papers.

Wanted, a healthy wet nurse without a child.

Wet nurse wanted. A wet nurse to go traveling; none but a white woman need apply.

To hire, a colored wet nurse, with a healthy child.

Wanted immediately, a wet nurse, white or colored, without a child. Good recommendations would be satisfactory.

Many of the advertisements ran for several days, likely indicating a dearth of replies. The notices also give evidence that many middle- and upper-class families considered both black and white nurses acceptable. If there was a preference, it probably reflected the racial composition of the domestic help the family had become most accustomed to in a period when a growing immigrant population made white help more accessible, at least in the cities. The primary concern, however, was the life of the newborn, and however specific the advertisement, many families would doubtless compromise to ensure the health and life of the baby. Milk supply, not race, was the main worry.[22]

Rachel Mordecai Lazarus, of Wilmington, North Carolina, attested to the problems of one southern family in finding a wet nurse. After the delivery of her baby, she suffered from malaria, and her baby had thrush. Her physician gave her quinine, but chills and fever left her supine. "A wet nurse the doctor declared was indispensable," Rachel wrote later, "and every exertion was instantly made to procure one—for ten days I saw no more of my sweet infant." Rebecca was obviously upset that her poor health forced others to make an important maternal decision. Even though the family resided in a city of some size and was relatively well known, it had trouble finding a wet nurse, if it found one at all.[23]

Alicia Middleton wrote to the Dehon family, of York County, South Carolina, about another difficult case:

A wet nurse has at length been procured, in rather an unsatisfactory way. Mrs. Girardeux, meeting a good natured healthy looking Negro woman in the street with an infant in her arms, inquired of her if she knew of a wet

22. Charleston *Courier,* July 1, 1834, July 28, 1851, July 14, 1859, July 27, 1859. Summer months were selected because more advertisements for wet nurses appeared then, probably as a result of a desire to avoid handfeeding during the season of cholera infantum.

23. Rachel Mordecai Lazarus to Ellen Mordecai, October 13, 1828, in Jacob Mordecai Papers.

nurse to be hired. She said she was one herself, and was in the hands of a broker for sale but did not know if she could be hired. Mr. T, with his usual alacrity, applied to the broker, and found that the woman was from Georgetown, and had been brought up in the family of Mrs. John Kirth, he obtained from Mr. R a pretty satisfactory account of her, and having had her on trial a few days, and finding her good tempered and anxious to please, they determined to purchase her, from the funds to be rec'd from the sale of the horses, and thus if possible to be relieved from the present, and perhaps future difficulties of the like kind. . . . I am sure you will wish success to the plan.

For the Lazaruses, for the family described by Alicia Middleton, and for many others, the search for a wet nurse, particularly during the critical early days of an infant's life, could create a good deal of anxiety.[24]

Southerners were generally satisfied with the women they selected to feed their infants. White women showed a wide range of reactions to their domestic servants, ranging from declarations of complete dependence to exclamations of annoyance, but most parents were surprisingly content with the substitute feeder. It is easy to become overly demanding with a servant so intimately involved with one's child, but complaints were rare. Pickens had only complimentary things to say about the black wet nurse at his sister's house. He described her as a "fine, healthy, careful Negro woman." Mrs. Norwood attributed her third child's robust health and large size to her black nurse, Eliza, and rhapsodized that "Eliza is a great help to me, as she has plenty of milk for the baby." Three years later she commended the woman for being "quite smart—has plenty of milk for her child and mine." Southern mothers were generally grateful for the help they received in caring for the health of their child. Yet one husband might not have been. Thomas Chaplin, of South Carolina, was relieved that his wife could breast-feed their newborn. "Hope to God it will not have to suck a bottle and what is ten times worse, a Negro," he grumbled.[25]

The role of black nurses in nourishing southern white babies has been exaggerated. That is partly because the travel accounts of nineteenth-century visitors to the South paid disproportionate attention to the

24. Alicia Middleton to Anne Dehon, n.d., in Dehon Family Papers, South Carolina Historical Society Library, Charleston.

25. Samuel Pickens to Selina Lenoir, April 26, 1836, Laura Norwood to Selina Lenoir, September 25, 1842, August 27, 1845, all in Lenoir Family Papers; Rosengarten, *Tombee*, 370. For southern women's unenthusiastic reactions to slavery, see Sudie Duncan Sides, "Southern Women and Slavery," *History Today*, XX (1970), 54–60, 124–30.

suckling of white infants by black mammies, since that was something largely unknown in the North and in Britain—and something that, in many cases, offended the racial sensibilities of the visitors. Historians at times mistake chronicles of the extraordinary for descriptions of the quotidian. Frederick Law Olmsted, the most famous observer of ante-bellum southern society and later a renowned landscape architect, was struck by the close relationships between blacks and whites, and he noticed that black mammies often carried white infants in their arms. He did not, however, mention breast-feeding, either because he saw none or because he found the subject embarrassing. Fannie Kemble, who abhor-red slavery, found domestic servants lacking in basic cleanliness. "This very disagreeable peculiarity does not prevent southern women from hanging their infants at the breasts of negresses," she sighed. Exactly how common it was that white children "hung" from the breasts of slaves she does not tell. This outspoken abolitionist was anything but disinterested. Her alertness to breast-feeding owed partly to the fact that her two young children—one still suckling—and a presumably capable white nurse accompanied her on her travels. Anyway, a writer would be unlikely to see large numbers of white mothers nursing their young, since breast-feeding was usually done in private. Even one white child at the breast of a slave would have been cause for comment, particularly by an observer like Mrs. Kemble, who believed black wet nurses far below her standard.[26]

Personal narratives by former slaves do little to contradict the idea that nineteenth-century southern mothers usually breast-fed their infants. In oral testimony gathered during the 1930s, few slaves mentioned serving as wet nurses. Only rarely did a child report that his mother "nu'sed de white babies from her own breas'" or that a woman "suckled all the master's children." Of course, many of the women interviewed were only children or teenagers when emancipation occurred, and not old enough to suckle infants. Perhaps others were reluctant to bring up a task they found distasteful. Or perhaps this maternal duty was so natural that it did not occur to them to speak of it. Still, the evidence is strong that when southern mothers used slaves, it was primarily for infant care rather than breast-feeding.[27]

26. Frederick Law Olmsted, *A Journey in the Seaboard Slave States in the Years 1853–1854, with Remarks on Their Economy* (1856; rpr. New York, 1904), I, 19, II, 28–29; Frances Anne Kemble, *Journal of a Residence on a Georgian Plantation in 1838–1839,* ed. John A. Scott (London, 1961), 61.

27. Principal sources of slave testimony are John W. Blassingame's *Slave Testimony:*

Reminiscences of southern white childhood romantically perpetuate the erroneous impression of the black wet nurse's role on the antebellum plantation. Susan Dabney Smedes recalled that "the mistress had wet-nurses for her babies chosen from among her Negro servants"; the implication was that most mothers gave up breast-feeding to their black servants. Reminiscences also dwell on the mammy's devotion to the white children, which is sometimes depicted as deeper than her feelings for her own family. Thomas Nelson Page, in his idealized social history of antebellum Virginia, recalled that the "careful and faithful" black nurse cared more for the master's children than for her own. After living through the humiliation of the Civil War and Reconstruction, Southerners developed a sentimental view of antebellum days, when selfless slaves served kind masters. The black mammy was elevated into a symbol of the congeniality between blacks and whites when allegedly both knew their place. Nevertheless, other reminiscences state with just as much conviction that white mothers hardly ever employed black wet nurses. Susan Eppes related that in her family of ten children and sixty-two first cousins a black wet nurse suckled only one child. She reported that "southern mothers nourished babes at the breast," for "they had time for all domestic duties and the care and training of their children came first." (It seems that nearly all the Eppes women were in abnormally good health after childbirth.) In the main, however, women's comments in letters and journals support the view that white mothers nursed their own infants.[28]

Keeping a newborn alive and healthy was such a critically immediate need that emergency measures often had to be taken. Most southern mothers had lost at least one child, and all knew that proper infant nutrition was essential. When a mother died or was too ill to breast-feed, it was not always possible to find a wet nurse. If the family wished to avoid hand-feeding, it might try to arrange for the sharing of breast milk. A female relative or friend might come to the rescue when a

Two Centuries of Letters, Speeches, Interviews, and Autobiographies (Baton Rouge, 1977) and George P. Rawick's *The American Slave: A Composite Autobiography* (41 vols. and index; Westport, Conn., 1972–81), 1st ser., II, III, 2nd ser., XII–XIV, 1st supp. ser., I, VI–X. I found very little information about wet-nursing.

28. Susan Dabney Smedes, *Memorials of a Southern Planter* (1888), ed. Fletcher M. Green (New York, 1965), 72; Thomas Nelson Page, *Social Life in Old Virginia Before the War* (New York, 1897), 57; Susan Bradford Eppes, *The Negro of the Old South: A Bit of Period History* (Chicago, 1925), 76. See also Deborah White, *Ar'n't I a Woman? Female Slaves in the Plantation South* (New York, 1986), esp. "Jezebel and Mammy," 46–61.

newborn's life hung in the balance. When Virginia Shelton, of Tennessee, noticed a motherless infant traveling with its father, she willingly fed it from her full breasts. After Mrs. Clitherall gave birth, she suckled both her new child and a newborn granddaughter whose mother was ill. She remarked that "it does not often occur, that the grandchild is suckled by the grandmother." In her younger years, she had employed a wet nurse, because her milk supply had been inadequate.[29]

Mrs. Gwynn was so ill after giving birth that she could not breast-feed. Her infant daughter was also weak. Her sister Sarah, who was attending her, wrote their mother that they "got one of her neighbors Mrs. Austin to come and nurse her yesterday and she came this morning and this evening." Mary Ann had a black wet nurse available, but because she had little milk, the family was afraid the infant would not get enough nourishment. Hand-feeding was never considered for a baby so delicate. "We expect Mrs. Austin to nurse her three times a day and let sister and Eliza keep her the rest of the time," Sarah continued. "I have been thinking that when baby got well enough, I would get sister to go over and stay several weeks, and we could try Sallie's milk, and if it answered, she could come over and do the washing." The options open to Mary Ann confused by their number, and Sarah finally confessed that she needed her mother's advice. "Think about it please!" she urged. "Desperate cases will occur and this is a desperate one. Mrs. Austin is so kind and good hearted. . . . She is more than willing to do all she can for sister's baby but you know it is very inconvenient for a woman with small children to leave home three times a day for an hour or so, and we can't expect her to do it long. Poor little creature you can't realize how very frail and delicate it is unless you could be with her awhile." Mary Ann was blessed to have an understanding and generous neighbor with an abundant milk supply, and fortunate as well to have a concerned family.[30]

Less common were cases where white women nursed black infants. Mary Jones, of Georgia, conveyed the news that her daughter Mary Jones Mallard was feeding a slave child. "Your dear sister has such an abundance of nourishment," she wrote her son, "that she has had to nurse one of the little Negroes." If she had to, that was not in order to

29. Virginia Campbell Shelton to Margaret Campbell, March 10, 1852, in Campbell Family Letters, Manuscript Department, William R. Perkins Library; Eliza Clitherall Autobiography and Diary, VII, 35.

30. Sarah to Selina Lenoir, August 1, 1854, in Lenoir Family Papers.

relieve pressure, for milk could have been removed manually or with a breast pump. A male slave described in the Smedes memoirs boasted that his white mistress nursed him. Robert Ellett, a Virginia slave, recalled seeing his mistress nurse one of his brothers as well as her own baby. One could argue that simple plantation economics led white women to feed slave children whose lives depended on getting safe milk. But it is likely that women who shared their milk were also motivated by the desire to keep any child alive and healthy, whether black or white. Here was another way that some southern mothers rose above racial prejudice.[31]

Feeding a baby was tiring, particularly for a mother whose health was already questionable or who suffered severely during labor and faced a long recovery. Often specific medical problems interfered with lactation. Anne Cameron could not nurse, for she had a painful abscess on one breast and admitted that "the operation of nursing dear little Mary drew tears almost every time." Her physician diagnosed the problem as a "stoppage of a milk vein" and recommended lancing, but Anne refused to submit to the knife, claiming her nerves would not tolerate the action. Temporary health problems could prevent nursing. Eliza Middleton wrote that a friend who suffered a "rising" between her breasts had hired a substitute because she could not feed her infant but that she expected to return to nursing soon. Medical advisers also cautioned women who were pregnant or menstruating not to breast-feed their babies. Some doctors apparently believed that suckling drew vital supplies away from the fetus; a greater number seem to have believed that milk from menstruating or pregnant women could be tainted. Dr. Alva Curtis thought that pregnancy decreased a lactating mother's milk supply, and Dickson called the milk of pregnant women an "unwholesome secretion." Southern women often heeded the medical advice, and as soon as they realized that they were pregnant, they ceased breast-feeding.[32]

Another antebellum idea was that a mother's milk transmitted cer-

31. Myers, *Children of Pride*, 415; Smedes, *Memorials*, 56, 198; Charles L. Perdue, Jr., Thomas E. Barden, and Robert K. Phillips (eds.), *Weevils in the Wheat: Interviews with Virginia Ex-Slaves* (Charlottesville, Va., 1976), 84.

32. Anne Cameron to Paul Cameron, December 26, 1845, in Cameron Family Papers; Eliza Middleton to Mary Hering Middleton, Tuesday the 18th, 1842, in Hering-Middleton Collection, South Carolina Historical Society Library; Alva Curtis, *Lectures on Midwifery and the Forms of Disease Peculiar to Women and Children* (2nd ed.; Columbus, Ohio, 1841), 42; Dickson, *Elements of Medicine*, 553.

tain characteristics of the lactating woman to the suckling infant. Any woman who was deranged, overexcited, nervous, or ill was therefore urged to cease feeding her infant. In Nathaniel Hawthorne's *Scarlet Letter,* Hester Prynne, overwrought and nervous, at one point requires professional assistance "not merely for Hester herself, but still more urgently for the child; who, drawing its sustenance from the maternal bosom, seemed to have drunk with it all the turmoil, the anguish, and despair which pervaded the mother's system." Lactating women who are tired or tense often have less milk, but there is no evidence that the nourishment alters in form.[33]

Mothers frequently continued to nurse when ill, though their husbands and other family members often expressed concern about the effects on the child and about potential problems for the woman. Paul Cameron, of Orange County, North Carolina, worried about his infant daughter's feedings. "Magey was more out of order than she has been since her birth," he fretted, "doubtless caused by feeding on the feverish milk of the mother." Henry Watson, an Alabama planter and merchant frequently away from home, was distressed that his wife was ill after childbirth. He inquired concerning their newborn, "Will not the health, if not the life of the child, be endangered by letting it suck its sick mother?" In neither case was anything said of looking for a wet nurse, nor did the mothers cease nursing. It appears that mothers usually made the final decision about breast-feeding, and those who wished to continue to suckle their newborn did so as long as they were able. At times mothers seem to have ignored the concerns of husbands and physicians, doing what they felt essential for the well-being of the child.[34]

A common belief of the nineteenth century was that the body contained limited natural forces and that drawing away vital liquids—such as milk—could deplete a woman's strength. Certainly many lactating mothers were tired. Recovering from the trauma of childbirth often took months, yet most southern mothers had to attend not only to the newborn but also to their other children and their domestic responsibilities as well. In 1858, Ann Rutherfoord wrote that constant infant care kept her "not only thin, but weak." Letitia Lewis, of Sedley, Virginia, explained that she was quite thin, for "Letty has gotten into a

33. Nathaniel Hawthorne, *The Scarlet Letter* (1850; rpr. New York, 1970), 96.
34. Paul Cameron to Duncan Cameron, July 18, 1848, in Cameron Family Papers; Henry Watson to Sophia Watson, May 18, 1848, in Henry Watson, Jr., Papers, Manuscript Department, William R. Perkins Library.

fashion of suckling just as often as she pleases." Mary Henderson wrote in her journal, "I grow weaker, nursing goes hard with me," and she later confessed, "I seem to have no time, for I feel so wearied after nursing."[35]

The North Carolina planter Thomas Bennehan worried that a sick woman on his plantation was nursing her baby, "for it must contribute to weaken her." William Elliott, upon hearing that his wife was ill with fever, at once diagnosed nursing as a cause. "From what you tell me of your sickness and nervous feeling," wrote the concerned husband, "I am persuaded that something must be attributed to your nursing so stout a girl as our daughter." One childless woman, who had no first-hand experience of breast-feeding, felt qualified to offer advice. She urged her sister, Adelle Allston, to forgo the pleasures of nursing and to put her own health first. "Recollect [that] your health and strength is of much more importance to her future well being," she cautioned, "than your nursing her can be, to nurse her when you are not at all able would be a selfish gratification entirely." Grandmothers, drawing on the memory of their own experience, knew what demands nursing placed on their daughters. Mary Hering in 1842 suggested to her daughter Eliza that she not breast-feed her baby at night. "I am sorry to find you allow the babies to disturb your night's rest so much as to make you ill," wrote Eliza's dismayed mother. "As she grows older she will become more ravenous and you will, I fear, suffer increasing fatigue." Mary encouraged Eliza to seek the assistance of a nurse for the nighttime feedings. In one case, an entire family opposed a mother's suckling her infant. Mary Curtis reported of Eliza Ann Wright that all the people in her family "dread her attempting to nurse—each time it has brought her to the grave."[36]

The nineteenth century ostensibly felt little concern about choosing a proper diet and limiting medication during lactation. In contrast to the

35. Ann Rutherfoord to John Rutherfoord, December 13, 1858, in John Rutherfoord Collection, Manuscript Department, William R. Perkins Library; Letitia Lewis to Letitia Floyd, June 14, 1841, in John Warfield Johnston Collection, Manuscript Department, William R. Perkins Library; Mary Henderson Diary, September 7, 1854 (Southern Historical Collection).

36. Thomas Bennehan to Duncan Cameron, January 1, 1845, in Cameron Family Papers; William Elliott to Ann Elliott, October 5, 1823, in Elliott-Gonzales Letters; Harriet to Adele Allston, January 8, 1838, in Allston Family Papers, South Carolina Historical Society Library; Mary Hering Middleton to her daughter Eliza, January 26, 1842, in Hering-Middleton Collection; [?] to Mary Curtis, July 16, 1847, in Moses Ashley Curtis Papers, Southern Historical Collection.

suggestions the advice books offered for the pregnant woman, there was a virtual silence on the dietary habits and foods desirable during breast-feeding. One can only assume that diet was adequate, even if lacking all the nutrients now considered optimal. In the improbable event that suggestions were given, they tended toward the curious and the cautious. Dr. Charles Delucena Meigs discouraged lactating mothers from a diet rich in fruits and vegetables, and Gunn contented himself with the observation that the maternal diet could alter the nourishment that a baby received. Southern women often had their own ideas. Mrs. Hall believed that green tea gave her strength, and she drank it religiously. Mary Henderson was remorseful over her young daughter's death, thinking that she had contributed to the tragedy. "To strengthen myself and increase her nourishment," she grieved, "I ought to have taken some nice gruel" while breast-feeding.[37]

Physicians were slow to realize that drugs taken by a nursing woman might affect the baby. D. Henry, a South Carolina medical student who based his dissertation on personal experience, discovered that lactating mothers who took opium or laudanum sometimes drugged their infants. Hydropaths shunned all drugs, and homeopaths warned patients of their deleterious effects. The majority of southern allopaths, however, did not understand that traces of a drug could be passed by a mother's milk into the baby's system. Whether physicians prescribed drugs or whether mothers just reached into the family medicine chest, drugs were readily available, and personal letters reveal that many mothers relied on them while breast-feeding.[38]

Mary Henderson drank wine whey, milk toddies, and brandy during her time of nursing, and she took Ayer's Pills, stimulants, and "blue mass," an opium derivative. When Anne Cameron suffered chills and fever, "wild delirium," headaches, and great sensitivity to light a month after parturition, the attending doctor admitted to being frightened out of his wits but prescribed leeching and bloodletting. Anne's husband, however, decided that "morphine, quinine, and calomel would accomplish our wishes," and the drugs were administered. During all this, Anne breast-fed her infant. It is no wonder that her husband perceived

37. Charles Delucena Meigs, *Observations on Certain of the Diseases of Young Children* (Philadelphia, 1850), 218; Gunn, *Gunn's Domestic Medicine*, 392; Rebecca Haywood Hall to Eliza Haywood, September, 1860, in Haywood Family Collection; Mary Henderson Diary, February, 1854.

38. D. Henry, "The Effects of Opium" (1847), in Waring Historical Library.

that the baby "was more out of order than she has been since her birth." Julia Howe, of Alabama, took quinine, and Nealy Lenoir laudanum. Emily Barrow's physician prescribed morphine, quinine, and "all stimulants the stomach will bear" while she was nursing. The effect these drugs had on nineteenth-century infants, and on their nursing mothers, can be imagined.[39]

In the correspondence of antebellum southern women, there was virtually no sharing of breast-feeding advice. When questions and problems arose, did these women turn to advice books and physicians for solutions, or did they rely on the wisdom and experience of the women close at hand? Medical advice books were full of practical information about dry and inverted nipples, breast abscesses, the proper formula until the mother's milk was ready, and the preparations necessary for nursing. One volume included the suggestion that a puppy be obtained to suck the breasts a few months prior to childbirth. Yet when the need for advice was urgent, women probably turned to other women, no doubt crossing race and class lines. Correspondence was too slow, and physicians did not provide the emotional sustenance that women could have from one another. Often, however, mothers could act in their baby's best interest only according to their own intuitions, retaining their distinctive rights as mothers.

39. Mary Henderson Diary, various entries in 1854; Paul Cameron to Duncan Cameron, July 8, 12, 17, 18, 1848, all in Cameron Family Papers; Nealy Lenoir to Walter Lenoir, February 1, 1858, in Lenoir Family Papers; Edwin Adams Davis (ed.), *Plantation Life in the Florida Parishes of Louisiana, 1836–1846, as Reflected in the Diary of Bennet H. Barrow* (1943; rpr. New York, 1967), 28, 30.

6 Sources of Comfort and Double Anxiety
INFANT ILLNESS AND MATERNAL CARE

"James has been ill," wrote an Alabama mother of her infant son, "and my inexperience and fear of relying on my own judgment, together with the heartrending task of watching a little sufferer who cannot tell its wants, all convince me that I am now beginning as a Mother and wife to experience trials I have hitherto been a stranger to—I often feel like giving up under the responsibilities of my station." She added, though, that she would "look above for strength to assist" her. A Georgia physician understood such apprehensions. "There is no anxiety like that of the fond mother who clasps in her arms her sweet and tender babe," commented Dr. Joseph Wright, "which she has but recently struggled and travailed to bring into the world yet knows not how to minister to its wants." The care of children was what southern ante-bellum society regarded as women's sacred occupation.[1]

The approach of southern doctors to infant therapy in the period before the Civil War provides some interesting contrasts to their practice of obstetrics. Children's health care often remained within the province of domestic and maternal medicine. Some physicians thought it enough that there were medical advice books on infant nurture. Several mothers apparently concurred. When her children became ill, Rebecca Haywood Hall frequently consulted Dewees' treatise, a book she found "excellent," and Jane Woodruff mentioned using an advice book when her children were sick.[2] These home guides directed infor-

1. Mary B. Hutchinson to Martha Jackson, March 1, 1837, in Jackson and Prince Collection, Southern Historical Collection, L. R. Wilson Library, University of North Carolina at Chapel Hill; Joseph F. Wright, *A Practical Treatise on the Management and Diseases of Infants and Children* (Macon, Ga., 1859), 8.
2. Rebecca Haywood Hall to Elizabeth Haywood, 1836, in Ernest Haywood Collection, Southern Historical Collection; Jane Woodruff Diary, 1829 (Clarkson Family Papers, Special Collections, J. Murrey Atkins Library, University of North Carolina at Charlotte).

mation toward parents, and especially mothers, who had traditionally tended to infant illnesses. Rural families were often far from a physician and had no choice but to be self-reliant, and doctors had not yet mounted a campaign to establish infant health as an area in which they could wield authority, for they had not yet recognized fully either the field's therapeutic possibilities or the opportunities in it for an expanded practice. Courses in medical school dealing with infant health held less interest for students than those directed toward female health problems did, and work in childhood medicine usually fell under the heading of "female and infant diseases." From a practical standpoint, doctors had good reason to avoid the field, for its results were mostly discouraging. Diagnosing children's illnesses was extremely difficult, particularly when youngsters could not talk or describe their symptoms. More important, the success rate in treating infants was extremely poor. Heroic therapy did little to improve small constitutions, babies being even less capable than adults of withstanding an onslaught of bleeding, purging, and drugging. Many doctors administered the same medications and dosages to infants that they did to other patients, frequently with fatal results. Infant mortality was frighteningly high (see Chapter 7), and contagious diseases were widespread among young children with few natural immunities. When some southern doctors began to urge greater professional involvement in child care, others were wary. Anyway, southern parents often had little confidence in medical professionals when young children were involved, preferring their own remedies to those of physicians. Parents often concluded that doctors did little to improve the health and survival of their offspring but merely brought death across the doorstep.

It was commonly recognized that the first two years of an infant's life were the most precarious. *The Maternal Physician,* an advice book devoted to infant care, did not discuss the years after the second, for its author considered anything later an "age requiring comparatively less attention." By two, a youngster had probably suffered several childhood diseases, survived dentition and weaning, and learned to walk and talk. In many cases, a younger sibling had superseded it within the family and needed its mother's attention.[3]

Steady good health escaped nearly all antebellum southern families.

3. *The Maternal Physician: A Treatise on the Nurture and Management of Infants, from the Birth Until Two Years Old* (Philadelphia, 1818), 272. See Charles E. Rosenberg's introduction to the Arno Press edition (New York, 1972).

Almost all experienced epidemics, illnesses, accidents, and accompanying high mortality. Most southern parents saw the death of at least one child, and infant illnesses recurred seemingly without end. The poor health of young children was so common that references to sickness often described a relatively vigorous family. Anne Cameron was pleased that her children had "upon the whole enjoyed good health," although one youngster had a sore throat and another was suffering from a disordered stomach. More strikingly, Fanny Lawrence reassured her husband that their children were well. She went into the condition of each, mentioning that one son had an ear that was oozing, one child had worms, another had an inflamed foot, and their newborn had an enlarged navel and "has not looked so well for a day or so." From Fanny's perspective, things could apparently have been much worse.[4]

In personal letters of the period, one is repeatedly struck by the preoccupation with the health of southern children. The subject was critical, because parents realized that much was at stake. Good health early in life implied a constitution better able to withstand problems later. It was also unspoken proof that the child came from good stock and evidence that a mother was attentive to her nurturing duties.

The topic made up a considerable portion of the domestic news shared by southern families. Only rarely did a child enjoy really blooming health, but obviously, when it did, it deserved special comment. Mary Burton, of Lincolnton, North Carolina, quietly boasted, "We are truly blessed with healthy children." One compliment was for a healthy young child to be compared to a miniature mountaineer. Julia Howe described her little daughter "as hearty, plump and healthy-looking as a mountain child." Fathers also expressed pride in their vigorous offspring. The Virginian Daniel Anderson boasted that their three-week-old son resembled a three-month-old baby and had "not had one hour's sickness since he was born." A month later, the happy father noted, "My sweet little boy is too well," implying that such good fortune may have been ill deserved, certainly abnormal. But comments like these were unusual, and many southern babies fell victim to illnesses almost immediately, even when placental and breast-milk immunities should have offered some protection.[5]

4. Anne Cameron to Paul Cameron, December 5, 1844, in Cameron Family Papers, Southern Historical Collection; Fanny Brashear Lawrence to Henry Lawrence, November 6, 1848, in Brashear Family Papers, Southern Historical Collection.

5. Mary Burton to Mira Lenoir, September 7, 1816, Julia Howe to Louisa Lenoir,

The ultimate responsibility for infant care usually rested on mothers. Sympathetic husbands, neighbors, relatives, domestic servants, and physicians provided assistance, but it was mothers who had their infants' needs at heart, could sensitively react to each mood and movement, and were deemed best suited to ensuring the soundness of the country's next generation. Society's glorified vision of motherhood notwithstanding, southern women found child rearing difficult, especially when their infants were ill. Mothers might spend days or even weeks attending sick children. Mahala Roach's diary chronicled ceaseless attention to her sickly family. On one occasion, with two children ill, she managed to find time for only a brief journal entry. "I have not been to bed at all," wrote the exhausted mother, "sat up and held John in my arms all night long." (This infant demanded constant care, for he had weighed only three and a half pounds at birth.) Several mothers mentioned all-night vigils, which could continue as long as two or three weeks. Nursing a sick child interfered with a mother's normal routine and sometimes absorbed her so totally that she had no time to herself even for sleep or writing letters. Typical of many young mothers was Letty Lewis, of Virginia, who wrote, "Today is the first time for near a week, my dear mother, that I have been able to put my poor little Letty out of my arms long enuf to commence a letter in reply to your last which I rec'd about ten days ago." Husbands might relate domestic news—as they often did after delivery—when their wives were burdened with a sick child. More likely, letters remained unwritten.[6]

Even under the best of conditions, women approached their maternal tasks with a good deal of trepidation, particularly in the case of a firstborn. "I cannot tell you what a trial it was and how awkward I felt when I first undertook the management of my baby," confessed an Alabama woman in 1837, "but now I am learning to wash, dress, and undress her without suffering half as much anxiety." Though the family owned slaves, this mother apparently did not have, or did not use,

September 11, 1841, both in Lenoir Family Papers, Southern Historical Collection; Mary B. Hutchinson to Martha Jackson, October 18, 1837, in Jackson and Prince Collection; Daniel Anderson to Duncan Cameron, August 21, September 11, 1801, both in Cameron Family Papers.

6. Mahala Roach Diary, July 3, 1856, July 23, 1858 (Southern Historical Collection); Letty Lewis to Letitia Floyd, June 14, 1841, in John Warfield Johnston Collection, Manuscript Department, William R. Perkins Library, Duke University.

domestic servants to assist with the tasks she spoke of. She probably learned what to do through trial and error, from sympathetic neighbors, or from advice books. Handling an illness was far more distressing but an almost constant concern. Hugh Clay, of Huntsville, Alabama, described the reaction of his wife, Celeste, to their newborn's bout with colic. "She has all a mother's apprehension—has had a cry or two—wishes her mother were here—and is nervous and unhappy," he admitted.[7]

Such reactions to tasks that society assumed women were naturally endowed to handle had several grounds. Some southern mothers blamed inadequate preparation. The growing number of educated middle- and upper-class young women found that training in foreign languages, geography, natural science, music, and velvet painting served them poorly when they needed to deal with a child's illness. Women sometimes concluded that their own mothers had failed to prepare them for the tasks at hand. Eliza McCorkle, of Alabama, murmured that her mother had "not trained [her] for householders." On several occasions, her children's poor health and behavior overwhelmed her. Although documents show that many mothers trained their daughters carefully in domestic and maternal matters, that was not always so, especially regarding certain aspects of infant care. Since mothers held the principal role in nursing sick infants, they may not have given their daughters enough practical experience in that area. Perhaps, too, the failure to instruct daughters adequately was more evident among the privileged, whose domestic slaves might handle some of the everyday but critical tasks associated with child care.[8]

A mother's own poor health could reduce her ability to nurse a sick infant. A weakened condition during a difficult pregnancy or following a delivery could make infant health care arduous or impossible. Anne Holmes commented that her cousin Ann Jones was again "in a family

7. Julia Howe to Louisa Lenoir, May 31, 1837, in Lenoir Family Papers; Hugh Lawson Clay to his sister, January 14, 1856, in Clement Claiborne Clay Letters, Manuscript Department, William R. Perkins Library.

8. Eliza McCorkle Diary, April 13, 1850 (William McCorkle Papers, Southern Historical Collection). On the educating of daughters for future maternal tasks, see Carroll Smith-Rosenberg, "The Female World of Love and Ritual: Relations Between Women in Nineteenth Century America," in Michael Gordon (ed.), *The American Family in Social-Historical Perspective* (New York, 1978), 334–58; Sally McMillen, "Education and Maternal Domesticity: Women in the Southern Social Order, 1830–1860" (M.A. thesis, University of North Carolina at Charlotte, 1980), 16–56.

way" and so sick that she could not nurse her one-year-old daughter, who had whooping cough. G. A. Wyche, of Alabama, described the postnatal condition of his wife Bettie as "high fever and great soreness of the womb and violent pain in the womb and all her limbs, so much so that she was perfectly helpless." Bettie was unable to roll over in bed without assistance, much less attend her newborn.[9]

The constant care of young children was often the very reason women's health declined. One husband sighed, "My wife's ill health has been much increased by the labours and cares and anxieties of a large family." Often other domestic duties added to the burdens of a mother with sick children. Mrs. P. M. Syme, of Petersburg, Virginia, nursed her baby, who had a severe case of croup. In a typical reaction of pure exhaustion, she confessed, "I am sometimes almost ready to give up, in despair, but a sense of duty urges me on." Her responsibilities had become heavier because her husband was incapacitated for three months and also required her attention.[10]

Mothers often had to act on their own with regard to infant health. Husbands might be away tending to business or political matters, leaving their wives without another adult they could turn to for comfort and assistance. As a rule, husbands, when home, did not take charge of nursing a sick child but might be consulted on medical problems or perform in certain medical or child-care capacities. Just as important, they offered a strong shoulder when their wives felt overwhelmed or exhausted. In the more remote southern settlements, plantation women missed the support that neighbors and friends could provide, especially in an emergency. Locating a doctor was often difficult. In a crisis, women often acted alone, making important decisions about the proper medical attention for their children.

Mrs. Hall's efforts to raise her children on the family plantation were poignant. Rebecca worked under the disadvantage of an unstable mental condition, a dependence on drugs, and an unsupportive and absent husband. Maternal duties overwhelmed her, and she frequently complained that she had no nearby relatives or friends or reliable domestic servants. She admitted that she was "almost worried out" by constantly

9. Ann Clinton Holmes to Betsy Blanks, July 8, 1843, in Elizabeth Holmes Blanks Letters, Manuscript Department, William R. Perkins Library; G. A. Wyche to Octavia Wyche Otey, October 24, 1856, in Wyche-Otey Collection, Southern Historical Collection.

10. William Anderson to Duncan Cameron, June 22, 1839, P. M. Syme to the Paul Camerons, February 14, 1844, both in Cameron Family Papers.

holding the newborn and that she never ventured off the plantation. Months later, she apologized to her sister for failing to write. "I am so engaged in nursing," she explained, "I cannot, and then after losing my sleep every night I have to be in attendance all day and no one to relieve me whilst I could take a few moments repose." The situation only worsened with time. Four years later, Rebecca was home alone with three young daughters. She blamed her "hysteria" on the "constant din of children." "Now I have to stand the fire and roar of their artillery, which I can never do without fleeing from them or trying to remedy their perturbed and violent passions," she wrote in a desperate vein. "I am almost worn out in the cause, when I have a baby, it can never lie like other people's, always must be in the arms or suckling, and the larger ones not much better." Rebecca's daughters suffered from worms and fevers, and except for occasional visits from a local physician, she saw to their health care. In the fall of 1841, her daughter Alice was fatally burned—in an accident that Rebecca's husband blamed on her inattention and carelessness. In her effort to save the child, she severely burned her own hand. For months thereafter, the frazzled mother left the family clothes unwashed and unmended. Rebecca herself died shortly after Alice's tragedy, never having achieved peace as wife and mother.[11]

Each addition to a large southern family brought new burdens. A Virginia woman, F. Brockenbough, commenting on her domestic situation to a friend, wrote, "I can hardly say my time is my own—six small daughters, I assure you, make me a complete bond woman, every moment is theirs." Some mothers scarcely weaned a child before becoming pregnant with the next. In raising a large family, southern mothers often had neither the time nor the energy to do more than look after the children who were ill. Family size prevented southern mothers from lavishing time and attention on each child. Even so, they worked overtime, undermining their own physical and emotional well-being.[12]

The southern climate, with its numerous epidemic and endemic diseases, made things worse. Typical were the Elliotts, of coastal South Carolina, who battled the unending parade of childhood illnesses and malarial fevers. Phoebe Elliott regretted the location of their plantation.

11. Rebecca Haywood Hall to her sister Elizabeth Haywood, 1836, September 19, 1836, September, 1840, May 9, September 30, 1841, all in Haywood Family Collection, Southern Historical Collection.

12. F. Brockenbough to Madge Dickins, March 27, 1840, in F. A. Dickins Papers, Southern Historical Collection.

"I begin now to feel great concern about the health of my family in the low country," she noted, as the family began its annual trek to cooling mountain springs. Southern mothers blamed the "mushetoes," "mus-ketos," or yellow flies for bothering their babies' sleep at night and interfering with their own rest. Humid malarial regions could be particularly devastating to young children's health, and when possible, families relocated temporarily to healthier regions.[13]

In accepting the miasmic explanation for diseases, southern mothers concluded that pure air was essential to good health. Trips to the mountains, the sea, and to cooling springs often figured in a privileged family's summer or fall plans. Mothers might leave home and husband temporarily to find an invigorating setting for their children. A North Carolina mother believed that city air might be more beneficial for her newborn than the malarial damp surrounding their plantation. When Anne Cameron's three-month-old daughter experienced severe chills and fever, the worried mother vowed to leave the family plantation to visit Raleigh, judging that "if she stays here, she will hardly get through this month." Southern mothers put their infant's health before other concerns, even if that meant dismantling part of the household and causing other inconvenience. Taking an active step probably eased a mother's anxiety as well.[14]

The poor health of the young could persuade southern families to move permanently. Families like the Whittles, of Richmond, Virginia, relocated to the countryside where the situation was "much better for children." Israel Pickens, a North Carolinian, moved his family to St. Stephens, Alabama, in 1818, presumably to make his fortune in cotton. After his youngest son suffered prolonged diarrhea, Pickens realized that the change had an unacceptable cost for his family's health. "This admonition which so long threatened the life of a fine child," he wrote, "and the fair prospect of having more thrown on my hands, has induced me to look a little higher up the country for a permanent situation where the prospect of health may be surer." In another instance, Mrs. Howe announced that the children's chronic ill health determined her family to relocate "from our sickly place in Alabama," and she ex-

13. Phoebe Elliott to William Elliott, July 26, 1833, in Elliott-Gonzales Letters, Southern Historical Collection.

14. Paul Cameron to Duncan Cameron, September, 1848, in Cameron Family Papers. Other examples: Jean Syme to Rebecca Cameron, July 6, 1811, in Cameron Family Papers; Letty Lewis to Letitia Floyd, June 14, 1841, in John Warfield Johnston Collection.

pressed optimism that in their new home, she would "see the children looking as rosy as the little ones in the country." Yet even after the Howes settled on the Mississippi prairies, good health escaped them. Within a few years, Julia persuaded her husband to move to Greensboro, North Carolina. She was thoroughly fed up with lonely frontier living and the children's illnesses. Julia at last realized her wish to be surrounded by "churches, physicians, and friends."[15]

Childhood health required mothers' constant vigilance. Table V (see Appendix One) lists the principal causes of death among antebellum children. These statistics, from the federal census for 1850, are not delineated by region, so it is impossible to determine accurately which diseases affected southern youngsters. But personal correspondence shows that fevers, malaria, and worms were common among southern infants. Probably contagious diseases like measles, exacerbated by urban living conditions and a colder climate, occurred more frequently in the Northeast. But every illness, however mild in form, could result in serious consequences and lead to severe health problems or even death.[16]

Women's letters reveal that diarrhea and dysentery were the most frequent complaints among southern children. Besides cholera infantum, discussed earlier, other intestinal problems proved worrisome. In part, this reflected antebellum society's fixation on proper bowel movement; the assumption was that any irregularity needed treatment. But health problems went beyond daily regularity. Mothers frequently mentioned that their infants suffered from "disorderd bowels," "inflammation of the bowels," or "violent" or "obstinate" dysentery and that immediate bold action was essential. On the recommendation of the family doctor, Anna King gave her infant "active medicines" for a case of dysentery. Mothers frequently administered calomel for disordered bowels. To parents and physicians, loose or constipated bowels indicated malfunctioning within the digestive tract and constituted an illness rather than a symptom. Intervention was essential, they thought, for such problems could affect other areas of the body.[17]

15. S. D. Whittle to his sister Jule, November 10, 1852, in Lewis N. Whittle Collection, Southern Historical Collection; Israel Pickens to William Lenoir, January 29, 1820, Julia Howe to Louisa Lenoir, July 15, 1844, August 10, 1849, all in Lenoir Family Papers.

16. Because illnesses were often misdiagnosed or identified by a variety of names (names often different from those in use today), one must use these figures with caution. Nevertheless, they suggest how parents and doctors perceived infant health problems.

17. Anna King to William Butler King, June 9, 1842, in Thomas Butler King Collec-

For dysentery and diarrhea, antebellum physicians recommended a bland diet. They suggested the consumption of vegetables, bread, and cow's milk and the avoidance of most fruits, spicy foods, and meats. Many also advised taking medicines. Dr. William Potts Dewees believed that when a child suffered nausea or loose bowels, "it will always be best to cleanse the stomach, as these symptoms are almost always sure to arise from the presence of a portion of whatever substance may have been offensive." He was not alone in recommending calomel or castor oil to purge the digestive tract. Dr. David Holmes recommended a mild cathartic to remove the irritation, followed by Dover's Pills or opium. Purging was believed critical for both nausea and diarrhea, since physicians thought internal agitation could rid the body of the problem.[18]

Worms were an ever-present health concern. The *Charleston Medical Journal and Review* observed that worms were more common in warm climates and "notorious on our plantations." Census statistics reveal that worms occurred most often in children over two years of age. One Alabama doctor extracted three hundred from a two-year-old. Mothers and physicians noticed that suckling infants rarely had problems with worms—perhaps one more argument for breast-feeding. A newborn's exposure to worms was limited by its diet as well as its relative immobility. But once youngsters learned to walk and began to consume a variety of foods, they became hosts to several intestinal parasites.[19]

In one particularly severe case, worms may have led to a young child's death. When two-year-old Duncan Cameron, of North Carolina, came down with chills and disordered bowels, his distraught father called him "hardly a good shadow of himself" and said that he was "without life." A week later, Paul Cameron diagnosed worms, purged the youngster with calomel, and urged his wife, Anne, to "commence the use of worm tea." After a week on medication, Duncan still remained "pale, feeble, and lifeless." The physicians and the parents continued their efforts to restore his health, but Duncan did not live to complete his third year. Worms were a serious concern, for they

---

tion, Southern Historical Collection; Rebecca Cameron to Duncan Cameron, September 3, 1805, in Cameron Family Papers.

18. William Potts Dewees, *A Treatise on the Physical and Medical Treatment of Children* (Philadelphia, 1847), 327; David Holmes, *The Child's Physician: A Popular Treatise on the Management and Diseases of Infancy and Childhood* (Providence, 1857), 157.

19. "Churchill and Condie on Diseases of Children," *Charleston Medical Journal and Review*, V (1850), 346.

depleted young bodies of essential nutrients, weakened constitutions, led to anemia, and increased the susceptibility to other illnesses.[20]

Southern parents treated worms in a variety of ways. Anna Garretson, of Virginia, suggested that "if Rosa complains of an itching in the anus, please to let one of your most careful female servants introduce the head of a pin and by twitching it around they will work out." She added that "Henry took out as many as seven" from the little girl. Mrs. Hall wrote of her daughter Betsy, "We have physicked her for worms and she has passed [one] and measured a foot in length." Eighteen months later, Rebecca recorded that another daughter had "discharged fifty odd worms." Still, Betsy's problem persisted, for she remained a "shadow, so pale and ematiated and under her clothes is a mere skeleton," according to her anxious mother. Rebecca finally consulted the family doctor, who employed heroic remedies including Pink Root, bleeding, and a body rub of turpentine. Nonetheless, the child remained "delirious with fever" three months later, still passing worms.[21]

Antebellum physicians began to understand the negative effect worms had on young bodies, but their knowledge came gradually. The medical understanding of these intestinal invaders developed considerably after the late eighteenth century. Dr. Benjamin Rush had conceived worms to have a cleansing effect in the removal of indigestible matter from the system. By the mid–nineteenth century, southern doctors were convinced that the parasites were harmful and needed expelling. But other ideas remained speculative. Medical empiricism led most doctors to suppose that a troubled digestive tract or feeble stomach brought on worms; they did not understand that the parasites caused the disorder of the intestines. The hydropath Joel Shew declared that if a child remained vigorous and healthy, worms would disappear. "Worms cannot exist in a truly healthy state of the system," Shew assured. Thomas Ewell concurred, confident that "worms rarely appear when the action of the bowels is vigorous." But not all doctors agreed. A Georgia doctor felt that even the healthiest children could carry worms. Most advice books urged parents and doctors to use purgatives such as calomel or castor oil to remove them. *The American*

20. Duncan Cameron to Paul Cameron, July 3, July 12, July 17, 1848, all in Cameron Family Papers.

21. Anna Garretson to her cousin, January 29, 1816, in Anna Garretson Papers, Southern Historical Collection; Rebecca Haywood Hall to Elizabeth Haywood, July 9, September 30, 1839, February 9, December 17, 1841, all in Haywood Family Collection.

Lady's Medical Pocket-Book suggested a regimen of purgatives followed by warm baths and leeches applied to the abdomen. Dewees advised the use of Pink Root, blistering, and calomel. Other doctors put the emphasis on prevention through better maternal care; perhaps they realized that few remedies were effective once worms were contracted. Advisers urged mothers to strengthen their infants' digestive tracts by close attention to diet, fresh air, and exercise—certainly sound advice for any child but poor protection against worms, since many youngsters ran barefoot in warm weather. No medical therapy of the time was successful.[22]

Like infants today, southern babies suffered from colic. It was typically one of the first illnesses southern mothers had to treat. Clay declared that his child's fretfulness could hardly be "called a disease" but that his wife, Celeste, was in a mild state of panic, fearful that colic might lead to croup. She tried various treatments and finally covered the poor infant's chest with a plaster of suet and turpentine. Nealy Lenoir applied brandy to her colicky baby's stomach and also gave him alcohol to drink. The combination of colic and constipation received blame for the death of one six-week-old infant. Mrs. McCorkle wrote that her newborn "suffered excruciatingly" from the two medical problems. The baby's suffering was "evidenced first by wailings—then by moanings, till utterance failed." Two physicians attempted to bring relief with heavy doses of oil, calomel, and morphine, but to no avail. Heroic therapies were often as devastating to a tiny baby as the illness itself. What Clay felt scarcely deserved the appellation of sickness was considered the cause of the McCorkle child's death.[23]

Of all the diseases surveyed in the federal census of 1850, croup caused the greatest number of deaths among young children, particularly among children under the age of one. Southern mothers mentioned the illness infrequently in their correspondence, and it may be

22. David Francis Condie, *A Practical Treatise on the Diseases of Children* (Philadelphia, 1844), 229; Joel Shew, *Children and Their Hydropathic Management in Health and Disease* (New York, 1852), 281; Thomas Ewell, *Letters to Ladies, Detailing Important Information, Concerning Themselves and Infants* (Philadelphia, 1817), 299; Paul F. Eve, "An Essay on Signs and Symptoms of Worms," *Southern Medical and Surgical Journal*, III (1839), 321–30; *The American Ladies' Medical Pocket-Book and Nursery Adviser* (Philadelphia, 1833), 280; Dewees, *A Treatise on the Treatment of Children*, 453.

23. Hugh Lawson Clay to his sister, January 14, 1856, in Clement Claiborne Clay Letters; Nealy Lenoir to Selina Lenoir, February 2, 1858, in Lenoir Family Papers; Eliza McCorkle Diary, 1855.

that southern youngsters were less prone to it than children living in colder parts of the country. Nevertheless, southern parents were concerned. Mrs. Clay made every effort to prevent her infant from contracting a case. A North Carolina girl knew enough about croup's dangers to refer to it as "that dreaded disease" when her infant brother suffered from it. Virginia Shelton's five-month-old firstborn caught an apparent case of croup, and the Tennessee mother gave her baby nothing stronger than sweet oil. A neighbor who had more experience with domestic remedies "rubbed him all over with mutton suet and gave him a mixture of mutton suet and molasses," and the child recovered. Since the Sheltons had reservations about consulting doctors for infant health problems, Virginia was probably relieved that domestic remedies availed.[24]

Whooping cough, or pertussis, a highly contagious bacterial disease characterized by a wheezing, rasping cough, was probably one of the most dramatic and frightening of all infant ailments. Frequently every young member of a family was affected, for its rate of contagion was 85 to 90 percent among children. The recovery rate was lowest for infants under the age of one. Whooping cough was a long-lasting disease, usually hanging on for six to ten weeks. One South Carolina woman believed that it was of even more protracted duration; she remarked that "if it is taken in the fall of the year, they don't get better of it until spring." When young children caught it, mothers spent anxious weeks in attentive nursing. But there was little that antebellum mothers could do apart from avoiding exposing their children and easing their suffering.[25]

The diary of Mary Henderson, of North Carolina, underlines the seriousness of whooping cough. Mary's frenetic state and her sorrow, anger, and bewilderment often make it difficult to follow the details of the tragedy that whooping cough visited upon her young family. But her stream-of-consciousness writing and her mental disorder make the

24. Becky Cameron to Anne Cameron, January 19, 1853, in Cameron Family Papers; Virginia Campbell Shelton to Mr. and Mrs. David Campbell, November 18, 1850, in Campbell Family Letters, Manuscript Department, William R. Perkins Library.

25. Catherine DeAngelis, *Pediatric Primary Care* (3rd ed.; Boston, 1984), 154; T. Fraser to Mary De Saussure Fraser, Monday the 8th, 1800, in Mary De Saussure Fraser Collection, William R. Perkins Library. Whooping cough can now be prevented by giving a vaccine to babies, but the disease has the potential to become a serious health problem once again, since the vaccine is implicated in rare instances of brain damage and its manufacturers face soaring litigation costs. Most states now require children to be vaccinated against whooping cough. See *Science News,* CXXVI (September 15, 1984), 167.

tale all the more moving. Apparently, when two of Mary's school-age sons caught whooping cough from a classmate, Mary did not remove them from school at once. After the deaths of the two youngsters, she reproached herself, saying, "My sad experience has taught me that whooping cough is one of the most formidable diseases." Unfortunately, the illness passed on to her infant daughter. Mary spent a total of eighteen months nursing the three of her children who caught the disease. In page after page of her journal, she poured out her despair, especially during the infant's suffering. When her efforts in behalf of the baby proved futile and the child died, Mary denounced everyone involved, including the attending nurse, whose teas and oils had produced no improvement. Not least did she censure herself, believing that "overanxiety and the dread of whooping cough" caused her to accept too readily the physician's heroic cures. The distraught mother criticized her own weakness in not forcing the doctor to stop medicating the infant. "I erred, erred, erred, terribly, fatally," she moaned. But the principal target of her anger was the physician himself, who had done nothing right in her eyes. She took exception to his dosing the baby with calomel and cupping her, and she decided that "a blister between shoulders with purgative and quinine" would have been far better, even if no less violent. She reproved the doctor for prescribing "depressing syrups" and "blue stone, which entirely destroyed her voice and I fear permanently injured her little palate." Mary assailed the "desperate and dangerous remedies" the physician thought suitable for a nine-month-old; she maintained that water, breast milk, flannel clothing, cool baths, and wool stockings would have served far better. "It is very wonderful that she lived a month under such treatment, actually taking poisons all the time," she charged.[26]

The young, seemingly inexperienced doctor who attended the infant typified the state of antebellum pediatrics. Mary, probably because of prior experience, had little trouble identifying whooping cough, but apparently the doctor misdiagnosed the illness in a desperate effort to appear knowledgeable. He called it thrush, the putrid sore throat, and even gangrene, before he finally acceded to Mary's identification.

Some antebellum physicians would not have bothered to treat the child, for they believed little could be done for whooping cough. Others would have left the job entirely in the hands of Mary. Wright noted

26. Mary Henderson Diary, various pages from fall, 1854, through summer, 1855, but esp. December 21, 1854, August 22, 1855 (Southern Historical Collection).

that "like most other contagious diseases, the whooping cough will run its course, in spite of all our exertions to cure it." Dr. Charles Delucena Meigs believed that therapeutic intervention was inappropriate, for no drug, in his opinion, could shorten the progress of the illness. Dr. James Ewell took the offensive, declaring that "no disease [is] more generally treated improperly by parents" than whooping cough. He recommended domestic medicines that parents could administer and articles that they could use, including an emetic, melted hog's lard to suppress the cough, and coarse flannel or a flesh brush for rubbing. Holmes too held mothers accountable for infant health. He asserted that the best remedy for whooping cough was attentive nursing. Looking back, Mary would probably have preferred any one of these physicians to the proponent of dramatic therapies whom she engaged.[27]

But Mary's doctor was not alone in his commitment to a heroic approach to whooping cough. A view that gained currency was that medical efforts might trim the course of the disease even if not actually cure it. In 1844, Dr. Francis Condie counseled a mild diet, belladonna, opium syrups, and blistering of the chest. Dewees believed that whooping cough did not have a "predetermined course," and he suggested measures that comprised bleeding, purgatives, an abstemious diet, blistering the lungs, leeching between the shoulders, and the regular use of calomel. A New Orleans doctor recommended arsenic, which—with grim truth—he claimed considerably diminished the duration of the disease.[28]

Young children often caught mumps and measles, which, like whooping cough, were recognized as having little, if any, effective treatment. Rarely was a fatal case of measles recorded, though Octavia Otey, of Alabama, claimed that her baby daughter "lay at the point of death" with the disease. Scarlet fever posed a greater risk. A form of this disease became more virulent by the first quarter of the nineteenth

27. Wright, *A Practical Treatise,* 106; Charles Delucena Meigs, *Observations on Certain of the Diseases of Young Children* (Philadelphia, 1850), 156; James Ewell, *The Planter's and Mariner's Medical Companion, Treating According to the Most Successful Practice* (Philadelphia, 1807), 265; Holmes, *The Child's Physician,* 214. For a good overview of antebellum therapeutics for whooping cough, see Benjamin Waterhouse, *An Essay Concerning Tussis Convulsiva; or, Whooping Cough: With Observations on the Diseases of Children* (Boston, 1822).

28. Condie, *The Diseases of Children,* 327; Dewees, *A Treatise on the Treatment of Children,* 412–15; John Eberle, *A Treatise on the Diseases and Physical Education of Children* (Cincinnati, 1833), 475; A. R. Nye, "On the Use of Arsenic in Hooping-Cough," *New Orleans Medical and Surgical Journal,* IX (1852), 282.

century, after existing in a milder form during the colonial period. Scarlet fever demanded constant nursing and could be a merciless killer of young children. Mary Custis, of Deep Creek, North Carolina, lost twins to the dreaded disease. Parents made every effort to keep healthy children from infected households to prevent exposure. When a Raleigh woman, Mary Polk, heard of neighboring children who had scarlet fever, she noted, "I live in constant dread that Catherine is to be the next victim" and did her best to keep her children at home.[29]

Given the endemic nature of malaria, it is surprising that only a few southern mothers mentioned in diaries and letters that their infants suffered from this debilitating ailment. Recent studies show that malaria can be congenital, though the placenta often acts as an effective barrier. If the placenta is damaged, however, the fetus can suffer. In Africa, where the disease is hyperendemic, it is estimated that malaria is responsible for 10 percent of all infant deaths, either directly or by breaking down the baby's immune system. Whether southern babies were at less risk, whether writers of letters and diaries chose not to dwell on problems that everyone had, or whether other health problems loomed larger is hard to tell.[30]

Southern infants were disposed to physical injury. Constant vigilance was needed. Especially recurrent were burns, falls, and accidental poisonings. Eliza Clitherall described a friend's infant who died by poison: "The sweet Babe was poison'd by the shameful mistake of the Apothecaries clerk, who sent a wrong phial—sent a Aconite, a deadly poison." Several southern mothers described their babies' near-fatal falls from beds and tables. Other infants swallowed foreign objects, ate

29. Octavia Wyche Otey Diary, May 17, 1852 (Wyche-Otey Collection); M. D. Wise to Frances Custis, April 25, 1835, in John Beauchamp Jones Papers, Southern Historical Collection; Mary Polk to Mrs. Lucius Polk, October 13, 1832, in Polk, Badger, and McGehee Papers, Southern Historical Collection. See also Barry B. Behrstock and Richard Trubo, *The Parent's When-Not-to-Worry Book* (New York, 1981). Behrstock (p. 224) claims that the disease was not widespread until the mid–nineteenth century. But family correspondence shows that cases were quite common by the 1830s.

30. I. S. Audu and W. R. F. Collis, "Malaria in Childhood: Modern Concepts of Immunity, Treatment, Prophylaxis," *Clinical Pediatrics*, IV (1965), 357–63; Robert M. Galbraith *et al.*, "The Human Materno-Foetal Relationship in Malaria," *Transactions of the Royal Society of Tropical Medicine and Hygiene*, LXXIV (1980), 52–72. Carol Laderman ("Malaria and Progress: Some Historical and Ecological Considerations," *Social Science and Medicine*, IX [1975], 587–94) states that where malaria was endemic, "it had no equal" as a killer of children.

unripe fruit and vegetables from the garden, received scaldings from hot water or burns from an open fire, and fell out of open windows.[31]

Yet no illness, epidemic, or physical calamity proved to be so distressing as teething. Some of the problems connected with dentition and weaning have already become evident, but the impact of dentition went well beyond infant nourishment and cholera infantum. The period of dentition covered roughly the time between six months and two years of age and came to assume major importance as a stage of human development, much like puberty and menopause. At least until 1860, the federal census included teething as a cause of death.[32] Few infants passed through this stage with ease. So critical was the period that some southern mothers kept written records of each child's progress—or lack of it. Sophia Watson, of Greensboro, Alabama, distraught that her six-and-a-half-month-old son still lacked teeth, poured out her distress to her absent husband. "I begin almost to despair of seeing one for some time to come," she lamented. But Ann Blank, of Leesburg, North Carolina, had cause for celebration. "Dear Henry . . . has two through and two almost through," noted the happy mother. Bringing infants through the period alive and in relative good health became a major challenge for southern physicians and mothers. As the most obvious and universal sign of bodily change during the early part of a child's life, teething was at one time or another held accountable for nearly every infant ill.[33]

Mothers assumed that this stage of human development meant infant distress and illness, so they were prepared to worry and to provide attentive nursing. Margaret Cameron resigned herself to the task ahead, commiserating, "I shall feel most anxious for her until she is done teething." She later held teething responsible for her infant's bout with a ten-week-long siege of spasms, high fever, and irritable stomach. Mrs. Shelton described the ailments accompanying her son's dentition

31. Eliza Clitherall Autobiography and Diary, XIII, 1854–55 (Southern Historical Collection).

32. For the importance of teething as a stage of infant development, see Charles Rosenberg's introduction to the Arno Press edition of *The Maternal Physician*. For the inclusion of teething in the list of diseases, see U.S. federal census mortality statistics for 1850 and 1860.

33. Sophia Watson to her mother-in-law, Mrs. Watson, May 22, 1847, in Henry Watson, Jr., Papers, Manuscript Department, William R. Perkins Library; Ann Holmes Black to Betsy Blanks, June 5, 1846, in Elizabeth Holmes Blanks Letters.

and bravely accepted the incommodity his teething imposed upon her. "Of course, I have much anxiety and have not slept for several nights," she wrote, knowing that her aunt would understand. When infants teethed without suffering, incredulity met their good fortune. Caroline Pinckney, of South Carolina, had the enviable experience of raising a daughter whom teething scarcely affected. "She looks so robust," wrote the puzzled mother, "that you would not suppose she had been cutting teeth thro' a Carolina summer."[34]

Southern mothers were always looking for ways to ease their infants' distress. Mrs. Clay recommended the healing waters of a local Alabama spring, vouching that they would "afford instantaneous relief to teething children." Mrs. Shelton followed a suggestion in many advice books and purchased an India-rubber tooth cutter for her baby to chew. Lancing the gums was advocated by the majority of southern physicians, who felt that it created a freer passage for the growing tooth, relieved swollen gums of excess blood, and prevented irritation from reaching the brain. Parents often took matters into their own hands and lanced their infant's gums. Rebecca Cameron expressed gratitude to her husband for doing the job, noting that it "was of the greatest importance" to their son. Anne Cameron believed her daughter Mary was much "relieved by having her gums scarified."[35]

But at times teething was so unpleasant that only medicines and physicians could provide relief. When Ann and William Elliott's son had three days of high fever while teething, the parents administered castor oil and then called in the local doctor, who lanced the boy's gums. When the fever persisted, the doctor returned and lanced the gums in four places. Margaret Devereux administered doses of calomel on the advice of her doctor and concluded that the purging was "decidedly beneficial" to her teething child. Mrs. Lenoir's baby vomited and suffered convulsions, and the doctor, certain that teething was the problem, lanced the baby's gums and administered morphine. Unfortu-

34. Margaret Cameron to Paul Cameron, 1849, in Cameron Family Papers; Virginia Shelton to William Campbell, March 16, 1851, in Campbell Family Letters; Elizabeth Blythe to Adelle Allston, September 21, 1833, in Allston Family Papers, South Carolina Historical Society Library.

35. Celeste Clay to her sister, April 15, 1857, in Clement Claiborne Clay Letters; Virginia Shelton to Margaret Campbell, September 11, 1850, in Campbell Family Letters; Rebecca Cameron to Duncan Cameron, May 6, 1810, Anne Cameron to Paul Cameron, January 10, 1845, both in Cameron Family Papers.

nately, the poor child never recovered, but whether because of an un-diagnosed illness or an overdose by the doctor is unclear.[36]

Teething and the disorders attendant upon it were a focus of south-ern medical journals and dissertations. Doctors prescribed a mild diet, exercise, fresh air, and bland liquids for a child with little pain, in order to counteract what Dewees called a "highly excitable state." They be-lieved that loose bowels were an advantage in teething, in that they could prevent potential problems by relieving internal pressure that might ultimately affect the child's digestive and nervous systems. "Many physicians think it much better for children to have diarrhea during dentition, so long as it does not emaciate them," noted Mrs. Watson in 1848. "It prevents their having fevers and their head from becoming affected." Perhaps here physicians were only justifying a naturally loose state of children's bowels during dentition. To prevent blood from flowing to the brain and triggering convulsions during teething, several physicians instructed mothers to keep the infant's head cool by cutting its hair and not letting it use feather pillows for sleeping or wear a cap. All doctors recommended purgatives, particularly the use of calomel, to keep the bowels open. They thought a narcotic useful for lessening pain. That any child might pass through the teething stage with little suffering was unbelievable to antebellum parents. That the medical remedies employed were less painful or harmful than the actual problem is perhaps more surprising today.[37]

Dewees, in his influential text on children's health, offered observa-tions on teething that were virtually ignored by his colleagues. Al-though he admitted that the perturbation could excite fever and increase the chance of disease, he saw that during the teething stage, "children are subject to many other complaints, to which they fall sacrifices" and that "it cannot be truly said that many diseases are necessarily connected with the acquisition of teeth." A doctor in Rutherford County, Ten-

36. William Elliott to Rhett Smith, July 23, 1832, in Elliott-Gonzales Letters; Mar-garet Devereux to Ellen Mordecai, January 4, 1845, in Margaret Devereux Papers, South-ern Historical Collection; Nealy Lenoir to Walter Lenoir, March 16, 1858, in Lenoir Family Papers.

37. Dewees, *A Treatise on the Treatment of Children,* 199; Sophia Watson to Henry Watson, Jr., Greensboro, Alabama, June 12, 1848, in Henry Watson, Jr., Papers. See also Eberle, *A Treatise on Diseases and Physical Education,* 29–62; James Ewell, *The Planter's and Mariner's Medical Companion,* 256–60; Holmes, *The Child's Physician,* 50–57; and Wright, *A Practical Treatise,* 95–98.

nessee, agreed, stating that dietary changes rather than teething should be blamed for illness during the period. But such views were in the minority; few doctors and parents paid heed to them. Even European doctors, generally in the vanguard of medical ideas, were unsure whether teething caused childhood diseases and ill health or whether something else was responsible.[38]

As a result of teething itself, most doctors believed, children increased their susceptibilities to fevers, convulsions, epidemics, nervous disorders, and diseases "of the most dangerous character." An Ohio physician, Dr. John Eberle, attributed 10 percent of all infant deaths to teething, and both he and Dr. Joel Shew, a hydropath, considered dentition one of the most precarious periods of a child's life. James Ewell concurred, remarking that teething "probably caused the death of more children than any one [disease] to which they are liable." Teething has always been an uncomfortable period for babies, but the belief that it was the primary cause of numerous severe disorders, high fevers, convulsions, and even death betrayed the medical unsophistication of antebellum doctors. If antebellum physicians had had a better understanding of infant health problems and the etiology of diseases, they would have attributed most illnesses during dentition to other changes in the baby's life. During the very time children were teething, natural immunities they acquired in the uterus and through breast-feeding declined. Furthermore, their diet and their exposure to infection altered considerably. Nonetheless, decades would pass before a majority of physicians correctly imputed the most common infant health problems to something else.[39]

Most people before the Civil War still believed that miasmic conditions caused illness, but some began to surmise that human beings were responsible for spreading certain diseases. By the 1850s, a few southern doctors, but probably a greater proportion of parents, were speculating that diseases such as whooping cough, measles, and scarlet fever could be spread from one individual to the next. John Jarrell, of Hot Springs,

38. Dewees, *A Treatise on the Treatment of Children*, 304; and John W. Richardson, "Remarks on the Diseases Which Prevail in Tennessee During Summer and Winter," *Western Journal of Medicine and Surgery*, I (1844), 112.

39. Eberle, *A Treatise on Diseases and Physical Education*, 128; Shew, *Children and Their Hydropathic Management*, introduction; James Ewell, *The Planter's and Mariner's Medical Companion*, 256; Behrstock and Trubo, *The Parent's When-Not-to-Worry Book*, 140. See also Harvey Kravitz *et al.*, "Teething in Infancy: A Part of Normal Development," *Illinois Medical Journal*, CLI (1977), 261–66.

Arkansas, described the death of three neighbor children who caught scarlet fever from a "young man who knew at the time he had it and entered the house after being forbidden to do so." Jarrell was livid, describing the man's conduct as "damning beyond description." Mothers often avoided visiting families with sick children or traveling to an area where illness had been reported. When a disease was epidemic, however, there seemed little sanctuary. Jessie Walton, of North Carolina, despaired of her children's escaping illness. "The whooping cough is all around us," she wrote in 1857. "I am very much afraid my children will take it." Her concerns lingered, and she postponed a visit to her mother: "If they take the disease with my willfully exposing them, I should regret it so much."[40]

Parents had little reason to doubt the communicability of certain diseases, but doctors vacillated. In 1841, Laura Norwood, of Hillsboro, North Carolina, commented on the medical disagreement over scarlet fever. "There is considerable panic prevailing. . . . Dr. Webb and Dr. Strudick think the disease *not* contagious, but Dr. Norwood thinks that it is." Medical advisers provided little consensus on the subject. Eberle ascribed scarlet fever to a "specific contagious miasma," and Meigs cautiously presented it as an "unmanageable affection" of diverse origins, so that "evidence of its contagion is imperfect." In 1857, Holmes uncourageously laid it to either a miasma or contagion. Doctors were beginning to consider the spread of disease among people but had come to no definite conclusions. Southern mothers, ever fearful for their children's lives, were in far less doubt and tried to limit exposure.[41]

The most significant change in infant health since colonial times was the widespread use of vaccination or inoculation to prevent, or ameliorate the prognosis of, smallpox. That disease had once had a devastating

40. John Jarrell to David Coverstone, April 23, 1859, in John Jarrell Collection, Manuscript Department, William R. Perkins Library; Jessie Walton to her mother, March 12, 1857, April 7, 1858, both in Walton Family Papers, Southern Historical Collection. William Buchan believed in the contagiousness of certain diseases, including whooping cough and scarlet fever, though his views were not accepted by many doctors even several decades later. For discussions of the contagion theory, see Charles E. Rosenberg, "Medical Text and Social Context: Explaining William Buchan's *Domestic Medicine*," *Bulletin of the History of Medicine*, LVII (1983), 38; George Rosen, *A History of Public Health* (New York, 1958), 103–107, 287–90; and E. H. Ackerknecht, "Anticontagionism Between 1821 and 1867," *Bulletin of the History of Medicine*, XXII (1948), 562–93.

41. Laura Norwood to Mary Ann Gwynn, August 24, 1841, in Lenoir Family Papers; Eberle, *A Treatise on Diseases and Physical Education*, 248; Holmes, *The Child's Physician*, 248; Meigs, *Observations*, 192.

effect on nonimmune or virgin populations and had been an important cause of high infant morbidity and mortality, killing as many as an estimated 10 percent of the infant population. In the early eighteenth century, variolation had been found effective against the disease. Edward Jenner, a British doctor, experimented with cowpox vaccine and in 1796 discovered that when properly given, the vaccine provided immunity. Smallpox thus ceased to be an epidemic killer among the white population.[42]

Most middle- and upper-class southern women were convinced that vaccinating their children was crucial. The main concern of antebellum mothers was how soon, rather than whether, the infant should be immunized. Rebecca Cameron wrote that she had had all her older children inoculated simultaneously but hesitated to have the prophylaxis performed on her three-month-old daughter. She consulted the family doctor and happily reported, "The doctor has assured me there is not the least danger to be apprehended from her taking it." Physicians generally recommended that a baby be at least a week old, but preferably a month old, before vaccination.[43]

Southern physicians also began to consider the impact that drugs and heroic remedies could inflict on small constitutions. Wright warned against bleeding youngsters but approved of cupping, opiates, and poultices. In 1850, a Louisiana doctor denounced the "injurious consequences of drugging" young children. Several physicians wrote that injudicious bleeding could lead to convulsions or even death, and they advised that bloodletting cease as soon as a pallor was evident on the child's lips and face. In 1849, a doctor writing in the *Charleston Medical Journal and Review* warned of calomel's potential to harm. He declared that "no article in the whole materia medica is prescribed more frequently, more continuously or more causelessly to children than calomel." The *Review* also noted that an "indiscriminate use" of opium in infant therapeutics had "opened the eyes of the profession to the dan-

42. On smallpox and vaccination, see *The American Ladies' Medical Pocket-Book and Nursery Adviser*, 206; Gunning Bedford, *Clinical Lectures on the Diseases of Women and Children* (4th ed.; New York, 1856), 506; Robert H. Bremner (ed.), *Children and Youth in America: A Documentary History* (Cambridge, Mass., 1970), 302–304; Thomas E. Cone, "Highlights of Two Centuries of American Pediatrics, 1776–1976," *American Journal of the Diseases of Children*, CXXX (1976), 765; DeAngelis, *Pediatric Primary Care*, 144–46; and John Duffy, *Epidemics in Colonial America* (Baton Rouge, 1953).

43. Rebecca Cameron to Duncan Cameron, July 14, 1811, in Cameron Family Papers.

gerous effects of the drug, and it is now prescribed with more caution than in former years."[44]

Yet the cautious attitude did not reflect the majority medical position. Doctors' reports of cases, account books, and family correspondence confirm that when doctors treated infants, the therapies they employed were generally dramatic. Recommendations of moderation in medical advice books were not usually followed when southern physicians entered the nursery. Many physicians and parents found nothing unusual in Dr. John Richardson's medication of a fourteen-month-old baby who had diarrhea. That physician from Rutherford County, Tennessee, mentioned using calomel, prepared chalk, acetate of lead, sulphate of morphia, and an emetic of ipecac over a fifty-one-day period. He summed up his account of the therapy by saying, "Our treatment in this case, we must confess, was purely experimental. We tried spirits of turpentine, muriatic and nitro-muriatic acid, iron, cathartics, sasparilla, quinine, and some domestic remedies." Other physicians lanced jugular veins to cure children's convulsions. Dr. Alfred Folger, of North Carolina, heralded calomel as "quite the most important of our medicines" for children, even though it caused a far stronger reaction than in adults. The heroic measures could have disastrous consequences. Extensive bleeding could permanently weaken a child's body, blistering could lead to gangrene, and purgatives could dehydrate a baby's body or upset its chemical balance. But when doctors entered the nursery, they had little to take the place of dramatic medicine, and to the physician, action was preferable to inaction.[45]

Interest in infant health issues, except for concerns about teething and contagion, remained minimal among southern doctors during the antebellum period. The dearth of journal articles and dissertations on pediatrics reflects a widespread indifference to it. Southern physicians readily agreed that children's health care was neglected by the profession, and some urged greater efforts in the field. Dr. Henry Miller, at the Louisville Medical College, solicited in behalf of babies the "profound study of the peculiarities of their organization and diseases to

44. Wright, *A Practical Treatise*, 43; Bedford, *Clinical Lectures*, 494; Holmes, *The Child's Physician*, 252; Shew, *Children and Their Hydropathic Management*, 180; Review of John Beck's *Essays on Infant Therapeutics*, in *Charleston Medical Journal and Review*, IV (1849), 190; Condie, *The Diseases of Children*, 63.

45. Richardson, "Remarks," 112; Alfred M. Folger, *The Family Physician, Being a Domestic Medical Work, Written in Plain Style, and Divided into Four Parts* (Spartanburg, S.C., 1845), 244; Behrstock and Trubo, *The Parent's When-Not-to-Worry Book*, 50, 140.

curtail the fearful mortality to which they are exposed." Other physicians feared that if they failed to act, quacks and even midwives might move in, but their territoriality was insufficient to overcome their wariness. Pediatrics would not become a medical specialty until the 1880s, and no antebellum doctors devoted their time and energy exclusively to the field. The doctors who cared for sick children were usually family practitioners or those interested in women's and allied diseases.[46]

All the same, advice books on children's health and maternal responsibilities abounded. If doctors were unwilling, reluctant, or ill prepared to undertake pediatric practice, they could at least provide direction to those they deemed in charge. And for some physicians, like Holmes, there was no doubt who had to accept blame for high infant morbidity and mortality. The poor state of infant health, he said, was "chargeable to circumstances, which to a degree lie within the control of parents and guardians; in other words, it is mainly attributable to ignorance and mismanagement." Dewees, lamenting that "the diseases of childhood have never until lately sufficiently engaged the attention of physicians," hoped that the trend toward the written word would continue. He encouraged American doctors to create their own advice books, with emphasis upon the specificity of American health problems, and no longer to rely on European efforts. American diseases have, he said, "a peculiarity of character, an intensity of force, and a rapidity of march altogether unknown to European climates." Some writers of advice books addressed mainly their inexperienced colleagues and medical students, hoping to generate greater interest in infant care. Other writers directed their advice primarily to mothers.[47]

Some women questioned the efficacy and appropriateness of heroic remedies for children. L. Petigru, of Cordesville, South Carolina, who had two physicians attend her son when he had worm fever, was grateful to them that her son lived, but could not check her amazement at the therapy. "I never saw anyone take such quantities of medicine," she exclaimed. The Sheltons reacted similarly. When their son was ill, the family physician applied "some very severe remedies for such a sweet

46. Henry Miller, "An Inquiry into Some of the Causes of Mortality of Infants," *Western Journal of Medicine and Surgery*, I (1840), 24; Thomas E. Cone, *History of American Pediatrics* (Boston, 1979), 70. The word *pediatrician* was not used until the late nineteenth century.

47. Holmes, *The Child's Physician*, iii; Dewees, *A Treatise on the Treatment of Children*, Part II, preface.

little fellow to endure." The doctor tried cupping, bleeding, and a dose of antinomial wine to induce vomiting. These measures, William Shelton decided, "prostrated [the boy's] whole system so that life itself appeared to hang by a very slender thread." Obviously Mrs. Henderson was skeptical about dramatic treatments for whooping cough. She concluded simply, "Babies should take no medicines."[48]

"We seem to lose faith in medicines," Susan Hutchinson, of Augusta, Georgia, wrote, "and though the Doctor visits and prescribes, we do not profit by his advice." Apparently the physician had done little to help her children and stepchildren. Often mothers preferred homemade herbal remedies to prescribed medicines.[49]

At times, women reacted emotionally. In one case, a Georgia mother—for reasons not entirely clear—dissolved into hysterics when the doctor prescribed heroic medicines for her baby. She could not breast-feed her infant, and the rich gruel she fed him caused dysentery. The mother feared for the youngster's life. On top of that, her sister and the family doctor kept insisting on radical therapies. The distraught woman, buckling under the pressure, reacted the only way she knew how. She ran weeping from the house, crying, "They are going to give him calomel, my child will be killed." In the end, she retreated to her room, where she stayed for several days. In this instance, the physician's will—bolstered by that of a family member—prevailed.[50]

Meigs acknowledged that some of his female readers might believe "that to put a young child into the hands of a physician is to expose it to considerable risk." He tried to dispel that perception, but many southern mothers remained unconvinced. Mary Anderson served as chief attendant to an infant with disordered bowels and fever. "I have a great aversion to Doctors for children," she announced, "and therefore ventured to doctor him myself." She boasted that her home remedies, including sweetened tea of blackberry leaves, made according to a recipe she had clipped from the newspaper, had "entirely relieved him." Mrs. Henderson concluded that "doctors seem not to understand children's constitutions"—a classic understatement by a woman who saw

48. L. Petigru to Adelle Allston, September 18, 1832, in Allston Family Papers; William Shelton to Margaret Campbell, March 23, 1851, in Campbell Family Letters; Mary Henderson Diary, December 21, 1854.

49. Susan Hutchinson Diary, March 27, 1827 (Southern Historical Collection).

50. Story related by the woman's sister, Martha Richardson, to James Screven, November 18, 1818, in Arnold-Screven Letters, Southern Historical Collection.

three of her children die under a doctor's care. Mrs. Lenoir noticed that the doctor who tended her daughter could do nothing beyond repeating the remedies she had already tried.[51]

It is interesting that the mistrust southern women felt concerning heroic therapies for children had not been prefigured by any mistrust of heroic obstetrics. Perhaps it was seeing radical things done to small and helpless bodies that raised doubts. Labor, after all, implied pain, and it was one thing to have nineteenth-century medicine inflicted on oneself but another to watch it ravage a beloved child. Anyway, many mothers had their own ideas about proper child treatment, which stood in a long tradition of home remedies and preventive medicine. Natural measures often seemed the most sensible and successful. It is also not insignificant that doctors probably did not project the same authority and confidence in child care that they did in the birthing chamber.

Fathers were at times as chary of professional medicine as their wives were. Paul Cameron, exasperated with a doctor's results, blustered that if he had been home to take charge of his sick child, matters would have improved. Evidently disgusted, he pilloried the idea that "a doctor is to be consulted with every sore finger." In another instance, a North Carolina father admitted that he looked after his infant daughter instead of calling a doctor, "partly because I thot they could do but little more than I could do myself." Henry Watson, absent from his Alabama home, worried that the physician who was caring for his sick baby was incompetent, and he suggested calling in another. When his wife was reluctant to act, Henry wrote sternly, "The life of our child is of more importance to us than any matter of delicacy or etiquette."[52]

But if love and concern drove a surprising number of parents to reject drugs and doctors for their children, it led others to accept them. Mothers administered calomel to their babies for diarrhea, dysentery, teething, and worms. Many liked the prestige of having a male professional attending family members and were themselves impressed with the practitioner's education, expertise, and credentials. Being beyond a physician's easy reach could cause parental worry. Phoebe Elliott com-

51. Meigs, *Observations,* 18; Mary Anderson to Rebecca Cameron, September 10, 1805, in Cameron Family Papers; Mary Henderson Diary, August 22, 1855; Nealy Lenoir to Walter Lenoir, March 16, 1858, in Lenoir Family Papers.

52. Paul Cameron to Duncan Cameron, July 3, 1848, in Cameron Family Papers; Isaac Avery to Thomas Lenoir, June 24, 1824, in Lenoir Family Papers; Henry Watson to Sophia Watson, May 28, 1848, in Henry Watson, Jr., Papers.

mented that when their little daughter became sick, "we suffered greatly from anxiety, being twenty miles from a Physician." In 1805, John Waddell admitted that for two years his family had "suffered very great uneasiness" by having no doctor nearby. Mothers who placed a lot of faith in doctors sometimes lost confidence in their own ability to handle infant illnesses. Rebecca Cameron sent for the family doctor when her infant came down with fever and ague, "afraid to give her any medicine without the Doctor's advice." And many parents accepted heroic cures for their children with no apparent reservations. P. M. Syme seems to have accepted with equanimity that his son, who had a severe case of the croup, was "hus'd, bled in the bone, and [given] a quantity of medicine, and today the doctors have applied a blister between his shoulders." Anne Cameron carried out without cavil a physician's order that her baby's liquid intake be severely restricted so long as he had fever, chills, and diarrhea.[53]

The role of southern fathers in nursing sick children is perhaps as variable as that of doctors. In some instances fathers became actively involved, but in other families they were reluctant child assistants. The time and energy of the father who appeared uninvolved may have been needed elsewhere, or he may have believed that child-care activities fell within the sphere of maternal responsibility. Some men found children bothersome and demanding and had no desire to be around them. In a letter written during one of his annual and lengthy sojourns in Saratoga Springs, New York, to restore his failing health, William Elliott questioned his wife about their plantation and crops, and then, as an afterthought, his children: "Tell me of my little ones that I love most at a distance—why? Can it be because they do not then plague me?" The peace that Elliott discovered away from juvenile noise may have been as soothing as the sulphur springs. The fathers who assumed parental duties normally believed their role a limited one. Frances Bumpas delineated the division of parental responsibility in her family. "I have taken charge of her for the first year," she wrote, "and Mr. Bumpas says he will afterwards take charge of her." *Taking charge* meant punishing the youngster, for Frances continued to attend to the girl's daily needs and nurse her illnesses when she was well beyond the age of one,

53. Phoebe Elliott to William Elliott, July 26, 1833, in Elliott-Gonzales Letters; John Waddell to Duncan Cameron, November 10, 1805, Rebecca Cameron to Duncan Cameron, May 22, 1804, P. M. Syme to the Camerons, February 14, 1844, Paul Cameron to Duncan Cameron, June 10, 1848, all in Cameron Family Papers.

but her husband assumed the duty of spanking the child. Any form of parenting at all embarrassed the father who perceived it as a maternal responsibility. Demonstrations of love and tenderness undermined the masculine image that southern men cultivated. Jean Syme told of visiting a friend and her new baby and inadvertently bursting in while the father was holding the newborn. "I went over last night and found him in the act of nursing it," she related, "and you can't think how much ashamed he was of being caught so effeminately employed, he instantly put it down and leaved himself."[54]

But some fortunate mothers received loving support and steady assistance from their husbands. Isaac Avery sat up all night when a newborn suffered a sudden seizure of the "livid disease of infants." When a young daughter became partially paralyzed, James Gwynn— who appeared to be a particularly solicitous father—slept in a downstairs room with her while his wife cared for their baby. During one absence Gwynn worried about their young daughter to the point of issuing constant reminders to his wife. "Take good care of her," he urged Mary Ann, "mind her to stand up a great deal and try and get her to use her limbs; it's time now she was sitting alone—toss and tumble her about a great deal and don't let her be carried about in persons arms too much. She has been nursed too much for her good, I think." James had a well-defined view of proper infant care.[55]

The public acceptance of paternal nurturing may have grown somewhat by midcentury, and some physicians encouraged fatherly involvement. In his advice book of 1857, Holmes referred to the "parental" management of children, rather than calling it maternal. Wright encouraged fathers to become active in tending their offspring, commenting that the father "has an equal interest in their welfare." It is hard to determine how widespread paternal participation in child rearing was in the rural South. It may have been essential in some plantation households. In others, slaves may have been able to give southern mothers what assistance they needed. The degree of paternal participation doubtless depended upon the demands of the father's occupation and the amount of free time it left him, upon the depth of the marital

54. William Elliott to Ann Elliott, August 17, 1828, in Elliott-Gonzales Letters; Frances Bumpas Journal, May 14, 1844 (Southern Historical Collection); Jean Syme to Duncan Cameron, December 16, 1804, in Cameron Family Papers.

55. Isaac Avery to William Lenoir, Swan Pond, November 27, 1827, James Gwynn to Sarah Lenoir, January 28, 1844, James Gwynn to Mary Ann Gwynn, June 20, 1842, all in Lenoir Family Papers.

relationship, upon his and his wife's physical conditions, and upon his attitude toward sharing what society viewed as a feminine duty. Whatever the situation, however, a number of fathers nurtured their infants out of love, concern, and the desire to become involved.[56]

The participation of other people who aided with infant nursing is less ambiguous. Female family members, friends, and neighbors proved to be an invaluable source of aid during difficult periods, particularly when infants were ill. Southern mothers wrote of friends and neighbors who sat with them during all-night vigils. Letty Lewis mentioned a neighbor, Mrs. Dunn, who spent four sleepless nights with her when her daughter had scarlet fever. She found it hard to "express the sympathy I felt, and feel, for the poor creature who seems never to weary in the discharge of kind offices towards myself and children." Mrs. Petigru described two neighbor women who "were very attentive and were a great deal with us" when her son suffered a case of worm fever. Susan Hutchinson's acquaintance, Mrs. Smelt, sat up with her baby until two one night. The women who helped were likely to be neighbors living near enough to provide a mother with immediate aid. Those who had prior experience in nursing specific illnesses were undoubtedly the greatest help. The sharing of time, emotion, and maternal advice proved to be an important way for women to support one another in moments of stress.[57]

The position that black nurses achieved within the southern family structure and the extent to which they shared power with southern mothers must have varied from family to family. Personal relationships between mistress and slave could be close, but distrust and distaste from the standpoint of either race were also possible. From limited data in slave narratives and white women's correspondence, it appears that slave women rarely assumed a primary role when infants were ill or raised a child as long as the mother could tend to her duties. Healthy white mothers did not readily leave nursing duties to black domestic slaves, or if they did, they rarely admitted it. Like breast-feeding, nursing a sick child remained a prerogative of the mothers, and white women were unlikely to turn these duties over to a family servant, particularly when a child's life was in danger.

56. Holmes, *The Child's Physician,* iii; Wright, *A Practical Treatise,* 13.

57. Letty Lewis to her mother, Letitia Floyd, December 28, 1841, in John Warfield Johnston Collection; L. Petigru to Adelle Allston, September 18, 1832, in Allston Family Papers; Susan Hutchinson Diary, March 15, 1827; Mahala Roach Diary, *passim.*

Perhaps the greatest contribution that black slaves made during a mother's nursing vigil was to look after other members of the household and to do domestic chores, thereby enabling the mother to concentrate on her ailing child. Slave narratives show too that a typical duty for slave children was as child-sitters or playmates for the master's children. Privileged southern mothers relied on black nurses and black children to assist mainly in the care of children who were well. Often youngsters of both races played and matured together on the plantation, though such interaction was mentioned more often in slave narratives than in white correspondence. Perhaps it was so common that it did not occur to women to write about it, or perhaps southern mothers were disinclined to admit their dependence on others' help.[58]

Childrearing, touted as a joyful duty, was often worrisome, exhausting, and difficult for mothers. Doctors played an uncertain role during these early years, while mothers, as long as they were healthy, retained ultimate responsibility for the well-being of their infants. In most instances, their attentiveness paid off, but in other cases, the reality of death had to be faced. Not even deep love and devoted care could forestall the reality of infant mortality.

58. See George P. Rawick, *The American Slave: A Composite Autobiography* (41 vols. and index; Westport, Conn., 1972–81); Eugene Genovese, *Roll, Jordan, Roll: The World the Slaves Made* (New York, 1974); Deborah White, *Ar'n't I a Woman? Female Slaves in the Plantation South* (New York, 1986); and Daniel Blake Smith, *Inside the Great House: Planter Family Life in Eighteenth Century Chesapeake Society* (Ithaca, N.Y., 1980).

7 *Their Sorrowing Hearts*

INFANT MORTALITY AND MATERNAL

BEREAVEMENT

"Pray heaven you may not like me know what it is to consign to the grave a darling and beloved child," wrote Mary Anderson to her brother and sister-in-law in 1807. "My sorrowing heart has three times had that sad and sorrowfull task to perform." Another grieving mother put her pain in a letter after visiting her baby's grave. "I feel my beloved Infant's loss so very sensibly," mourned Priscilla Bailey from her eastern North Carolina plantation. "Dear little Innocent, how fondly does my heart cling to her and how often is the tear of sorrow shed to her memory." The death of a child was an experience nearly all antebellum southern mothers knew. Illness, disease, or an accident—often at first seeming innocuous—could suddenly end a young life. Women lived with the constant awareness that their own child might be the next victim. The good health and survival of their children became an end in behalf of which mothers gave their time and energy and sometimes lost their health, and even mental stability. Yet regardless of what they did, death was omnipresent.[1]

Antebellum physicians were well aware that infant mortality was alarmingly high, both in America and abroad. In 1851, statistics issued by the registrar general of England showed that children under the age of one accounted for one-third of all deaths in that country. In the United States, both Dr. Joel Shew and Dr. David Holmes speculated that a third of the entire race perished before attaining three years of age. Holmes, in an understatement, called this a "fearful mortality among children." A decade earlier, Dr. Charles Delucena Meigs had suggested that half of the world's deaths occurred to children under the

1. Mary Anderson to Duncan Cameron, September 30, 1807, in Cameron Family Papers, Southern Historical Collection, L. R. Wilson Library, University of North Carolina at Chapel Hill; Priscilla Browning Bailey to John Bailey, November 30, 1824, in John L. Bailey Collection, Southern Historical Collection.

age of six. A writer for the *New Orleans Medical and Surgical Journal*
noted that half of all deaths in New York and Philadelphia—but only
30 percent of those in New Orleans—were of children under five years
of age. Even professionals who were ambivalent about the practice of
children's medicine acknowledged that infant mortality was serious.
For some doctors, that was reason enough to become involved in infant therapeutics; for others, it was cause to steer clear, for the area was
not likely to show off their medical skills to best advantage. Nor did
the situation appear to be improving. The consistently high infant
death rate continued until the Civil War and had an important bearing
on demographics, family structure, and most important for this study,
southern women.[2]

Mortality statistics, like other forms of statistics, were becoming
increasingly important to Americans. The 1850 federal census, directed
by Dr. Edward Jarvis, of Massachusetts, was the first nationwide effort
to determine systematically the death rate and the causes of death
among Americans. The introduction to the census report remarked,
"The federal census of 1850 furnishes the first instance of an attempt to
obtain the mortality during one year in all the States of the Union." The
editor also admitted that problems beset the survey. Because a severe
cholera epidemic affected the United States beginning in 1849, mortality figures were unusually high in urban areas where the disease was
rampant. The editor also admitted that census takers at times gathered
data haphazardly, and "at least one-fourth of the whole number of
deaths, have not been reported at all."[3]

Nevertheless, the data-gathering efforts delineated mortality for the
nation by age, sex, race, state, and cause. Table VI (see Appendix One)

2. "Churchill and Condie on Diseases of Children," *Charleston Medical Journal and
Review*, V (1850), 201; Joel Shew, *Children and Their Hydropathic Management in Health and
Disease* (New York, 1852), introduction; David Holmes, *The Child's Physician: A Popular
Treatise on the Management and Diseases of Infancy and Childhood* (Providence, 1857), iii;
Charles Delucena Meigs, *Observations on Certain of the Diseases of Young Children*
(Philadelphia, 1850), 17; Review of John Eberle's *Treatise on the Diseases and Physical
Education of Children*, in *New Orleans Medical and Surgical Journal*, VII (1850), 790. Infant
mortality does not seem to have improved from the colonial period.

3. *U.S. Federal Census, Mortality Statistics of the Seventh Census of the United States,
1850*, ed. J. B. D. De Bow (Washington, D.C., 1855), 8. Beginning with the federal
census of 1850, statistics included the cause of death. The *New Orleans Medical and Surgical
Journal* referred to the "new science of vital statistics" (VII [1850], 790) in presenting
numerical information to its readers. For the importance of data collection and analysis to
the medical establishment, see also James H. Cassedy, *American Medicine and Statistical
Thinking, 1800–1860* (Cambridge, Mass., 1984).

indicates that American children under the age of one year accounted for nearly 17 percent of all deaths in 1850, and those under five years of age, more than 38 percent. The figures for 1860 are even more startling, showing that greater than 20 percent of all deaths occurred among infants and almost 43 percent among those five years and under. Table VII calculates infant mortality by state, relative to both the total number of deaths and the total number of live births. It is apparent from the 1850 and the 1860 censuses that the first twelve months of a child's life were the most precarious. According to the figures, regional differences were minimal. Perhaps the negative effect of the southern climate and the region's endemic illnesses balanced the devastating effects of cholera and other contagious diseases that hit northeastern and midwestern urban areas. Readers were cautioned not to view the census as "showing the respective pretentions to healthfulness or the degree of un-healthfulness of the several States." Certainly the figures caused a good deal of alarm among physicians and in the public. Neither doctors' calculations nor federal statistics supported the idea that infant health was improving.[4]

Southern families needed neither doctors nor census figures to inform them of the frightening infant death toll. Children's deaths were common, and often recurrent within a family. "In four years I have known little else but the most heartrendering affliction," wrote a disconsolate Mary Henderson, "having buried four bright, lovely, beautiful children." In 1852, Selina Lenoir recorded that her friend Adeline attended another family burial. "It is the fifth interesting little babe she has buried," she commented. A young South Carolina mother, Henrietta Down, stoically wrote her aunt that she had been "blest with three fine little Comforts—my eldest who was named Henrietta Tommer I had the misfortune to lose at the age of two, my second I still thank God am blest with . . . my third who would have been a twelve-month old last April, I had the misfortune to lose last June with an inflammation in his bowels." In a particularly tragic case, Caroline Mordecai Plunkett, of Wilmington, North Carolina, lost two children within the space of three days. Eight months later her husband died. She bore a child three months after that, and her baby lived only nine months. It may be little wonder that Caroline spent her final days in a mental institution. In another unfortunate situation, a daughter of Isaac

4. *U.S. Federal Census, Mortality Statistics*, 9.

Avery died suddenly in 1825 from "inflammation of the brain, the same unsparing disease that took Theodore from us." Two years later, the same disease caused a newborn's death in the same family, and the following year another child died from it. Isaac mourned, "This is the fifth child we have lost by sudden and acute diseases."[5]

Today, psychiatrists agree that the death of a child can be the most traumatic experience in a parent's life. From a late-twentieth-century perspective, it seems a wonder that southern mothers could endure the emotional suffering, particularly when infant death recurred frequently within a family. Isaac Avery remarked that after a third child died, his wife Harriet "appear[ed] to sink more under it than under any former trial." There is no record of Harriet's bereavement after she lost two more babies, but her sorrow must have been intense and prolonged. Carrie Roberts, helping a close friend who had just buried the last of her three infants, sympathized, "It was worse than anything she ever had to come before her." Martha Richardson, of Savannah, was disconsolate when another of their infants died. "Oh, James," she wrote her nephew, "may I never see another child die. I should like to die before them all." In later months, she frequently recalled her "dear darling little boy" and thought of herself as a "wretched mother." "I do believe," she sighed, "I would put an end to my existence, for what is my life, one continued scene of sorrow." Even a single loss had a profound impact. When the two-year-old son of Mrs. Roberts died from whooping cough, she fully understood some of the pains of motherhood. "I never thought I could stand it," she confessed.[6]

Devastating too were times when the baby was stillborn or died shortly after birth. A Georgia woman, Sarah Screven, described her feelings of loss. "I am a child of sorrow and never do I expect happiness on earth," she wrote. "I was the mother of one of the sweetest babes I

5. Mary Henderson Diary, July 1, 1855 (Southern Historical Collection); Selina Lenoir to Sade Lenoir, March 18, 1852, in Lenoir Family Papers, Southern Historical Collection; Henrietta Down to her aunt, May 13, 1802, in Edward Down Papers, Manuscript Department, William R. Perkins Library, Duke University; Ellen Mordecai to Sam Mordecai, May 18, 1828, in Jacob Mordecai Papers, Manuscript Department, William R. Perkins Library; Isaac Avery to Thomas Lenoir, July 8, 1825, February 24, 1828, both in Lenoir Family Papers.

6. Isaac Avery to Thomas Lenoir, July 8, 1825, in Lenoir Family Papers; Carrie Roberts to Mary Bailey, November 13, 1856, in John L. Bailey Collection; Martha Richardson to her nephew James Screven, February 3, 1819, in Arnold-Screven Letters, Southern Historical Collection; Carrie Roberts to Mary Bailey, November 13, 1856, in John L. Bailey Collection.

ever had—the day after 'twas born he was taken ill, lingered for a week and died, dear little fellow." Even though Sarah had other children, they afforded little consolation at that moment, for she wrote, "I do not wish to live out this year." Sophia Watson's friend Clara delivered a stillborn baby, and both she and her husband were deeply affected. Sophia related that, five days after the death, "when she saw me she burst into tears and wept for some time." Even if parents had not had time to bond with their infants and perceived them as "temporary travelers in a world of sorrow," their death was a cause for intense grief.[7]

Some scholars of family history have conjectured that a high infant mortality rate and a high birthrate deterred parents from investing themselves in their children. According to the theory, the child-centered family and affectionate parenting emerged only with the decline in infant mortality rates and the concomitant rise in the preference for smaller families. The idea seems to be that the death of a child has less impact on parents of a large family than it does on parents of a small one. It also seems to suppose that a mother possesses a finite amount of love which she has to apportion among her children, so that the more sons and daughters there are in the family, the less she can love each child and the less she will mourn her loss if a child dies. The idea is incorrect when considering the emotional investment antebellum southern mothers made in their offspring. Despite the region's high infant mortality rate and high birthrate, southern mothers had seemingly limitless love and inexhaustible nurturing to offer.[8]

Mothers did not mind saying that their very existence was wrapped up in their children. A Virginia woman wrote in 1858, "I imagine nothing, no relation in life, makes one feel so differently as that of being a Mother. To woman, I have always heard it said, the gift of a child was a joy all other joys above." Another Virginia woman had been absent from her baby for only a month but found the experience wrenching:

7. Sarah Screven to James Screven, March 16, 1820, in Arnold-Screven Letters; Sophia Watson to Henry Watson, Jr., May 21, 26, 1848, both in Henry Watson, Jr., Papers, Manuscript Department, William R. Perkins Library.

8. See Lawrence Stone, *The Family, Sex, and Marriage in England, 1500–1800* (New York, 1980), 81–82, 410–21, 651–57; and Louise A. Tilley and Joan W. Scott, *Women, Work, and Family* (New York, 1978), 58–59. For another point of view emphasizing deep love and concern, see Jane Turner Censer, *North Carolina Planters and Their Children* (Baton Rouge, 1984), 24–25; and Darrett B. Rutman and Anita H. Rutman, *A Place in Time: Middlesex County, Virginia, 1650–1750* (New York, 1985), reviewed by Edmund S. Morgan in *New York Review of Books,* January 17, 1985, pp. 44–45.

"My poor heart felt like bursting under the cumbrous weight—in short, I feel all that a doating mother could feel at the absence of that better part of her existence, an idolized infant." Ella Clanton Thomas felt a new sense of happiness with the arrival of a baby and echoed the feeling of many southern mothers. "A mother's love, there is no sounding its depths," she wrote. "Oh how strongly are the chords of affection woven around this precious wee bit creature."[9]

Whether maternal instinct is naturally or culturally based is an undecided sociological and anthropological question. By the first half of the nineteenth century, mothers had assumed child nurturing as their principal role. Motherhood became middle- and upper-class women's primary occupation, which society elevated not merely to a duty but to an enviable vocation. Finding few options outside the home for their energy and emotions, antebellum southern women turned to their children and sought satisfaction in a role honored by their society. Southern women achieved status through motherhood. Whether in this they were different from women elsewhere in the nation is not clear, but it is possible that mothers in the antebellum South developed a deeper commitment than women in other regions to family and maternal responsibilities. Existing in a class-defined, male-dominated society and precluded from nearly all public activities, they had no choice but to devote their lives to mothering. In addition, the presence of slaves who could handle some of the ordinary and less agreeable tasks of child rearing may have opened to privileged and healthy mothers a greater number of opportunities for concentrating on the profounder aspects of child nurturing—particularly on duties where emotional ties could strengthen. Often living in relatively isolated settings, plantation women had few outlets beyond the home and family. Their deepening commitment to the family thus became self-feeding. The more involved they became with their infants, the more they depended on their children and maternal duties for personal satisfaction and emotional comfort. Consequently, the death of a child meant not only the loss of something treasured but also the fracture of the self.[10]

9. Jean Syme to Rebecca Cameron, April 27, 1811, in Cameron Family Papers; sister to Elizabeth Harrison, February 6, 1850, in Elizabeth Seawell Harrison Letters, Southern Historical Collection; Ella Clanton Thomas Diary, November, 1857 (Manuscript Department, William R. Perkins Library).

10. See Elisabeth Badinter, *Mother Love: Myth and Reality—Motherhood in Modern History* (New York, 1980); Maxine L. Margolis, *Mothers and Such: Views of American Women and Why They Changed* (Berkeley, Calif., 1984); and Jan Lewis, *The Pursuit of*

Still, southern mothers could not surrender to their grief. Anticipatory bereavement, the recognizing of a loss before it occurred, sometimes eased the moment when the infant died. A mother who had been
nursing her sick child for several days or even weeks—as was often the
case—may have gradually accepted the idea that death was inevitable. In
a few cases, mothers seem to have handled their grief by ignoring it.
Martha Screven observed that her mother-in-law bore the "loss of her
infant much better than I expected." She attributed this to the fact that
two other daughters were seriously ill, demanding their mother's attention. "She had no time for useless grief—fears and anxiety for the
living," Martha commented. Apprehensive of additional deaths and
overwhelmed by the nursing of other sick children, she had little time,
energy, or emotion for the one she had just lost—at least according to
Martha's perception.[11]

Southern mothers developed a viewpoint that incorporated the possibility of children's deaths. Mary Boulware, of South Carolina, despaired for her sister's newborn when the infant became ill. "I do not
think they ever can raise her," Mary wrote in her journal. Fortunately,
her prediction proved inaccurate, at least concerning that sickness. After
the birth of a first child, Jean Syme prayed that "Providence in its
wisdom and goodness see fit to spare my darling boy to me." She
plainly entertained the possibility of his death. Joseph Norwood observed his wife's stoic attitude toward their healthy infant's possible
demise. "She says she would not grieve after him and does not ever
expect to raise him," he related. Another pessimistic mother, Martha
Richardson, lamented that her children's lives might be cut short because they had inherited her husband's weak constitution. She confided
to a friend that even if each child lived through childhood, "I may still
look for their death at 11 or 13 or 15, so I am to live in torture." For
Martha, there was to be little peace in motherhood. Perhaps sharing

---

Happiness: Family and Values in Jefferson's Virginia (New York, 1983), 184. Lewis argues
that nineteenth-century southern parents saw children as their sole comfort rather than as
one of many, as they did during the colonial period.

11. Martha Screven to James Screven, December 2, 1821, in Arnold-Screven Letters.
There are many current studies on grieving and loss. See, for example, Judy Tatelbaum,
The Courage to Grieve (New York, 1980); Linda Edelstein, *Maternal Bereavement: Coping
with the Unexpected Death of a Child* (New York, 1984); Richard A. Kalish, *Caring Rela-
tionships: The Dying and the Bereaved* (Farmingdale, N.Y., 1980); Barbara A. Backer *et al.,
Death and Dying: Individuals and Institutions* (New York, 1982), 1–44, 135–70; and Bernard
Schoenberg *et al., Anticipatory Grief* (New York, 1974).

with others the thought that one's children might not survive provided strength and comfort and lessened the impact of death if that occurred.[12]

When a child died, mothers found that an open grief was healing. Antebellum southern society could not offer mothers psychiatric counseling, institutionalized support groups, or the swift travel that might let women talk out their sadness face to face with distant family members. But it did allow mothers to mourn, and many women willingly shared their pain and sorrow with relatives and friends. Death was not a subject to be avoided, as it became in the twentieth century, but rather a topic to discuss—often in detail. It was not unusual for mothers' letters to describe the last, rather grim moments before their infants succumbed. It is likely that bereaved mothers also spoke about their feelings with nearby friends and relatives.

Southern mothers grieved privately as well, perhaps sensing the importance of written expression for ultimate psychological recovery. Charlotte Beatty, of Louisiana, gave full voice to her sorrows and even composed a poem to her dead infant that began, "My fairest sleeps within the tomb." After four children died, Mary Henderson released many of her emotions into the privacy of her journal. "I am in despair and for that my life is so wretched," wrote the distraught mother. "I can *never* pass another happy hour." Daily entries in women's diaries often included the birth dates of children long since deceased, evidence that the infants were not forgotten. Mothers mentioned visits to family grave sites, where miniature stones marked the birth and death dates of each child. Each loss left an indelible mark.[13]

The religious beliefs of women were just as important during infant rearing as during pregnancy and childbirth. In nursing a sick child or dealing with their own or a friend's bereavement, they found reassurance in their deep belief in God's ultimate wisdom. Religion sustained women through the daily hardships they encountered. When Mary Bethell lost a six-month-old baby—eighteen months after the

12. Mary Boulware Journal, April 18, 1855 (Boulware Family Papers, Archives and Special Collections, Ida Jane Dacus Library, Winthrop College, Rock Hill, S.C.); Jean Syme to Rebecca Cameron, January 30, 1811, in Cameron Family Papers; Joseph Norwood to Sarah Lenoir, November 24, 1854, in Lenoir Family Papers; Martha Richardson to James Screven, October 4, 1819, in Arnold-Screven Letters.

13. Charlotte Beatty Pocket Diary, 1843 (Southern Historical Collection); Mary Henderson Diary, July 1, 1855. Eliza Clitherall and Lucilla Gamble McCorkle both noted their dead children's birthdays each year.

death of another child—she wished that she could "feel a perfect resignation to the Lord's will." With incomplete conviction but ultimate hope, she added, "I hope this affliction will work out for my good." Southern mothers believed that God could support them through their sorrow. A La Grange, Georgia, woman described the miserable moments she endured without her husband when her infant died. "I must have sunk under my affliction, but I do believe the Lord sustain'd me, and blessed be his holy name." She added that life without this child held little meaning, beyond the comfort God provided: "I have but little to desire [in] life but to become holy."[14]

Hope existed for mothers who believed that the hereafter provided ultimate happiness. In heaven, one could be reunited with loved ones long removed from the sorrows of life on earth. Eliza Jane DeRosset, like many southern women, had as her goal to "meet our darling ones in Heaven." Often mothers lived with the idea that their children would be happier in heaven than in what often seemed a world of sorrow. The I. J. Whittles, of Virginia, tried to convince themselves of this after their daughter died: "We ought to rejoice that the sweet little girl has gone to a better world." Margaret Dickins' cousin Emma attempted to cheer her cousin after her baby died. She assured Margaret that the infant was "not dead, but a pure, bright angel." When another Dickins baby died three years later, Ellen Harin observed, "She is safe, she is happy, she is another link in the chain to bind your heart to heaven." It was easier to accept infant death if one believed that the loved one was enjoying peace and an existence superior to what life offered.[15]

Southern mothers often mentioned their nurturing with a degree of tentativeness, anticipating that infant death might intervene. Yet it was reassuring to acknowledge that, whatever happened, God's infinite wisdom ruled. In part this was a self-protective reaction toward the inevitable; in part it was an expression of the strong religious faith of southern women. They were remarkably free of anger in their mourning. They were taught to accept their lot, and they seldom complained.

14. Mary Bethell Diary, April 11, 1854 (Southern Historical Collection); Nancy Walton to cousin Jane Gurley, January 16, 1836, in Jane Gurley Letters (Southern Historical Collection).

15. Eliza Jane DeRosset to Kate DeRosset Meares, June 3, 1855, in DeRosset Family Papers, Southern Historical Collection; I. J. Whittle to Lewis Whittle, October 25, 1847, in Lewis N. Whittle Papers, Southern Historical Collection; Emma to Margaret Dickins, October 12, 1849, Ellen Harin to Margaret Dickins, August, 1852, both in F. A. Dickins Papers, Southern Historical Collection; Lewis, *The Pursuit of Happiness*, 66, 79.

In one instance, a mother realized that she had overstepped propriety by protesting her lot. As she and her family moved from their home, leaving reminders of her dead children behind, the woman apologized, "God has afflicted me and it is a sin to murmur. I do not mean it as such only I cannot forget my babes." Kate DeRosset Meares owed no apologies. She moved from a week of intense mourning to a trusting acceptance of her infant's death. "I am happy, yes, very happy to have a little cherub in that happy land," she told her mother, "because I know that she is where there will be no more pain nor sorrow and God will wipe away all the tears from her eyes." This was a mother who grieved but accepted her fate and, through faith, made the best of her loss. Her words did not, however, imply a complacent fatalism about death. Southern mothers gave themselves totally to sustaining their infants' lives, nursing their sick children, and forestalling in any way they could their offspring's end. Their sacred occupation was to bear and raise healthy children, and they did not bow easily to the inevitable.[16]

Parents rarely blamed the Deity for their loss. They regarded the divine will kindly and accepted God's ultimate wisdom. Martha Jackson, of rural Georgia, admired how her aunt and uncle mourned their infant's death. "They express entire resignation to the dispensation of providence," she observed. Avery, whose unemotional words seemed to reflect a parent all too accustomed to infant death, commented when another child died, "It has pleased the Almighty again to lay his afflicting hand on us." A belief in the ultimate soundness of God's judgment made it easier to deal with the cruelties of life and the pains of motherhood. Southern parents drew on their faith in God not only for support but for making sense out of what seemed to be an unjust world.[17]

Mothers might blame themselves for a young death, thinking that they had overindulged the child. "It has pleased our heavenly father to take the dearest pledge of my affections," wrote a Charleston woman to her sister. "I had forgotten my duty and placed my whole affections on that dear child—which we are so strictly forbidden by our Bible." Letty Lewis, of Millwood, South Carolina, delighted in her daughter's antics

16. Sister to Mrs. James Screven, August 8, 1819, in Arnold-Screven Letters; Kate DeRosset Meares to Eliza DeRosset, June 5, 1855, in DeRosset Family Papers.
17. Martha Jackson to Henry Jackson, June 6, 1834, in Jackson and Prince Collection, Southern Historical Collection; Isaac Avery to Thomas Lenoir, July 8, 1825, in Lenoir Family Papers.

but realized she needed to hold her maternal affection in check. "I have often felt superstitious about indulging such an extent of feeling toward the little angel as I do," she wrote her mother, "and I often turn from contemplating the bare possibility of losing her with the self-abandoning tenets of Christian faith. I have so frequently sat and watched her thousand little capers, her bright rosy face." William Walker, of Norfolk, Virginia, had a definite idea of God's reaction to strong parental affection. "It is very difficult to restrain our attachments to our children; within proper bounds and to avoid making devils of them," he stated. "But our merciful God certainly knows how to make one allowance for *this* weakness of our nature," he commented, implying that death was the surest means to limit such love. According to Walker, God is willing to teach mortals a lesson.[18]

During bereavement, female friends and family members once again proved to be a source of strength and comfort to mothers. Husbands shared their wives' grief and provided empathy and affection, but because of their own pain, they often could not provide the support the wives required. It was other women, particularly those who had experienced similar losses, to whom mothers turned for comfort. Recent studies on grieving show that it is important for a bereaved parent to have a support group outside the family. Relying on the spouse often puts a destructive pressure on the marital relationship and on the grieving partner. Southern mothers instinctively turned to women who had been empathic on other occasions. It was a mixed blessing that there were so many who could sympathize with their pain. Studies have also shown that grieving mothers believe that their sorrow is unique in that only those who have been through a similar experience can understand the dislocation of what has happened. After Mrs. Anderson's baby died, the mother felt that "Him and a Parent can only tell how hard was my struggle." Mrs. Roberts, who had lost a child, observed with the wisdom of experience, "No one knows the feelings of a Mother when she sees her child in its last moments but those who have gone through with it."[19]

18. Anna Porter to her sister Elizabeth Ann Yates, July 17, 1822, in Yates Family Papers, South Carolina Historical Society Library, Charleston; Letty Lewis to Mrs. Niketti Floyd, December 30, 1839, in John Warfield Johnston Collection, Manuscript Department, William R. Perkins Library; William Walker to John Rutherfoord, October 5, 1855, in John Rutherfoord Collection, Manuscript Department, William R. Perkins Library.

19. Mary Anderson to Duncan Cameron, September 30, 1807, in Cameron Family

Another support—or escape—for southern women dealing with grief was narcotics. Sometimes dependence resulted from drug use following childbirth or a bout with a serious illness. Physicians administered opiates, often for temporary relief during and after delivery. An occasional prescription might not lead to addiction, but it could seem a convincing argument for using narcotics in other circumstances, particularly for relieving physical pain, mental stress, and depression. At times, a dependence developed from a woman's desire to withdraw from demanding, lonely, or unhappy straits. Laudanum, an opium derivative, may have been to the nineteenth century what diazepam (*e.g.,* Valium) became to the late twentieth century. Some southern women used it whenever physical or emotional problems overwhelmed them. Lucilla McCorkle and Susan Hutchinson frequently took the drug and mentioned being "languid and lifeless." At such times, they found themselves unable to cope with daily activities or to focus coherently in their personal writing.

In several documented cases, drug dependence followed upon the loss of a child or the stress of nursing children through prolonged illnesses. If women lacked the emotional strength to deal with their daily responsibilities after the death of a child, drugs offered them sanctuary. In the haze of opium or morphine, some southern women found they could forget their sorrows. When Mrs. Henderson lost four children, her doctor prescribed Cooke's Pills, containing an opiate powder, for her mental anxiety. Livinia, a cousin of Octavia Otey's, described the "history of the desolation of my very soul" in the period following the loss of her young daughter, whom she continued to call "my dearest tie to earth" long after the child had died. Livinia, who had nursed her child for eleven weeks through a serious illness, wrote that during that time, "every eye [was] closed in sleep but mine," for no one else thought the child's life endangered. To her cousin, Livinia admitted acquiring a drug habit: "For months after her death I was kept under the influence of morphine, and if I ever slept, I did not know it, my mind in a complete wreck."[20]

Papers; Carrie Roberts to Mary Bailey, November 13, 1856, in John L. Bailey Collection. See also Tatelbaum, *The Courage to Grieve,* 72–82; and Edelstein, *Maternal Bereavement,* 89–91.

20. Mary Henderson Diary, September 13, 1855; Cousin Livinia to Octavia Wyche Otey, December 14, 1856, in Wyche-Otey Collection, Southern Historical Collection. Morphine is particularly effective in relieving the symptoms of depression and melancholy. See John C. Kramer, "The Opiates: Two Centuries of Scientific Study," *Journal of Psychedelic Drugs,* XII (1980), 89–103.

Martha Screven described the condition of a family acquaintance, Mrs. Bagland, whose doctor gave her black drops, a form of opium. "Here we behold the consequences of a bad habit," Martha decided. "When she first commenced the use of it—to relieve her mind after the loss of her son, little did he think future existence and tolerable comfort would render its use absolutely necessary." Her husband moved the family to a new community, presumably to escape reminders of their loss and of maternal comportment embarrassing to the Bagland children. But his wife's drug habit worsened with the passing months, and Mrs. Bagland eventually lost all interest in her family. Martha sympathized with the poor woman, noting that "death to me would be a happy release, and under present circumstances would be preferable." Perhaps it was fortunate that the woman died shortly afterward.[21]

Anne Cameron took morphine, opium, and laudanum during a significant number of her childbearing years. Apparently she at first took drugs to relieve her frequent headaches and debilitating recurrences of malaria, but she soon discovered that narcotics could also ease her worries and sorrows. Her husband, Paul, at times desperate over her condition, was afraid to leave Anne in order to go away on business. Anne often could not care for their children or even arise from bed. Paul at times had to assume a number of his wife's maternal duties as well as that of chief correspondent.

Anne's situation is freighted with pathos and detail, perhaps helping us to comprehend better the difficulties many southern mothers confronted. Recall that Anne was the daughter of a North Carolina supreme-court justice and the wife of one of the state's most prominent and wealthy citizens. But money and status did little to deter her addiction. In 1850, while pregnant for at least the seventh time, Anne wrote her husband,

> The clock has just struck three and I have been tossing on my bed since eleven, and not one wink of sleep have I had. . . . Anxiety about my darling little Mary—impatience to see her once more—the *weight* of affairs *here* and the fear that I shall have to remain here during the summer, almost run me crazy. You will I know think me very unreasonable but you will remember it is not a common thing *for me to be as I am* three years in succession. I feel my health—and spirits have suffered by it, and I now tell you I *need* rest and quiet. . . . Last year was one of so much *mental* suffering, to say nothing of my bodily ailments, that I have determined to find composure by opening my heart to you. . . . I beg you will not get provoked with me—it is

21. Martha Screven to James Screven, July 22, 1821, in Arnold-Screven Letters.

altogether uncontrollable. . . . At this moment my head and face feel as if they were on fire. If you think it wrong for me to express my feelings to you, say so, and I will bury them all in my bosom.

Anne's desperation is not transparent to interpretation. Because very few family letters exist for 1849, it is impossible to shed light on her mental and physical suffering. But this appears to be the year their two-year-old son, Duncan, died. Anne had given birth in June of 1848, and the child was sickly throughout 1849.[22]

Peace was to elude Anne for some time. Shortly after this letter, she spent ten weeks nursing their youngest daughter through a grave illness. She suffered frequent chills and fevers, as well as rheumatism, and her doctor time and again prescribed quinine and morphine. Whenever her physical ailments and depression became hard to bear, Anne increased her dependence upon drugs. Her husband finally found the courage to admit to his sister that Anne could no longer rise from bed but was "now without the syrup of morphine, as she took a large part of what she had." He avowed his shame in writing so intimately. "I feel so desolate that I cannot bring my thoughts into any sort of frame," he confessed, adding that the doctor continued to prescribe the drugs. A week later, Paul felt momentary elation when he perceived that Anne's condition "both as regards her mind and body" might be improving. That she had slept "without the aid of opium in any form" elicited an exclamation point. By late summer, Anne had resumed some of her domestic activity and showed increased interest in her children. Yet by fall, Paul was in despair again, aware that Anne's mind had "not yet regained its powers." How long her habit continued beyond 1860 the documents do not tell.[23]

With numerous illnesses, high infant mortality, a large family, and questionable personal health, some southern women welcomed a palliative. Unfortunately, dependence brought serious consequences and interfered with the performance of the very duties that caused the women anxiety. Still, most southern mothers did not develop drug habits but discharged their maternal and domestic responsibilities with

22. Anne Cameron to Paul Cameron, Fairntosh, 1850, in Cameron Family Papers. I am grateful to Dr. Sydney Nathans, of Duke University, for bringing this case to my attention.

23. Paul Cameron to his sister, M. B. Cameron, April 21, 1853, undated 1853, May 16, August 2, September 15, 1853, all in Cameron Family Papers.

dedication and commitment. The business of raising healthy, sturdy, and virtuous young citizens was daunting at times, but southern mothers were usually successful. Child rearing had become their sacred occupation, to which they dedicated their lives. The rewards and risks were many, but most southern women accepted them all.

Conclusion

Lydia Sigourney may have been convinced that women in becoming mothers had reached a "higher place in the scale of being." Her cheerful pronouncement, however, deserves footnotes. A study of antebellum southern women during pregnancy, childbirth, and infant nurture, and an acquaintance with the approach of antebellum doctors to medical therapy, make it apparent that in the Old South motherhood was difficult and demanding. Many of the experiences associated with childbirth and infant rearing in the Old South paralleled those of rural women living elsewhere, but it is apparent that southern women faced a particularly perilous and demanding situation. Though women dedicated themselves to their maternal duties and discovered rewards in family life, many would have concurred with an Alabama woman who defined the experience of motherhood as the "greatest trial of our suffering sex."[1] Women approached labor in fear of pain and their own and their infant's death. Southern mothers emerged from their repeated confinements with physical ailments, infection, and debilitating illnesses. Southern families were large, increasing a woman's physical risks and expanding the responsibilities and demands of nurturing. Southern diseases, such as malaria, heightened the dangers of each pregnancy. Many of the region's doctors remained wholly committed to heroic therapeutics up to the Civil War. Infant death was all too common during this period, placing demands on mothers to exert every effort to ensure their offspring's health. In the process women's own physical and mental state often suffered. No other role in the antebellum South could match the risks and physical and emotional hardships of women's "sacred occupation."

Long-established myths that perpetuate the illusion of the leisured

1. Julia Howe to Louisa Lenoir, March 31, 1837, in Lenoir Family Papers, Southern Historical Collection, L. R. Wilson Library, University of North Carolina at Chapel Hill.

life-style of middle- and upper-class southern mothers need recasting. Observers of the Old South often remarked upon the languid manner of privileged southern women. It was easy to conclude that these women led indulged and easy lives. But exhaustion and ill health can be mistaken for laziness. Endemic diseases and chronic maladies took their toll on all Southerners but especially on expectant women. Frequent confinements were debilitating, the suckling of infants was tiresome, and the nursing of sick children depleted women's strength. The large size of southern families only increased the perils and demands.

During the antebellum period, Americans became particularly concerned about rearing a sound national citizenry for the future. Doctors began in earnest to work at enlarging the authority and prestige of their profession, and one way to do that was by widening their sphere of activity. Gradually they came to assist women during labor, to determine the existence of pregnancies, to attend to prenatal and postnatal health problems, and—though more reluctantly—to look after the endless string of diseases afflicting young children. Motivated partly by humanitarian considerations, they at the same time saw no better means for gaining legitimacy, increasing their income, and expanding their individual practices than to earn the gratitude of wives and mothers.

At this juncture, at least in the South, the movement of the medical profession into maternal and infant care did not signify a gain for women. Whatever psychological benefits accrued from having male attendants were offset by the dramatic but often baneful medical therapies employed. Doctors of the period lacked knowledge of sound procedures and of the causes and cures of diseases. Medical intervention frequently led to infection, for physicians were unaware of sepsis. In seeking to ease women's and children's sufferings, the profession at times meddled in ways that led to the anxiety, poor health, and even death of its patients.

The larger number of antebellum southern doctors remained committed to heroic medicine, with its stress on bleeding, drugging, and surgical measures. Pure empiricism—*ad hoc* experimentation, and guesswork and reactive observation, rather than theoretically founded and scientifically regulated research—determined the direction of treatments. Action was generally preferred to inaction, and thus the best of intentions could bring dire consequences for mother and child. What was especially lamentable was the way doctors resisted reassessing unsuccessful methods and adjusting their approach. Competition within the medical profession and pressure from without were too keen, however, for doctors to admit errors. Because every action performed in the name of medical science was in part spurred by a wish to enhance the reputation of the profession, the time was not right for asking whether dramatic therapies made sense or not.

Public pronouncements endlessly glorified the pure, submissive, and maternal nature of women. Perhaps the paeans emanated from a fear that women and society were changing, perhaps from hope that the ideal woman would evolve. But public statements unanimously restricted southern women to the home, where they were expected to serve with dignity, in silence, and with satisfaction. The unusual southern woman who chafed under such limitations found it best to leave the South entirely.

One body of historical opinion argues that the sphere of influence allotted to women invested them with a degree of power and status in the end. A nationwide decline in fertility signaled the control women were taking over their own destinies, according to this view. Yet in the antebellum South, families remained large and women secondary. Southern mothers bore more children than women living in other regions of the country; this reflected not only the economic opportunities available in a rural and thriving region but also southern women's acceptance of their lot in life. Few dared to assert their power, and others seemed unaware that they had any power to assert. Birth control would have done the most to improve southern women's physical and emotional well-being, since the frequency with which confinements occurred was an important cause of the poor health of southern women and of the region's high maternal mortality rate. But that was moot, for few Southerners even associated the declining vigor of mothers with multiparity. Only the natural end of their childbearing years, a severe physical disorder, or death brought them surcease.

It would be unfair, though, to hold men wholly accountable for the hardships wrought by childbearing and infant rearing. What may at first blush look like nothing but male control or at least lack of male concern involved two parties. If one of them controlled, the other accepted, at least to a degree. Southern women did little to protest their portion in life, apart from complaining in letters or describing their loneliness and sorrow in journals. At least publicly, southern women rarely questioned their duty to bear and rear numerous children or dwelled on the cause of their exhaustion and poor health. It is doubtful that they kept quiet because they were content with their situation, though people of the antebellum period certainly were hardened to sorrow, physical and emotional strain, poor health, and death. Truly joyful moments were treasured just because they were exceedingly rare. Perhaps the southern patriarchy was so strong and male attitudes so ingrained that protest seemed impossible. Or perhaps women were so accustomed to the idea of male superiority and to masculine perspectives that they would not, or could not, ask the questions that needed answering. And for southern women to assert some degree of power could have torn the social fabric. If women became independent, might not slaves seek some of the same freedoms? It was far easier to control all levels of southern society than to allow selective liberties. Most southern women had been properly brought up to accept their position and to veil their protests. They generally accepted their rigidly defined role and devoted their time and energy to maternal and domestic duties, making the best of their hardships. Only the political and social upheaval caused by the Civil War and Reconstruction would begin to erode their traditional acquiescence.

The changing perceptions of childbirth and infant care in the urban Northeast had an impact on privileged southern women, who gradually welcomed male attendants into the birthing chamber. For middle- and upper-class women to have a choice of assistant marked a significant change from colonial practices. The medical profession was growing, and more doctors were available. Physicians made an effort to advertise their skills and convince women that they could serve their needs best. Male accoucheurs won acceptance partly because a trained or educated doctor carried far more status than a midwife. The profession's instruments and scientific procedures transformed an experience that had previously been regarded as natural and ordinary. Childbearing achieved an important place in medicine as women moved onto center stage for a group of professionals who were seeking to improve their own status. Feminine modesty scarcely retarded women's consent to male attendants, and male doctors gradually established their place in a historically feminine ritual.

Yet southern women did not take to male physicians unquestioningly. Some, for practical reasons or out of preference, continued to rely on midwives. Not all medical innovations were desirable, and some were no better than traditional practices. Southern women and their families reacted ambivalently toward bringing in doctors to attend to infants. Some were enthusiastic and desired a trained physician in that capacity, but others felt doubt or caution, and still others were openly critical of the poor success record and dangerous therapies of physicians. Hence, mothers often continued in their traditional reliance on domestic medicine.

In some cases, doctors carefully, and perhaps wisely, selected the areas in which they wished to be active. They knew the importance of prenatal care but in the main encouraged expectant women to monitor their own health by following the medical advice in guidebooks for home use. Physicians wanted pregnancy to be considered a natural rather than a pathological condition, for treatments were lacking for the myriad health problems that arose in connection with it. They were also apprehensive that seeing pregnancy as an illness might alter women's daily habits. Childbirth, on the other hand, they were willing to deem pathological. Despite the fact that the majority of births were normal, medical intervention altered labor by introducing drugs and instruments and reshaping many traditional practices that had stood the test of time. Ironically, a majority of southern physicians opposed or were indifferent to the administration of anesthetics in childbirth, though it would have accorded male attendants a more prominent place. The opposition of some doctors stemmed from fear of new methods in general. Other doctors believed that mothers should suffer when bearing a child, for pain and struggle, they thought, promoted maternal love and a commitment to nurturing the child. The medical profession was least inclined to involve itself in infant health care, shying from a losing battle against high infant mortality. Here physicians encouraged dependence upon the written word—and maternal nurturing.

Four million slaves must be seen as a boon to southern mothers and an assistance to privileged plantation families. But again, myth blurs reality. Although there is little doubt that domestic servants played an important role in housekeeping, in child sitting, and in helping with routine tasks in the nursery and birthing chamber, personal accounts prove that healthy southern mothers rarely surrendered their maternal duties to black slaves. White women felt responsible for their children and deeply committed to caring for their health and well-being. The frequency of infant illnesses, the unhealthy southern climate, and a frighteningly high infant mortality rate fortified maternal commitment rather than sparking a desire to pass on these duties. Most healthy southern mothers assumed the exhausting but rewarding task of breastfeeding each child. In contending with childhood diseases and life-threatening illnesses, mothers retained primary responsibility for the care of their infants, and they spent many sleepless nights and kept seemingly endless vigils. Black slaves rarely served as surrogate mothers so long as the natural mother survived and retained a semblance of good health.

But childbearing and infant rearing offered black and white women opportunities to interact on a very personal level. White mistresses occasionally assisted with slave women's confinements, and black midwives sometimes attended white women. The dependence must have encouraged a feeling of intimacy and trust, even if momentary. Black and white women might breast-feed each other's babies as circumstances required. Each woman contributed to the future of the other's child and earned maternal and family gratitude. Slave women also played an important role in looking after household and family matters when white mothers were ill or were busy nursing sick children. Perhaps a better understanding of women will eventually illuminate the general nature of black-white relationships as well.

The new medical perception of childbirth did not, fortunately, sap all meaningful traditions. The events surrounding paturition and infant rearing continued to afford married women their best opportunities for bonding with other women. In a close, feminine sphere, women shared concerns about pregnancy, offered mutual advice, and expressed their fears to one another. Female family members and friends gathered for each confinement and assisted during the long postnatal recovery. If this bonding lacked the political overtones that sometimes developed from northern women's involvement in reform, it proved significant all the same. Not even the presence of male doctors could undermine such closeness. In fact, female support may have become even more important once male attendants took charge. Doctors were forced to adjust, accepting a female support system during delivery and altering their own bedside manner.

Many a southern husband played an important role during his wife's pregnancies and the events surrounding labor and infant nurturing. Usually men in the family remained outside the birthing chamber, but most husbands stayed at home during the delivery and welcomed each newborn. They spread the news of the birth, and some even assumed a limited role in child rearing. Though their involvement varied, husbands were rarely central figures at delivery or in child nurturing. But personal accounts reveal that the southern woman needed her husband's love and devotion when she was tested.

A deep belief in God provided women with an enormous amount of strength, consistent with the importance that religion had in the lives of most southern women. Expectant women dreaded their coming confinement, all too aware of its pain and perils, not least of which was maternal or infant death. They turned to God for support, depending on divine mercy for a successful outcome and giving their Lord credit for a job well done. Yet God was not accountable if problems occurred. When mothers suffered or their children died, women blamed themselves or viewed their loss as part of God's plan. They learned to believe that the peace death brought their infant was worth more than any sorrowful life on earth.

Even if women could adjust mentally to the grim realities, they encountered infant death with startling frequency. Most families could anticipate losing at least one child. Whether it was young or old, part of a large family or a small one, its death caused profound despair. Mothers' grief was often prolonged, and the sympathy of others was essential. Women occasionally turned to their husbands for this but more often to female friends, family members, and God. They needed others to talk to in order to relieve their sorrow and find strength in what seemed like an unjust world. Each loss left an enormous void. Most mothers found that the passage of time and an ability to express their grief freely lessened the pain. But suffering could be intense, and in some instances women lacked the strength to move forward without resorting to drugs.

The unhealthful southern climate and the numerous endemic and epidemic illnesses of the region increased the difficulties for women, infants, and physicians. The general poor health and the numerous diseases of the antebellum South were behind the high maternal mortality rate. Malaria could contribute to stillbirths and miscarriages and could cause debilitation and long-term health problems. Nineteenth-century diseases, such as scarlet fever, whooping cough, and cholera infantum, and persistent parasites like worms, had severe effects on young children. Southern physicians felt well justified in using heroic efforts to combat such diseases. But medical solutions often exacerbated a situation. Heavy bleeding of pregnant women or young babies depleted their strength and ability to fight diseases. Drugs were often overprescribed, with injury to the fetus, the pregnant woman, or the nursing infant. Medications were frequently too strong for any constitution to withstand; the result then was death.

Women's sacred occupation was anything but easy. Yet the majority of southern mothers survived and raised their children—a testimony to their inner strength under difficult, lonely, and insalubrious conditions. Southern women were all too aware that anxiety, exhaustion, sorrow, and poor health accompanied their maternal office. But they also knew that the rewards justified their sacrifices. Elizabeth Roberts, reflecting on her maternal role, expressed what most mothers have always believed. "It is a woman's place to raise her children herself," she stated, "and though to do this faithfully she must make some sacrifices and many a time deny herself amusements and pleasures, I am grateful I have given up everything else for those duties—they were sometimes irksome—but as far as my children are concerned, I am paid back with interest." Lucilla McCorkle gazed upon her one-year-old and noted in her journal, "Now my little bud of promise is repaying me amply for all the pain I suffered." The overall picture of the southern mother's life may not be particularly cheerful, but maternal love and dedication made all its difficulties worthwhile. Women devoted themselves to raising their infants and found meaningful emotional rewards in watching their family evolve and grow.[2]

This study ends with infancy. But the demands of motherhood continued long after that. New mothers might have felt that the first two years of a child's life were the most precarious and exhausting; others with experience to guide them saw this period as only the beginning. With the wisdom that comes from raising several children, Henry Watson's mother told her daughter-in-law, who had just borne her first child, "From this time forward, he will be a source of anxiety of which you know little—You may take more pleasure in him the first twelve years of his life than ever after." And E. Wingfield, a Virginia woman, remarked ruefully, "We all think our children are very sweet and good while they are small, some of them grow up very bad and give their parents more pain than pleasure." Antebellum southern mothers, like all mothers, were embarking on a lifetime of anxiety, commitment, and devotion to their sacred occupation.[3]

2. Elizabeth Roberts to her brother James Bailey, March 24, 1856, in John L. Bailey Papers, Southern Historical Collection; Lucilla Gamble McCorkle Diary, December 17, 1846 (Southern Historical Collection).

3. Mrs. Watson to Sophia Watson, January 26, 1847, in Henry Watson, Jr., Papers, Manuscript Department, William R. Perkins Library, Duke University; E. Wingfield to Margaret Dickins, August 8, 1842, in F. A. Dickins Papers, Southern Historical Collection.

Appendix One

TABLES

TABLE I *Preference of Medical Attendant at Childbirth*

Years	Number of Women Who Used Doctor	Number of Women Who Used Midwife	Number of Women Who Used Both
1800–1820	2	0	0
1820–1840	4	8	1
1840–1860	13	19	3

These figures were extracted from the letters and journals consulted for this study.

TABLE II *The Medical Profession in 1850*

State	Number of Doctors	Population	Number of People per Doctor	Number of Inhabitants per Square Mile
Maine	659	583,169	885	12.52
New Hampshire	523	317,976	607	39.60
Vermont	663	314,120	474	39.26
Massachusetts	1,643	994,514	605	137.17
Rhode Island	217	147,545	680	122.95
Connecticut	560	370,792	662	78.06
New York	5,060	3,097,394	612	67.33
New Jersey	608	489,555	805	71.46
Pennsylvania	4,071	2,311,786	568	49.19
Delaware	114	91,532	803	43.17
Maryland	990	583,034	589	53.00
District of Columbia	104	51,687	497	1033.74
Virginia	2,163	1,421,661	657	23.17
North Carolina	1,083	869,039	802	19.1
South Carolina	905	668,507	739	23.87
Georgia	1,295	906,185	700	15.62

Florida	135	87,445	648	1.48
Alabama	1,264	771,623	610	15.21
Mississippi	1,217	606,526	498	12.86
Louisiana	912	517,762	568	12.52
Texas	616	212,592	345	0.65
Arkansas	449	209,897	467	4.02
Tennessee	1,523	1,002,717	660	22.79
Kentucky	1,818	982,407	540	26.07
Ohio	4,263	1,980,329	464	49.55
Michigan	854	397,654	466	7.07
Indiana	2,170	988,416	455	29.24
Illinois	1,402	851,470	607	15.37
Missouri	1,351	682,044	505	10.49
Iowa	512	192,214	375	3.77
Wisconsin	581	305,391	526	5.66
California	626	92,597	148	0.49
Total	40,381			

SOURCE: *Nashville Journal of Medicine and Surgery*, VII (1854), 410–11.

TABLE III   *White Women Who Died in Childbirth in 1850*

State	Number of White Women Who Died	Number of White Women Who Died in Childbirth	White Childbirth Deaths as a Percentage of White Women's Deaths
Alabama	1,946	62	3.2
Arkansas	956	32	3.3
Connecticut	2,794	38	1.4
Delaware	452	8	1.8
Florida	205	11	5.4
Georgia	2,068	104	5.0
Illinois	5,269	117	2.2
Indiana	5,783	94	1.6
Iowa	897	17	1.9
Kentucky	4,907	75	1.5
Louisiana	1,950	55	2.8
Maine	995	48	4.8
Maryland	3,180	64	2.0
Massachusetts	9,354	168	1.8
Michigan	2,078	66	3.2
Mississippi	1,549	36	2.3
Missouri	4,728	95	3.2
New Hampshire	2,190	26	1.2
New Jersey	2,818	48	1.7
New York	20,765	312	1.5
North Carolina	2,706	104	3.8
Ohio	12,956	199	1.5
Pennsylvania	12,637	303	2.4
Rhode Island	1,044	14	1.3
South Carolina	1,265	48	3.8
Tennessee	3,877	78	2.0
Texas	941	47	4.9
Vermont	1,592	24	1.6
Virginia	4,870	147	3.0
Wisconsin	1,318	38	1.9

SOURCE: *U.S. Federal Census, Mortality Statistics of the Seventh Census of the United States, 1850*, ed. J. D. B. De Bow (Washington, D.C., 1855).

TABLE IV *Infant-feeding Practices*

Decade	Number of Mothers Who Commented	Number of Breast-Fed Infants	Number of Infants Using a Wet Nurse	Number of Hand-Fed Infants
1800–1809	5	5		
1810–1819	4	3	1	
1820–1829	7	7		
1830–1839	10	8	3	2
1840–1849	24	22	4	2
1850–1860	23	19	6	3
Total	73	64	14	7

These data were extracted from comments in the manuscript sources listed in the bibliography.

TABLE V *Principal Causes of Mortality Among Children in 1850*

Cause of Death	Number of Deaths of Children Under One Year of Age	Number of Deaths of Children from One to Five Years of Age
Bronchitis	999	902
Cholera[a]	1,417	4,283
Cholera infantum	1,842	1,999
Cholera morbus	177	402
Consumption	1,294	1,834
Convulsions	2,824	1,579
Croup	4,728	4,934
Diarrhea	1,467	2,184
Dysentery	2,311	8,164
Enteritis	645	733
External causes	1,567	2,334
Fever	1,719	3,633
Fever, scarlet	989	5,156
Fever, typhoid	391	1,276

(continued)

TABLE V   (*Continued*)

Cause of Death	Number of Deaths of Children Under One Year of Age	Number of Deaths of Children from One to Five Years of Age
Measles	487	1,564
Pneumonia	2,042	2,518
Smallpox	366	550
Teething	836	1,585
Whooping cough	2,103	2,659
Worms	306	2,049
Unknown	15,256	7,635
Total*b*	54,265	68,713

SOURCE: *U.S. Federal Census, Mortality Statistics of the Seventh Census of the United States, 1850*, ed. J. D. B. De Bow (Washington, D.C., 1855), 17–18.

These figures include white, slave, and free black children. Census statistics record that zymotic, or contagious or infectious, diseases caused the greatest number of deaths among children, followed by diseases of the brain and nervous system, respiratory diseases, and digestive diseases.

*a*Because there was a cholera epidemic in 1849–1850, these figures are probably higher than for a typical year of the period.

*b*These are the census totals and not the totals of the deaths listed in this table. Many causes of death were left out here because their significance was less profound.

TABLE VI   *Children's Deaths by Age in 1850 and 1860*

Age	Number of Children's Deaths in 1860	Children's Deaths as a Percentage of All Deaths in 1860	Children's Deaths as a Percentage of All Deaths in 1850
0–1	81,274	20.74	16.90
1–2	38,236	9.76	
2–3	23,646	6.04	21.41
3–4	14,650	3.74	
4–5	10,479	2.67	
Total		42.95	38.31

SOURCE: Joseph C. G. Kennedy, *Preliminary Report on the Eighth Census* (Washington, D.C., 1862), 29.

Includes "white and colored" children.

TABLE VII *Mortality Among Children in 1850*

State	Number of Live Births	Number of Deaths	Number of Deaths of Children Under One Year of Age	Number of Deaths of Children from One to Five Years of Age	Children's Deaths as a Percentage of All Deaths		Children's Deaths as a Percentage of All Live Births	
					Children Under One Year of Age	Children up to Five Years of Age	Children Under One Year of Age	Children up to Five Years of Age
Alabama	12,265	4,411	833	811	18.8	37.2	6.8	13.4
Arkansas	5,481	2,160	390	453	18.0	39.0	7.1	15.3
California	273	905	36	38	3.9	8.2	13.2	27.1
District of Columbia	1,248	789	143	148	18.1	36.9	11.4	23.3
Connecticut	7,646	5,781	705	905	12.2	27.8	9.2	21.0
Delaware	2,495	1,188	239	184	20.1	35.6	9.6	16.9
Florida	1,322	491	62	120	12.6	37.1	4.7	13.8
Georgia	15,239	4,592	868	830	18.9	37.0	5.7	11.1
Illinois	26,681	11,619	2,204	2,530	18.9	40.7	8.3	17.7
Indiana	32,296	12,808	2,213	2,748	17.3	38.7	6.8	15.4
Iowa	6,099	2,044	446	539	21.8	48.2	7.3	16.2
Kentucky	23,805	10,840	1,803	2,074	16.6	35.8	7.6	16.3
Louisiana	7,292	6,083	724	762	11.9	24.4	9.9	20.4
Maine	13,995	7,582	919	1,584	12.1	33.0	6.6	17.9
Maryland	14,036	8,109	1,545	1,555	19.1	38.2	11.0	22.0
Massachusetts	23,192	19,404	2,930	4,380	15.1	37.7	12.6	31.5

(continued)

TABLE VII (Continued)

State	Number of Live Births	Number of Deaths	Number of Deaths of Children Under One Year of Age	Number of Deaths of Children from One to Five Years of Age	Children's Deaths as a Percentage of All Deaths		Children's Deaths as a Percentage of All Live Births	
					Children Under One Year of Age	Children up to Five Years of Age	Children Under One Year of Age	Children up to Five Years of Age
Michigan	10,898	4,515	856	995	18.9	41.0	7.9	16.9
Mississippi	8,687	6,083	796	746	13.1	25.3	9.1	17.7
Missouri	19,632	12,121	1,634	2,179	13.5	31.4	8.3	19.4
New Hampshire	6,111	4,231	451	760	10.6	28.6	7.4	19.8
New Jersey	13,556	6,454	1,081	1,282	16.7	36.6	7.9	17.4
New York	76,337	45,585	6,705	9,758	14.7	36.1	8.8	21.6
North Carolina	16,648	6,028	872	743	14.5	26.9	5.2	9.7
Ohio	56,884	28,949	4,381	6,553	15.1	37.8	7.7	19.2
Pennsylvania	64,331	28,551	4,791	6,683	16.8	40.2	7.5	17.8
Rhode Island	3,610	2,241	353	437	15.7	35.2	9.8	21.9
South Carolina	6,607	2,879	380	466	13.2	29.4	5.7	12.9
Tennessee	23,090	7,825	1,537	1,318	19.6	36.5	6.6	12.4
Texas	4,765	2,219	369	401	16.6	34.7	7.7	16.2
Vermont	6,594	3,129	301	479	9.6	24.9	4.5	11.8
Virginia	25,153	10,608	1,585	1,707	14.9	31.0	6.3	13.1
Wisconsin	10,424	2,903	645	770	22.2	48.7	6.2	13.6

SOURCE: U.S. Federal Census, Mortality Statistics of the Seventh Census of the United States, 1850, ed. J. D. B. De Bow (Washington, D.C., 1855).
Includes both white and free black children.

Appendix Two

SOUTHERN WOMEN AND THEIR FAMILIES

Adele Petigru Allston (1810–1896)

Adele was married to Robert Allston, of Charleston, South Carolina. She had two adopted children, born in 1833 and 1834, and eight of her own, two or three of whom died shortly after birth.

The Badger Family

The three wives of George Badger were Rebecca Turner, Mary Brown Polk (1808–1835), and Delia Williams. George Badger, of New Bern, North Carolina, was born in 1793, attended Yale College, and was admitted to the North Carolina bar in 1814. He was elected to the state house of commons and served as a judge on the state superior court, and as a Whig in the United States Senate from 1846 to 1855.

The John Lancaster Bailey Family

The Bailey family lived in Pasquotank County, North Carolina, and moved to Hillsboro and, in 1859, to Asheville. John married Priscilla Browning, of "Wingfield," near Edenton, North Carolina, in 1821. While in Hillsboro, they lived at "Eno Lodge." John was a superior-court judge, a member of the state legislature (1827–1831), and a representative to the state convention of 1835. They had only two children. Their son, Thomas, married Sarah Harris, and they lived in Mississippi, Tennessee, and South Carolina. Their daughter, Sarah Jane, married Dr. William Cain, of Orange County, North Carolina, in 1846. The letters of both generations reveal an elite family that interacted with socially and politically prominent North Carolinians.

Charlotte Beatty

Charlotte lived near Thibodaux, Louisiana. Her son, Taylor, became an attorney and judge and owned several sugar plantations.

The Bedinger Family

Henry Bedinger III, of Virginia, married Caroline Browne Laurence, of Flushing, New York, in 1847. Henry was an ambitious Virginia lawyer, elected once to Congress, in 1845. Failing as a lawyer in New York, he returned to Sheperdstown, Virginia, in 1849, where he struggled with his law practice. After extensive work with the Democratic party, Henry was appointed chargé d'affaires to Denmark. While he was abroad, Caroline returned to her New York family home to give birth to their child. Henry died in 1858, after returning to the United States, and Caroline moved to "Poplar Grove," a Bedinger family home in Virginia.

Mary Jeffreys Bethell

Mary was born in 1821 near Raleigh, North Carolina, the daughter of Phereba Hinton and George Jeffreys. Several of her ten siblings died during childhood. Her mother died when only twenty-seven years old, and her father remarried and became a Methodist minister. Religion played a central role in the family. Mary received a good education through tutoring and at a girls' school in Milton and the renowned Salem Academy. In 1840, she married William D. Bethell. They resided briefly with his mother but soon established their own residence in Rockingham, North Carolina. Mary raised their seven children and four orphans. She and William journeyed to Louisiana, Tennessee, and Arkansas with the idea of moving—which Mary opposed. Mary began her diary in 1853.

The Samuel Biddle Family

Samuel Biddle's two wives were Mary B. Williams, whom he married in 1837, and Mary E. V. Powell, in 1846. Samuel (1811–1872) received his education at the University of North Carolina, from which he graduated in 1832. He was a wealthy merchant and planter in Craven County, North Carolina, who grew cotton and corn, raised livestock, and owned as well as leased numerous slaves. Samuel, a confirmed Baptist, had an interest in local politics and served as president of the Whig convention in 1846. His father made a considerable fortune in mercantile pursuits.

Elizabeth Holmes Blanks (1810–1861)

Elizabeth was born in Fayetteville, North Carolina, and in 1833 married William Blanks (1804–1844), of Bolivar, Tennessee, despite strong objections from her family. They resided briefly in Tennessee and then moved to Carrollton, Mississippi, where his family lived. In 1841, beset by a ten thousand dollar debt, declining markets, and poor health, the family moved to Taylor's Bridge, North Carolina. Despite efforts to recover his fortune, William eventually declared bankruptcy. Elizabeth bore children in 1834, 1835, 1836, 1839, and 1841.

Mary Jane Vinson Boulware (1832–1912)

Mary Jane married Thomas McCullough Boulware (1829–1889) in 1849. He was the son of Elizabeth McCullough and Musco Boulware II, of Rossville, South Carolina. Mary Jane and Thomas, a farmer, lived near Blackstock, Chester County, South Carolina, and had nine children.

Frances Moore Webb Bumpas (1819–1898)

Frances was born in Halifax, Virginia, and was tutored by her parents and private teachers in North Carolina. She taught school in Greenville County, Virginia. In 1842, she married the Reverend Sidney Bumpas, a Methodist, and they spent their early married years moving from one congregation to the next, including churches in Raleigh, Pittsboro, and New Bern, North Carolina. They were not among the southern elite financially, though his position gave him some status. Owing to Sidney's low salary, Frances taught school periodically. In 1847, the church appointed him a trustee of the Greensboro school district and Greensboro Female College. Frances and Sidney began publishing the *Weekly Message* in 1851 for North Carolina Methodists. Sidney caught typhoid fever in December, 1851, and died. Frances decided to continue publishing the newspaper despite public criticism that such activity was unseemly for a woman. The paper flourished until 1872, when the church began its own paper. Frances bore four children. Both she and her husband disliked slavery.

The Cameron Family

The Camerons became the wealthiest and one of the most influential families in antebellum North Carolina. Duncan Cameron (1777–1853) was born in Virginia, one of seven children of an Episcopalian priest. He studied law in Virginia and entered the North Carolina bar in 1798. Establishing himself as a successful attorney in Hillsboro, he eventually turned from law to other endeavors. He became a planter, a judge and clerk of the North Carolina Supreme Court, and president of the State Bank of North Carolina. He was a founder of St. Mary's School, in Raleigh, and served in the North Carolina house and senate. Duncan was one of the largest plantation owners in the South, with property in North Carolina and Alabama that exceeded thirty thousand acres. He averaged over a thousand slaves. In 1804, he built the family plantation home, "Fairntosh," and in 1835, constructed a large family home in Raleigh on ten acres of land.

Duncan married Rebecca Bennehan in 1803 after fighting a duel for her hand. Rebecca (1778–1843) was the only daughter of Mary Amis and Richard Bennehan, merchant, planter, builder, and pioneer of the tobacco industry. Richard started out in humble circumstances but became a successful merchant, purchased hundreds of acres northeast of Hillsboro, North Carolina, and acquired dozens of slaves. He was instrumental in getting Raleigh named capital of the state and in establishing the University of North Carolina. Rebecca brought Duncan three hundred acres as part of her dowry.

Rebecca and Duncan had eight children, two sons and six daughters. Four of their daughters died between 1837 and 1840, a fifth never married, and the sixth, Margaret, married George Mordecai. The Camerons' first son died without marrying, and their second son, Paul, received almost all the family property.

Paul (1808–1891) attended school in Middleton, Connecticut, the University of North Carolina, and Washington (now Trinity) College, in Hartford. He read law but never practiced it, being occupied with business and plantation matters. He was the wealthiest man in the state, at one time owning more than nineteen hundred slaves. He was also a railroad promoter. Anne Ruffin, whom he married in 1832, was the daughter of Thomas Ruffin, judge of the supreme court of North Carolina. They had ten children, but three died in childhood.

Other family members mentioned in the text include two of Duncan's sisters: Mary Read, of Petersburg, Virginia, who married Daniel Anderson; and Jean, who married the Reverend Andrew Syme, of Petersburg.

Mary Eliza Eve Carmichael

Mary Eliza was married to John Carmichael. They lived in Augusta and on their Georgia plantation, "Summer Hill." They had thirteen children between 1808 and 1831, four of whom died.

Mary McDowell Chaplin (1822–1851)

Mary was the wife of Thomas B. Chaplin (1822–1890), of St. Helena Island, South Carolina. She was from a wealthy Charleston family. Thomas, a planter, was socially involved with life on the sea island. Prodigality and poor management caused a decline in the family fortune, forcing Thomas to sell property, dozens of slaves, and his wife's assets. Mary died at the age of twenty-nine, after bearing seven children. She spent her final few years in declining health and addicted to snuff. Her half sister Sophy, who lived with the family, married Thomas in 1852.

Mary Boykin Miller Chesnut

Mary was the daughter of Mary Boykin and Stephen Decatur Miller, of Camden, South Carolina. Her father had passed from being a small farmer to being a wealthy planter, lawyer, congressman, governor, and senator. She was educated in local schools and sent to the renowned Madame Talvande's School, in Charleston. She was a lively, bright, and well-liked girl, who became a special favorite of the headmistress. At thirteen, Mary was introduced to James Chesnut, the uncle of a schoolmate. James, ten years her senior, was studying law in Charleston, and he was eventually to be the only surviving son of one of up-country South Carolina's wealthiest and most influential patriarchs, who owned more than five square miles of land and over five hundred slaves. Mary's father feared the man's intense interest in his young daughter and insisted that she leave school and join the family, now residing on a Mississippi plantation. Mary's removal from Charleston did not quell James's interest, however, and Mary returned a year later. After her father's death and a brief residence with her family when it returned to Camden, Mary married James at the age of sixteen.

For several years, Mary and James resided with his parents and his two unmarried sisters, and Mary often found her domestic situation stifling. She and her husband were not able to have children of their own, but Mary often cared for young nieces and nephews. Her husband was a planter who became involved in politics and in 1859 was elected to the United States Senate, where he served until South Carolina's secession. Mary's Civil War diary is a unique and valuable document. The Chesnuts suffered reduced circumstances after the war, and Mary had to supplement the family's income by selling eggs, running a dairy business, and writing. She was a strong-willed and outspoken woman who was often critical of slavery.

Virginia Caroline Tunstall Clay (1825–1915)

Virginia was born in Nash County, North Carolina, the daughter of Anne Arrington Tunstall and Dr. Peyton Randolph Tunstall. In 1828, her mother and sister died, and at the age of six, Virginia journeyed to Alabama to be cared for by relatives. She lived near Tuscaloosa and graduated from the Nashville Female Academy in 1840. In 1843, she married Clement Claiborne Clay in a lavish wedding in Tuscaloosa and brought at least ten slaves to the marriage. The Clay family was socially and politically prominent. Clement's father, Clement Comer Clay, had moved to Alabama from Tennessee in 1811. He was a lawyer and planter, as well as a Democratic congressman (1829–1835), the governor of Alabama (1835–1837), a United States senator (1837–1841), and the first chief justice of the Alabama Supreme Court. He owned two plantations, more than twenty-seven hundred acres of land and at least seventy slaves. Part of his wealth was due to his marriage to Susanna Claiborne Withers, daughter of a prosperous planter.

Virginia's husband, Clement (1816–1882), received a bachelor's and a master's degree from the University of Alabama and graduated from the University of Alabama Law School in 1839. He joined his father's law firm and became editor of the Huntsville *Democrat,* a member of the state legislature, judge of Madison County, and a member of the United States Senate in 1852 and again from 1856 to 1861. The only child he and Virginia had was stillborn. They lived on their plantation, "Wildwood," near Huntsville. Virginia was a brilliant and popular socialite in Washington and a famous flirt who enjoyed spending extravagantly. She made valuable contacts for her husband and was regarded as intelligent but superficial. After her first husband's death, Virginia married Judge David Clopton. She was the author of *Memories of Mrs. Clay of Alabama; or, A Belle of the Fifties.*

Carolyn Elizabeth Burgwin Clitherall (1784–1863)

Eliza was the daughter of John Burgwyn, of Wales, who established himself on "The Hermitage" plantation, near Wilmington. Her mother died when Eliza was three, and she spent most of her childhood in England, where she attended boarding school. After returning to North Carolina, Eliza met Dr. George Campbell Clitherall, of Charleston. After their marriage, they settled near Charleston, where he practiced medicine, but they later moved to "Thornbury," a rice plantation on the Cape Fear River near Smithville, North Carolina.

Summers were often spent in Hillsboro for cooler weather. Eliza ran a plantation school in 1814, and after her husband died in 1829, she moved to New Bern and, later, Alabama in order to teach and to manage female academies.

The Cornish Family

John Cornish was reared in Connecticut and Illinois, and he attended Washington (now Trinity) College, in Hartford, and the Episcopal Theological Seminary, in New York. In 1839, he. moved to South Carolina for health reasons, became a schoolmaster on "Seabrooke" plantation, Edisto Island, and took his Episcopal orders in 1842. That same year he married Martha Jenkins, daughter of Colonel Joseph E. Jenkins, a planter. John remained an Episcopalian priest and served as rector of St. Thaddeus Church, on Edisto, from 1846 to 1869. Martha died in 1862, after the birth of their eighth child.

Mary Jane DeRosset Curtis (1813–1903)

Mary Jane, of Wilmington, North Carolina, was the daughter of a wealthy and well-educated physician and slave owner. She married Moses Ashley Curtis in 1834. Moses was an Episcopalian priest and teacher born in Massachusetts and educated at Williams College. His profession caused the family to move frequently; it lived in Wilmington (1834–1836), Raleigh (1836–1839), Society Hill, South Carolina (1847–1856), and Hillsboro (1841–1847, 1856–1872). Moses was a noted botanist, with a particular interest in fungi, and he maintained an active correspondence with other scientists and wrote many articles. Mary Jane corresponded with her sisters Catherine, in Charleston, and Eliza, in Charleston and Philadelphia. The family owned slaves.

The DeRosset Family

Kate DeRosset was the daughter of a prominent and wealthy family in Wilmington, North Carolina. Her grandfather Armand John DeRosset (1767–1859), a French Huguenot, was a well-educated slave owner and physician, who attended Princeton and the University of Pennsylvania. Kate's father, Armand John DeRosset, Jr., attended the University of North Carolina, graduated at the age of seventeen, and then attended the Medical College of South Carolina (1826–1827) and the University of Pennsylvania (1828). In 1829, John, Jr., married Eliza Jane Lord (1812–1876), and their marriage lasted forty-seven years. Eliza Jane produced eleven children, five of whom died; she bore her last child at the age of forty-four. Dr. DeRosset did not derive satisfaction from his medical practice, especially when a young girl with diphtheria died under his care. He retired to a family plantation briefly until he was called back into the profession. He then became involved in the lumber business and adopted that as his full-time occupation in 1839. He was a promoter of railroads and became a director of the Wilmington and Weldon Railroad Company.

Kate received her education at St. Mary's School, in Raleigh, from 1842 to 1846, and had a relatively relaxed and indulged upbringing. She then attended Madame Chegaray's School, in New York City. She married Gaston Meares, a merchant, in 1850. Gaston was a partner in the mercantile firm of Watson and Meares and was elected to the North Carolina House of Representatives from Brunswick County. Kate bore six children, three of whom died. Gaston was killed while serving in the Civil War.

Mary Jane DeRosset Curtis was Kate's aunt, her father's sister.

Margaret Mordecai Devereux (1824–1910)

Margaret was the daughter of Anne Lane and Moses Mordecai. Her father, from a well-educated Raleigh family (*see* The Mordecai Family), died two months before Margaret was born, and her mother died while she was an infant. She was educated at a Philadelphia school, and in 1842 married John Devereux (1819–1893), of North Carolina. John was the only son of Catherine Ann and Thomas Devereux. Thomas, a wealthy lawyer and planter in Halifax County, owned several plantations and more than a thousand slaves. After John graduated from Yale in 1840, he practiced law and managed several of the family estates. He and Margaret resided on "Runeroi" plantation, which John purchased from his father in 1846. He fell into a large inheritance from his grandfather during the same year. The Devereux family summered in Raleigh, in the home that Margaret inherited from her mother's family. By the 1850s, the Devereuxs were mired in debt, for like many southern elite families, they were land and slave rich but cash poor. Margaret bore two sons and six daughters. One of her principal correspondents was Ellen Mordecai, her half sister.

Margaret Randolph Dickins

Margaret was the daughter of Thomas Mann Randolph, of Goochland County, Virginia, and his first wife, Harriet. Margaret married Francis

Asbury Dickins, a lawyer and agent for claims of the United States Treasury Department. They resided at "Ossian Hill," in Fairfax County, and Francis maintained a Washington office. Margaret bore nine children, five of whom lived to maturity.

Ann Hutchinson Smith Elliott

Ann was the only daughter of Ann Skirving and Thomas Rhett Smith, of South Carolina. Engaged when she was only fourteen, she married William Elliott, Jr., in 1817. William (1788–1863), the son of Phoebe and William Elliott, was a wealthy Harvard-educated planter who served in both the state house and the state senate but resigned over the issue of nullification. The Elliotts, growers of rice and cotton, owned several plantations in lower and coastal South Carolina. William's grandfather raised the first commercially successful crop of Sea Island cotton in America. The grandson was a sportsman, the author of *Carolina Sports by Land and Water* (1846), and an agricultural reformer. He had numerous health problems, and between 1823 and 1859 spent at least six months of every year at spas, mineral springs, and other points of interest. Because Ann never accompanied him, his travels created a lonely existence for her but gave her the opportunity for a substantial correspondence.

Mary De Saussure Fraser (1772–1853)

Little is known of Mary, of Charleston; the letters represent three generations of family correspondence. She was married to Frederick Fraser. Her son, Frederick Grimke Fraser, and his wife, Isabel, wrote her many letters from their home in Beaufort, South Carolina.

Anna Maria Deans Garretson

Anna married Isaac Garretson around 1815. Isaac worked for the United States Navy in Washington and Baltimore and ran farming operations in Gloucester County, Virginia. Anna and Isaac resided at "Middleway" plantation and later moved to Mathews County, Virginia.

Rebecca Haywood Hall

Rebecca was one of twelve children of Eliza Williams and John Haywood (1755–1827). Her father served as North Carolina state treasurer, a member of the board of trustees of the University of North Carolina, and the first mayor of Raleigh. There is some indication that John was implicated in the misuse of state funds. Rebecca met Albert G. Hall in 1834 and married him at the end of the year despite warnings about his character. Time revealed that the cautions had a basis, for Rebecca's letters make plain the tragedies and unhappiness of her married life. She and Albert lived at "Woodbine Retreat," near South Washington, North Carolina. She bore three children before her early death.

Mary Steele Ferrand Henderson

Mary married Archibald Henderson II (1811–1880), and they lived in Salisbury, North Carolina. Both her father-in-law and her son were lawyers and served in the United States Congress. In 1865, the Hendersons owned at least 108 slaves.

Julia Pickens Howe (1815–1898)

Julia was the daughter of Martha Lenoir and Israel Pickens, of Alabama, and the granddaughter of General William Lenoir (*see* The Lenoir Family), of North Carolina. Her father, who was a lawyer, a congressman, the governor of Alabama, and a senator, died in 1827. Her mother, Martha (1792–1823), died when Julia was young. Julia was well educated and attended school in Hillsboro and Pittsboro and at Salem Academy. She was raised by an aunt who lived at the family plantation home, "Fort Defiance." In 1836, Julia married Chilib Smith Howe, a graduate of the United States Military Academy. He resigned from the military in 1838 and became a merchant and planter. They lived on a plantation in Marengo County, Alabama. Julia bore three children.

Susan Nye Hutchinson

Susan was born in New York in 1790 but left the state to teach at a girls' school in Raleigh, North Carolina. She later moved to Augusta and opened a girls' school herself. In 1825, she married a widower, Adam Hutchinson, forty-four years old and the father of three children. Adam lost property in the cotton trade, and Susan reopened her school to assure the family an income. She bore four children. Adam died in 1834 of poor health. Susan then taught school in Salisbury and Charlotte, North Carolina, opening her own school in Charlotte in 1839.

The Jackson Family

Martha Rootes Cobb, the widow of Captain Howell Cobb, married Henry Jackson in 1819. They had three children. Henry was born in Devonshire, England, and emigrated to America in 1790. He graduated from the Medical College of Pennsylvania in 1802, became a professor of mathematics at the University of Georgia, and served as chargé d'affaires in Paris until 1818, when he returned to Georgia. In 1828, he retired to his plantation, "Halscot," near Athens, Georgia. James, his brother, served as a congressman, a senator, and the governor of Georgia. Serena Rootes Lea was Martha's sister; she was married to Henry C. Lea, of Alabama.

Nicketti Floyd Johnston (1818–1908)

Nicketti married John Warfield Johnston (1818–1889) in 1841. John was the son of a physician and was educated at South Carolina College and the University of Virginia. He practiced law in Tazewell County, Virginia, and was elected to the state senate and, after the Civil War, the United States Senate. Letitia Floyd, Nicketti's sister, married Colonel William Lewis, of Columbia, South Carolina; many of the Floyds and Lewises eventually moved there.

The Charles Colcock Jones Family

The Joneses were a wealthy and intellectual family of Liberty County, Georgia. They owned three rice plantations south of Savannah and dozens of slaves. Charles, Sr. (1804–1863), attended Andover, Andover Theological Seminary, and Princeton Theological Seminary and became a Presbyterian minister. He was best known for his efforts to evangelize slaves. He served the church in Columbia, South Carolina, and in Philadelphia but retired to his plantations because of poor health. In 1830, he married his cousin Mary Jones (1808–1869). Mary was from a wealthy planter family of Liberty County and was well educated, having attended girls' academies for seven years. She was esteemed for her energy, strength of character, and cheerfulness. She bore four children, one of whom died.

Charles, Jr. (1831–1893), attended South Carolina College, Princeton University, and Harvard Law School. He practiced law in Savannah, was mayor of the city from 1860 to 1861, and joined the Confederate Army as a lieutenant. He later returned to practice law, and he wrote several history books. He married Ruth Barrien Whitehead (1837–1861), of Bath, Georgia. Ruth bore two children, one of whom died of scarlet fever when only two years old. Ruth died of puerperal fever after her second confinement and the Jones grandparents helped raise this child. Charles later married Ruth's cousin Eve Barrien, who had been a bridesmaid at their wedding.

Joseph (1833–1896) attended South Carolina College, Princeton University, and the Medical College of the University of Pennsylvania, after which he taught at various medical schools in South Carolina and Georgia. He served in the Confederate Army and conducted medical research in Confederate prison camps. He gained an international reputation for his studies in tropical medicine and hygiene. In 1859, he married Caroline Smelt Davis (1832–1868), of Augusta, and they had four children. After her death, he married Susan Rayner Polk, daughter of Leonidas Polk. They had three children.

Mary (1835–1889) attended a seminary in Philadelphia. In 1853, after a long courtship, she married the Reverend Robert Quarterman Mallard (1830–1904), a Presbyterian minister. She bore five children. Robert served in Georgia churches and, after the Civil War, in New Orleans. Mary was much beloved, highly poised, and loving toward all who knew her.

Sally Graham Lacy

Sally was the daughter of a prominent Scotch-Irish Presbyterian family that settled in Virginia during the Revolution. Her father, Edward Graham, was a lawyer and a professor of science and astronomy at Washington (later Washington and Lee) College, founded by his brother William. Her mother, Margaret Alexander Graham, a voluminous correspondent, was responsible for sustaining close family ties. Sally married the Reverend William Lacy, and they lived in Virginia, Tennessee, and Missouri.

Caroline Olivia Laurens

Caroline married John B. Laurens, of South Carolina. They lived at "Mepkin," near Charleston on the Cooper River, a plantation that had been owned by Henry Laurens. In 1827, after her husband's death, Caroline moved to "Cedar Hill" plantation.

Frances Emilly Brashear Lawrence

Fanny, born in 1819, was the youngest daughter of Margaret and Walter Brashear. Her father was a physician, merchant, and sugar planter, and a member of the Louisiana state legislature beginning in 1834. She received her education in Lexington, Kentucky. In 1844, she married Henry Effingham Lawrence, son of Ann and Effingham Lawrence, of Long Island, New York, and they lived on the Brashear family plantation, in the Attakapas region of Louisiana. Henry joined two of his brothers, who had also moved south, in their mercantile activities, and he spent much of his time in New Orleans. Fanny bore seven children, five of whom were deaf mutes.

The Lenoir Family

Thomas Lenoir (1780–1869) was the son of Ann Ballard, daughter of a wealthy planter, and General William Lenoir, of Haywood County, North Carolina. William (1751–1839), who had been a Revolutionary War soldier and a member of the North Carolina Convention, was a wealthy landowner and land speculator. Thomas and his wife, Selina Louisa Avery, of Swan Ponde, North Carolina, lived on a plantation on the Pigeon River from 1806 to 1824 and eventually moved to the Lenoir family home, "Fort Defiance," on the Yadkin River in Caldwell County, after William's death. Selina and Thomas had eight children.

Their oldest child was William Avery Lenoir, who became a colonel. Selina, the oldest daughter, married Samuel Pickens, brother of Israel Pickens. They lived in Alabama. Laura Leah Carolina (1815–1894) married her cousin Joseph Caldwell Norwood (1815–1889) in 1836. They lived at "Oak Lawn" plantation, near Lenoir. Thomas Isaac Lenoir married Mary Elizabeth Garrett. Mary Ann (1819–1899) married James Gwynn (1812–1888), her cousin. They lived in Wilkesboro and, from 1852 on, at "Green Hill," a Gwynn family plantation that James had inherited. Sarah Joyce, known as Aunt Sade, remained unmarried. Walter (1823–1890) married Cornelia (Nealy) Christian, of Staunton, Virginia, who brought extensive property to the marriage. Their daughter, Anna Tate, died, and Nealy died in 1859. Walter never remarried. He was the founder of Lenoir College. The youngest Lenoir child, Rufus Theodore, married Sarah Leonara Gwynn, his cousin and sister-in-law, in 1856.

Thomas' sister Martha (1792–1823) married Israel Pickens in 1814. She was known for her beauty and charm, and was always the family favorite. Her daughter Julia married Chiliab Smith Howe. Harriet, another of Thomas' sisters, married Isaac Avery, of "Swan Ponde" plantation, in Burke County, North Carolina.

Lucilla Gamble McCorkle

Lucilla was the daughter of a Virginia minister, the Reverend James Gamble, and Sarah Ramsay. She married Alexander B. McCorkle, a Presbyterian minister, in 1841. Alexander was born near Lexington,

Virginia, and was educated at Washington College, Union Seminary, and Hampden-Sidney. Lucilla bore six children, two of whom died in infancy. She and Alexander lived in Virginia and Georgia and finally settled in Talladega, Alabama. Alexander helped found a synodical college for women there and became the first president of its board of trustees. The McCorkles owned slaves. Lucilla kept her diary between 1846 and 1858, during the years when her children were young.

The Mordecai Family

The Mordecais were a distinguished, brilliant Jewish family of North Carolina. The family patriarch, Jacob, was born in 1762 and attended school in Philadelphia. In 1784, he married Judith Myers, of New York, and they moved to Warrenton, North Carolina, in 1792 to conduct a mercantile enterprise. Judith died in 1796, leaving six children, and two years later Jacob married her half sister Rebecca Myers. His involvement in tobacco speculation brought financial reversals, and in 1809, Jacob opened a girls' school in Warrenton. Facilities were rebuilt after a fire destroyed the institution in 1811. He sold the school in 1818, and the funds he realized allowed him to retire to "Spring Farm" plantation, near Richmond, Virginia. The school had an outstanding reputation. Between his two wives, Jacob sired thirteen children. He died in 1838.

A son, Moses, married Margaret Lane, a member of a prominent and wealthy Raleigh family. Margaret bore three children but died after childbirth in 1821. Three years later, Moses married her sister Anne, causing some outcry from his family. Moses died in September, 1824, and their daughter Margaret (*see* Margaret Mordecai Devereux) was born in October of that year. Her mother died while Margaret was an infant.

Rachel Mordecai (1788–1838) was reared by a Richmond aunt after her mother died. She was described as well educated, brilliant, and serious, and she was one of the principal teachers in her father's school. In 1821, she married a widower, Aaron Lazarus, who had seven children. Rachel and Aaron had four. Her half sister Eliza lived with them to help care for the children. Aaron was a merchant in shingles and naval stores, but a fire in 1835 destroyed almost his entire business. Rachel died suddenly in 1838 while visiting her brother Samuel in Petersburg.

Ellen Mordecai (1790–1884) was also a teacher in her father's school and instructed several nieces and nephews. She fell in love with John Plunkett, a son of the music teacher and widower Achilles Plunkett. She planned to marry John in 1823, but her brother Moses objected so strongly that she changed her mind and apparently never regretted her decision. Ellen seemed to play the archetypal spinster sister, appearing for births, helping rear and educate nieces and nephews and keeping house for her brothers. She also opened a small school, in 1826. Her deep affection for her brother Solomon appeared somewhat unusual and created some tension between her and Solomon's wife.

Caroline Mordecai (1794–1862) also taught in her father's school. She fell in love with Achilles Plunkett. Despite her brothers' and father's protests, she married him, for they accepted the inevitability of her decision when her physical and mental stability seemed threatened. Caroline lost her husband and all three of their children between 1823 and 1825. Her last child was born after Achilles died. Caroline continued teaching in Warrenton. She died in a mental hospital.

Octavia Aurelia James Wyche Otey

Octavia was the daughter of Mary Ann Rebecca and William H. Wyche, of Alabama. She married William Madison Otey in 1849, and they lived in Madison County, Alabama, but also owned cotton plantations and slaves in Yazoo County, Mississippi.

Jane Petigru

Jane's husband was an attorney, a writer, and a South Carolina state representative. They lived in Charleston and the Abbeville district.

Ann Shepard Pettigrew

Ann was the daughter of a Whig congressman from New Bern, North Carolina. She married Ebenezer Pettigrew, a planter, North Carolina state senator, and United States congressman. Ebenezer (1783–1848) was also a North Carolina native and a graduate of the University of North Carolina. Their plantation, "Magnolia," was located in Tyrrell County. Ann bore a son, James Johnston Pettigrew, in 1828, and she died in childbirth in 1830. In 1864, the daughter who survived this tragic birth also died in childbirth.

Mahala Eggleston Roach

Mahala was the wife of James Roach, of the banking house of Wirt Adams and Company, in Vicksburg, Mississippi. She was Jefferson Davis' niece.

Anne Gales Root

Anne was a member of a prominent Raleigh, North Carolina, family. Her grandfather, Joseph Gales, founded and edited the Raleigh *Register*. Her father, Weston Raleigh Gales, became the paper's editor, and her mother, Love Freeman Gales, of Sandwich, Massachusetts, was the sister of George Freeman, an Episcopalian priest in Raleigh. Anne married Charles Root and bore three children, one of whom died.

The Thomas Ruffin Family

Thomas (1787–1870) was born in Virginia, attended Princeton, studied law, and was admitted to the North Carolina bar in 1808. The following year he married Anne Kirkland, who bore him fourteen children, including Anne, who was to marry Paul Cameron. Thomas, a Democrat and a devout Episcopalian, served in the North Carolina house and as judge and chief justice of the state supreme court. After he resigned in 1852 to return to planting, he became president of the Agricultural Society of North Carolina.

Ann Seddon Roy Rutherfoord (1832–1906)

Ann was the daughter of William H. Roy, who owned the estate "Green Plains," in Mathews County, Georgia. She married John Coles Rutherfoord (1825–1866), a lawyer, planter, and member of the Virginia House of Delegates. They lived at "Rock Castle," in Goochland County near the James River, an estate owned by John's father, who was also a planter and had served as governor of the state. John frequently rode the circuit, and he worked as a country lawyer in addition to assisting his aging parents and managing his slaves and plantation.

The Screven Family

James Proctor Screven (1799–1859) was a graduate of South Carolina College and Jefferson Medical College, in Philadelphia. He married his cousin Georgia Bryan in 1826 and gave up his medical practice to devote full time to planting. He was mayor of Savannah and president of the Savannah, Albany and Gulf Railroad. James and Georgia had four children. The Screven rice plantations, near Savannah, included "Proctor's," "Screven's Ferry," and "Brewster Hill." James's father, John, had had two wives: Hannah Proctor, who bore him three children, and her sister Sarah. Martha Richardson, widowed sister of Hannah and Sarah, lived with the John Screvens.

Virginia Campbell Shelton (1812–1867)

Virginia Tabitha Jane was one of seven children of a Tennessee merchant, David Campbell, and his wife, Catherine Bowen. Called Tabby as a child, she was born near Knoxville and was early recognized as precocious. Virginia had limited schooling in Tennessee. In part because of her father's business failures, she went to live with her aunt and uncle, Virginia and William Bowen, of Abingdon, Virginia. William served as governor of the state. He took special pride in his niece's mind and oversaw her education. The Bowens, having no children of their own, officially adopted Virginia, but she was always free to return home. In 1838, she accompanied her adoptive parents on a trip to the North.

In 1849, at the age of thirty-seven, Virginia married William Shelton, a Baptist minister whom she met in Clarksville, Tennessee. William was on the faculty at Union College, in Murfreesboro, and in 1856 established Brownsville Female Academy. He eventually became president of West Tennessee College, in Jackson. Virginia occasionally assisted as a teacher in her husband's schools. She bore seven children, one of whom died in infancy.

Virginia's brother, William Bowen Campbell (1807–1867), served as governor of Tennessee.

Ella Gertrude Clanton Thomas

Ella was born in 1834, the daughter of Colonel Turner C. Clanton, a prosperous plantation owner who lived near Augusta, Georgia. She and her sister received their education at Wesleyan College, in Macon, from which Ella graduated when she was seventeen. She began keeping her journal when she was fourteen. In 1851, she converted during a local Methodist revival and remained deeply religious all her life. When she attended her own debut in 1852, she refused to dance, for religious reasons.

In 1851, Ella became romantically interested in Jefferson Thomas, who was studying medicine. They married in December, 1852. After their son Turner was born in 1854, Jefferson and Ella lived on a small plantation, "Belmont," six miles from Augusta and a mile from her father's plantation. Jefferson oversaw several Clanton and Thomas plantations in nearby counties and spent some time away from home. They also resided at the Clanton home in Augusta. The Thomases owned approximately ninety slaves, many of them part of Ella's dowry. Ella expressed very modern feelings, for a southern woman. She abhorred miscegenation and desired equal education for women. The Civil War brought severe hardship to the family. Despite poor health, Ella had to teach in a county school, often begging for students in order to keep the struggling institution alive. She also sold wood and took in boarders.

Rebecca Allen Turner (1823–1917)

Rebecca was raised in Pittsburgh and attended a girls' seminary in Steubenville, Ohio. Her father, Edward Allen, worked as an engineer and contractor for railroad companies. She married Jesse Turner in 1855. Born in Orange County, North Carolina, in 1805, he was educated at the University of North Carolina and became a lawyer. He migrated to Arkansas, seeking better opportunities, and had made his permanent home in Crawford County by 1838. Elected to the state legislature as a Whig, he served as president of the Whig convention and was appointed United States attorney general of the Arkansas federal district.

Lydia Parish Turrentine

Lydia was educated in Sparta, Georgia. She lived in Wilmington, North Carolina, and Tuscaloosa, Alabama. She died in Wilmington in 1847.

Sarah Lois Wadley

Sarah lived near Monroe, Louisiana, during her diary-writing years. Her father, William Morrill Wadley, was a well-known railroad executive.

Sophia Watson

Sophia was born in the Northeast and attended schools in Hartford, Connecticut, and New York City. She married Henry Watson, Jr. (1810–1891), a Connecticut native who attended Washington College and Harvard. He moved to Alabama for his health when only twenty-one, with the idea of teaching. He returned north to study law and returned to Greensborough, Alabama, where he established a successful law practice, purchased land and slaves, and founded the Planter's Insurance Company. Sophia bore several children. Their plantation was located near Newbern, Alabama, and contained approximately a thousand acres. They owned 110 slaves. Henry's estimated worth in 1860 was $325,000. Owing to ill health, he retired from law practice in 1849 and devoted himself to farming.

The Whittle Family

Lewis (1820–1888) was an engineer and lawyer who settled in Georgia in 1836. He married Sarah Powers, the daughter of John Powers, of Monroe County, Georgia, in 1842. The majority of their children died when young.

Sarah Frances Hicks Williams (1827–1917)

Sarah was a New York girl who, at the age of twenty-six, married Benjamin Franklin Williams (1820–1890). Benjamin studied medicine in New York and North Carolina. He became a licensed doctor but spent the greater part of his time as a planter. He and Sarah lived in rural North Carolina.

Jane Campbell Harris Woodruff (1788–1834)

Jane was the daughter of a wealthy Charleston family. In 1816, she married an Army officer and paymaster who owned slaves and land in Georgia and Florida. The family moved to Florida to seek a fortune in agriculture but had little success. Jane's husband died in 1828.

Glossary

ACCOUCHEUR. A birth attendant.

ACONITE. A poisonous drug from a dried tuberous plant.

ALLOPATHY. The principal form of therapeutics in the antebellum period. Doctors who practiced HEROIC MEDICINE were called allopaths or regular doctors.

ALOE. A succulent plant whose juices contain PURGATIVE properties.

AMENORRHEA. Suppression of the menses.

ANTIMONY. A crystalline metallic element forming a medicinal and poisonous salt.

ANTIPHLOGISTIC. Counteracting inflammation and fever.

BELLADONNA. The "deadly nightshade," a perennial plant whose leaves are both a narcotic and a diuretic.

BLISTER. Any agent capable of irritating the skin when applied to it, such as mustard, garlic, or ammonia. The irritation usually became infected; the pus was seen as drawing out the infection. The word is also used as a verb.

BLUE PILLS. Pills of powdered mercury and gum arabic, sometimes laced with opium to increase secretions of the body. They were of the same nature as CALOMEL but not so effective.

BLUE STONE. Cupric sulfate.

BLUNT HOOK. A long instrument with a hook at the end, used like a FILLET to draw out the fetus.

CALOMEL. Mercury chloride, a heavy, white, odorless powder with the properties of a CATHARTIC. It increases salivation and causes teeth and hair to fall out.

CATHARTIC. A purgative, causing diarrhea.

CINCHONA BARK. Dried bark from a South American tree, used as a drug to treat malaria. It can be toxic.

COLIC. Infantile abdominal pain, a common problem during the early weeks of an infant's life.

COOKE'S PILLS. Pills developed by an American physician, John Esten Cooke, as a CATHARTIC. They contained CALOMEL, with rhubarb and ALOE.

CRANIOTOMY. The process of destroying the fetal head in order to facilitate delivery. The procedure was used when the mother's life was endangered.

CROCHET HOOK. A hook used to extract the fetus after a CRANIOTOMY.

DOVER'S PILLS. Pills created by an English doctor, Thomas Dover, to allay pain. They contained IPECAC and opium powder.

DYSENTERY. A disorder related to the inflammation of the intestines, often accompanied by abdominal pain and frequent and loose stools, sometimes containing blood or mucus.

ECLAMPSIA. Convulsions associated with pregnancy and resulting from high blood pressure, usually occurring during the last trimester. The condition often led to death.

EMETIC. Bringing on or causing vomiting.

ERGOT. A fungus derived from rye that can generate uterine contractions. It was used to hasten delivery.

FILLET. A bandage of muslin, linen, or soft leather to be cast around the legs or head of a fetus, often used in breech births. It is perhaps the oldest instrument employed to assist with delivery.

FORCEPS. Tongs or an instrument with two blades used for extracting the fetus.

HEROIC MEDICINE. Aggressive, daring therapeutic procedures popular in the first half of the nineteenth century. This form of medicine was based upon Benjamin Rush's idea of balancing vascular tension through depletion and accretion.

IPECAC. A mild EMETIC drug from dried roots of a tropical plant. It was used for DYSENTERY.

JALAP. A PURGATIVE drug of a tuberous plant.

LAUDANUM. A popular tincture of opium that can produce sleep and reduce pain. An overdose can cause convulsions or death. It was generally used until drowsiness occurred.

LEECHING. The application of leeches to draw blood. It was a favorite remedy of HEROIC MEDICINE.

LOBELIA. The dried leaves and tops of *lobelia inflata,* an herb with properties resembling nicotine's. The herb was the basis of the Thomsonian form of botanic medicine.

MIASMIC THEORY. The belief that a noxious emanation from the earth or air is the cause of certain diseases.

PAREGORIC. A camphorated tincture of opium.

PARTURITION. The act of giving birth to a child.

PERFORATOR. An instrument used to open the head of the fetus in the uterus in order to diminish its size. It was employed when the extraction of the fetus was necessary for saving the mother's life.

PESSARY. A device placed in the vagina to support the uterus. It was usually made of wood, metal, or leather.

PLASTER. A pastelike mixture applied to the skin as a counterirritant.

PROLAPSED UTERUS. A uterus that protrudes through the vagina, as a result of a weakening of the pelvic support tissue. It was a common problem of antebellum women.

PUERPERAL FEVER. A fever developing after childbirth and caused by infection. It was often spread by medical attendants who assisted at successive deliveries.

PURGATIVE. An agent or medicine that brings on or causes diarrhea.

QUININE. An alkaloid of CINCHONA BARK, used to suppress malarial parasites.

REMITTENT (INTERMITTENT) FEVER. Malaria.

SINAPISM. A PLASTER or paste of ground mustard seed, used to produce redness and as a counterirritant.

SUET. The hard fat from the abdomen or around the kidneys of cattle or sheep. It was used as an ointment.

THRUSH. An infection of the mouth caused by a fungus. It usually forms whitish spots.

VECTIS. A long, narrow instrument of wood or metal with a triangular, open, spoonlike end, curved to fit a small head in order to help extract the fetus.

VENESECTION. The opening of a vein in order to draw blood. It was used to relax the parturient woman and to ease labor. The procedure was prescribed for many other medical problems as well during the antebellum period.

VERSION. The manipulation of the fetal head or body in order to ease delivery.

VESICOVAGINAL FISTULA. An abnormal opening extending from the bladder into the vagina, caused by tearing during a difficult delivery.

Selected Sources

The debate over the South's regional distinctiveness continues among historians. This study on pregnancy, childbirth, infant care, and the southern medical profession in the antebellum period demonstrates that the South had some unique concerns, and sometimes its own solutions—giving a regional definition to women's "sacred occupation" and the medical profession's approach to that experience.

That there is a "southernness" to be reckoned with became evident as I read books on the history of childbirth, the medical profession, women's health, and the maternal role. Nothing in the books quite fitted the experiences of southern women and their families. Even accounts by the region's doctors were sometimes at odds with published medical advice. But that is probably to be expected, for on many subjects the South does not quite fit the norm and has been ignored or regarded as an aberration—and sometimes just left out. In this study, secondary sources have been useful as a framework (and the most important books and articles can be found in this bibliography), but my conclusions are often based upon what southern sources reveal rather than on what other medical and historical studies uncover as national trends. Historians who have studied childbirth and the medical profession have generally emphasized change, for that is what history is all about. But times can also be static or even regressive, and rarely does history move forward smoothly. The antebellum period does not appear to have been a time of radical therapeutic innovation in obstetrics, for physicians were struggling to establish a place in the birthing chamber and to gain and maintain the position of a profession. Improving women's health, exploring and accepting new means to ease delivery, and expanding the medical understanding of infant and female diseases do not seem to have been foremost in the minds of southern doctors.

This study would have been impossible without the availability of hundreds of southern manuscript collections. The diaries and letters of southern women and their families say more than any history book, and many evoke more emotion than the finest novel. These collections constitute some of the richest treasures of nineteenth-century southern literature—and are virtually untapped except by scholars. Individual journals and letters range from highly literate compositions, such as those by the well-educated Mordecais, to scribblings full of misspellings and awkward phrases. But all have an immediacy and personal tone that touch an inquisitive reader. One senses the suffering of a sick infant, a mother's stupor and mental haziness after a dose of laudanum, the lethargy brought on by another bout of "fever and ague," and a parent's joy over a newborn. The most extensive collection of antebellum material is at the Southern Historical Collection, in the L. R. Wilson Library, at the University of North Carolina at Chapel Hill. It holds a large number of nineteenth-century manuscripts spanning the South. The Manuscript Department of the William R. Perkins Library, at Duke University, also has a large, well-organized, and well-cataloged collection. Important too for this study were the South Carolina Historical Society Library, in Charleston, which includes letters of many wealthy low-country elite families; the South Caroliniana Library, at the University of South Carolina, in Columbia; the Tennessee State Library and Archives, in Nashville; and the Arkansas State History Commission Archives, at the Arkansas State Library, in Little Rock.

Antebellum southern diaries and letters are slowly being published as their value is recognized and as historians undertake the painstaking work of editing them. Published sources that were useful for this study include *Children of Pride: A True Story of Georgia and the Civil War,* ed. Robert Manson Myers (New Haven, 1972), which comprises the lengthy, rich, and cultured collection of letters of the Charles Colcock Jones, Sr., family of Liberty County, Georgia; C. Vann Woodward's recent reediting of Mary Boykin Chesnut's diary, *Mary Chesnut's Civil War* (New Haven, 1981); James C. Williams' "Plantation Experiences of a New York Woman," *North Carolina Historical Review,* XXXIII (1956), 384–412, 529–46, a collection of letters written home by the lonely wife of a North Carolina planter and doctor; "The Diary of Frances Baylor Hill" in *Early American Literature,* II (1967), 6–53, containing a graphic description of a southern woman giving birth; *The Pettigrew Papers,* Vol. I, *1685–1818,* and Vol. II, *1819–1843,* ed. Sarah Lemmon (Raleigh, N.C., 1971–88), which is a valuable collection of an influential North Carolina family; *Plantation Life in the Florida Parishes of Louisiana, 1836–1846, as Reflected in the Diary of Bennet H. Barrow*, ed. Edwin Adams Davis (1943; rpr. New York, 1967), a diary by a wealthy Southerner with over two hundred slaves, whose wife died after the birth of their eighth child; and Theodore Rosengarten's *Tombee: Portrait of a Cotton Planter, with the Journal of Thomas B. Chaplin* (New York, 1986), an intimate study and diary of the South Carolinian Thomas Chaplin and his family.

Medical dissertations and physicians' account books proved to be invaluable sources for understanding the southern medical profession. Medical dissertations of the period were far different from what they are today. Most were twenty- to thirty-page handwritten essays submitted by students to meet a requirement for graduation from medical college. Students usually compiled secondhand information from a variety of contemporary (and often unacknowledged) sources, including books, treatises, class notes, professors' remarks, and their own insights. Topics were wide-ranging and included medical quackery, malaria, typhoid fever, infant health, surgical procedures, the diseases of pregnancy, and medical responsibility. Dissertations consulted for this study came from the Waring Historical Library Annex, at the Medical University of South Carolina, in Charleston, and from the Special Collections at the Vanderbilt University Medical Center Library, in Nashville, which possesses more than four hundred. Doctors' individual account books were found in manuscript collections at the Southern Historical Collection and at the Manuscript Department of Duke's Perkins Library, under the name of a particular doctor, within a family collection, or without attribution. The accounts provide a cryptic but useful overview of individual practices, fees, medications, and treatments. A published primary source on southern medical views that was an asset is *Letters of Richard D. Arnold, M.D.*, ed. Richard H. Shryock (New York, 1929); this is a collection of letters from a Savannah doctor who served as the city's mayor and as first secretary of the American Medical Association.

Articles in antebellum southern medical journals were another important source of information. Some journals were short-lived; others, like the conservative *New Orleans Medical and Surgical Journal*, lasted for decades. These periodicals were published in conjunction with a medical institution, and their principal contributors were physicians associated with the sponsoring college as well as urban and rural practitioners who sent articles describing arresting cases and unique remedies. Authors mentioned both successful and unsuccessful therapeutic efforts. Southern medical journals that were consulted for this study include the *Nashville Journal of Medicine and Surgery* (1851–61); the *Nashville Monthly Record of Medicine and Physical Science* (1858), which became the *Nashville Medical Record* (1859–61); the *New Orleans Medical and Surgical Journal* (1844–61); the *Savannah Journal of Medicine* (1858–61); the *Southern Botanic Journal* (Charleston, S.C., and Forsyth, Ga., 1838–41), a Thomsonian organ and very critical of allopathic medicine; the *Southern Journal of Medical and Physical Sciences* (Nashville, 1853); the *Southern Journal of Medicine and Pharmacy* (Charleston, S.C., 1846–47), which became the *Charleston Medical Journal and Review* (1848–60); the *Southern Medical and Surgical Journal* (Augusta, Ga., 1836–39, 1845–61); the *Southern Medical Reformer and Review* (Macon, Ga., 1852–60); *Southern Medical Reports* (New Orleans, 1849–50); the *Virginia Medical and Surgical Journal* (Richmond, 1853–55), which became the *Virginia Medical Journal* (1856–60); and the *Western Journal of Medicine and Surgery* (Louisville, Ky., 1840–55). Also consulted were proceedings of some of the state medical societies such as those in Louisiana and Tennessee.

Published information and advice concerning childbirth, obstetrics, and infant health were important for understanding medical perceptions, though southern physicians generally did little book writing. From the North and from Europe came dozens of advice books and medical treatises every decade. Some writers approached the subject academically and geared discussion to a classroom audience, while others spoke directly to mothers and families and tried to simplify their accounts of diseases and therapies. Plagiarism was rampant. European treatises consulted for this study include one of the most popular of the time, *Advice to Mothers on the Subject of Their Own Health,* by William Buchan, of the Royal College of Physicians, Edinburgh (Boston, 1809); a bestseller complete with illustrations and technical information, *On the Theory and Practice of Midwifery,* by Fleetwood Churchill, an Irish doctor at the Lying In Hospital, with notes and additions by Robert M. Huston (3rd American ed.; Philadelphia, 1848); and a French manual, *Midwifery Illustrated,* by J. P. Maygrier (New York, 1833).

Advice books written in the North include probably the first such text by an American and directed toward midwives, *A Compendium of the Theory and Practice of Midwifery,* by Samuel Bard (New York, 1807); a book written solely for physicians, *Clinical Lectures on the Diseases of Women and Children,* by Gunning Bedford, professor of obstetrics at the

University of New York (4th ed.; New York, 1856); *A Compendious System of Midwifery,* by William Pott Dewees, professor of midwifery at the University of Pennsylvania and highly esteemed in the early antebellum period (Philadelphia, 1828); a dissertation and an early defense of bloodletting by the same writer, *Essay on the Means of Lessening Pain and Facilitating Certain Cases of Difficult Parturition* (Philadelphia, 1806); two volumes by Charles Delucena Meigs, professor of midwifery and the diseases of women and children at Jefferson Medical College, Philadelphia, and one of the most influential, though conservative, physicians of the period, *Females and Their Diseases: A Series of Letters to His Class* (Philadelphia, 1848) and *Obstetrics: The Science and the Art* (3rd ed.; Philadelphia, 1856); *Elements of the Principles and Practice of Midwifery,* by David Tucker, doctor of obstetrics and the diseases of women and children at Franklin Medical College, Philadelphia (Philadelphia, 1848); and *The Obstetric Catechism, Containing Two-Thousand, Three Hundred and Forty-Seven Questions and Answers on Obstetrics Proper,* by Joseph Warrington, principal of the Obstetric Institute of Philadelphia (Philadelphia, 1853).

In the South, James Ewell, a Virginia and Savannah physician, produced *The Planter's and Mariner's Medical Companion* (Philadelphia, 1807); Thomas Ewell, a Virginia doctor who wanted to establish a hospital for poor women and tried to instruct women in the skills of midwifery, wrote *Letters to Ladies, Detailing Important Information, Concerning Themselves and Infants* (Philadelphia, 1817); and Alfred M. Folger, who practiced at the Cherokee Hospital, in North Carolina, wrote *The Family Physician, Being a Domestic Medical Work* (Spartanburg, S.C., 1845). The most popular southern medical advice book was *Gunn's Domestic Medicine; or, Poor Man's Friend, Shewing the Diseases of Men, Women, and Children,* by John C. Gunn (Madisonville, Tenn., 1834). Gunn's advice, which covered more than obstetrics and child care, included an appealing combination of recommendations of home remedies, common sense, drugs, and reliance on doctors. The most reputable southern treatise on obstetrics was considered to be *A Theoretical and Practical Treatise on Human Parturition,* by Henry Miller, professor of obstetric medicine at the University of Louisville (Louisville, Ky., 1849). It had limited circulation because the original publisher went bankrupt, and the volume was reissued as *Principles and Practice of Obstetrics* (Philadelphia, 1858). Two other important southern works were *Woman's Own Book: or, A Plain and Familiar Treatise on All*

Complaints and Diseases Peculiar to Females, by Rev. D. L. Saunders, M.D. (Little Rock, Ark., 1858), and *The Planter's Guide and Family Book of Medicine,* by J. Hume Simons (3rd ed.; Charleston, S.C., 1848), both of which advocated a heroic approach. Two articles especially useful to this study for their details about southern obstetrics and obstetrical surgery were William P. Hort's "Report of the Committee on Midwifery and the Diseases of Children," *New Orleans Medical and Surgical Journal,* IX (1853), 472–84, 567–80; and John M. Watson's "A Treatise on Obstetric Surgery," *Nashville Journal of Medicine and Surgery,* XII (1857), 92–112.

Primary source material on alternative forms of medicine include *The Botanic Physician, or Family Medical Adviser,* by J. E. Carter (Madisonville, Tenn., 1837); *Valuable Vegetable Medical Prescriptions for the Cure of All Nervous and Putrid Disorders,* by Richard Carter, the son of an Indian mother and British father, who claimed to be trained by "herbs, barks and roots" (Cincinnati, 1830); *Lectures on Midwifery and the Forms of Disease Peculiar to Women and Children,* by Alva Curtis, a botanic but an opponent of Thomson, in part because Curtis promoted the value of medical education, edited the *Thomsonian Recorder,* and founded the Botanico Medical College of Ohio (2nd ed.; Columbus, Ohio, 1841); *Treatise on the Diseases of Married Females: Disorders of Pregnancy, Parturition, and Lactation,* by John C. Peters, a homeopath (New York, 1854); *Water Cure in Pregnancy and Childbirth,* by Joel Shew, an exponent of the power of hydropathy (New York, 1854); *The Family Physician and Guide to Health,* by Daniel H. Whitney, an advocate of a botanic approach (New York, 1833); *A Treatise on the Botanic Theory and Practice of Medicine,* by Alfred Worthy, a professor at the Southern-Botanico Medical College who directed his counsels to both parent and medical student (Forsyth, Ga., 1842).

Infant health was the subject of numerous treatises as well, though few related directly to problems in the South. European texts consulted for this study include Mrs. J. Bakewell's *The Mother's Practical Guide in the Physical, Intellectual, and Moral Training of Her Children* (3rd American ed.; New York, 1846), a popular work, and unusual because it is one of the few by women and because it includes advice concerning pregnancy; William Buchan's *Domestic Medicine; or, A Treatise on the Prevention and Cure of Diseases, by Regimen and Simple Medicines* (Boston, 1809), a best seller in America and abroad; William Cadogan's *An Essay upon Nursing and Management of Children* (London, 1748), the first formal treatise on child therapy from a medical perspective, written by an English doctor and reprinted in *Source Book of Medical History,* ed. Logan Clendening (New York, 1942); Andrew Combe's *The Management of Infancy, Physiological and Moral, Intended Chiefly for the Use of Parents* (Edinburgh, 1846); and Michael Underwood's *A Treatise on the Diseases of Children* (Rev. ed.; Philadelphia, 1818). Combe was a doctor at the Royal College of Physicians, in Edinburgh; Underwood was an English doctor. Many of the doctors were reacting against wealthy Europeans who seemed to show a parental indifference and aloofness by sending their children away to the countryside for nursing and nurturing. These practices, however, were becoming less common by the late eighteenth century.

Published American works on infant health include *The American Ladies' Medical Pocket-Book and Nursery Adviser* (N.p., 1833); David Francis Condie's long and detailed *Practical Treatise on the Diseases of Children* (Philadelphia, 1844); William Potts Dewees' best seller, *A Treatise on the Physical and Medical Treatment of Children* (9th ed.; Philadelphia, 1826); John Eberle's *A Treatise on the Diseases and Physical Education of Children* (Cincinnati, 1833); David Holmes's *The Child's Physician: A Popular Treatise on the Management and Diseases of Infancy and Childhood* (Providence, 1857); *The Maternal Physician: A Treatise on the Nurture and Management of Infants from Birth Until Two Years Old,* by an American Matron (2nd ed.; Philadelphia, 1818), unusual because of its maternal perspective; Charles Delucena Meigs's *Observations on Certain of the Diseases of Young Children* (Philadelphia, 1850); his son John Forsyth Meigs's *A Practical Treatise on the Diseases of Children* (Philadelphia, 1848); Joel Shew's *Children: Their Hydropathic Management in Health and Disease* (New York, 1852); Daniel H. Whitney's *The Family Physician and Guide in Three Parts* (New York, 1833); and from the South, Joseph Wright's *A Practical Treatise on the Management and Diseases of Children* (Macon, Ga., 1859).

Recent historical studies on antebellum medicine and the role of medical professionals are numerous, though the majority focus on urban and northern developments. For material useful in the present study, see Alex Berman, "The Heroic Approach in Nineteenth-Century Therapeutics," in Judith Walzer Leavitt and Ronald L. Numbers (eds.), *Sickness and Health in America: Readings in the History of Medicine and Public Health* (Madison, Wis., 1978), 77–86; James H. Cassedy, *Medicine and American Growth, 1800–1860* (Madison, Wis.,

1986), especially helpful for its regional approach; John Duffy, *The Healers: The Rise of the Medical Establishment* (New York, 1976), a comprehensive overview; Joseph F. Kett, *The Formation of the American Medical Profession: The Role of Institutions, 1780–1860* (New Haven, 1968; Westport, Conn., 1980), emphasizing licensing, education, and sectarian medicine; Lester King, *Medical Thinking: A Historical Preface* (Princeton, 1982); Charles E. Rosenberg, "Medical Text and Social Context: Explaining William Buchan's *Domestic Medicine,*" *Bulletin of the History of Medicine,* LVII (1983); Rosenberg, "The Therapeutic Revolution: Medicine, Meaning, and Social Change in Nineteenth-Century America," in Judith Walzer Leavitt and Ronald L. Numbers (eds.), *Sickness and Health in America: Readings in the History of Medicine and Public Health* (2nd ed.; Madison, Wis., 1985), 39–52; William G. Rothstein, *American Physicians in the Nineteenth Century: From Sects to Science* (Baltimore, 1972), which shows the impact of sectarian medicine on regular doctors; Paul Starr, *The Social Transformation of American Medicine* (New York, 1982), a fascinating and controversial Pulitzer Prize–winning study of the medical profession, though dealing mostly with the post–Civil War period; and John Harley Warner, *The Therapeutic Perspective: Medical Practice, Knowledge, and Identity in America, 1820–1885* (Cambridge, Mass., 1986), which presents an interesting examination of medical therapy, a thorough analysis of specificity, and justification for the practice of nineteenth-century medicine.

For studies on medical education, see Charles Donald O'Malley, *History of Medical Education* (Berkeley, 1970), a collection of essays; O'Malley, *Medical Education in the United States Before the Civil War* (Philadelphia, 1944); and Frederick C. Waite, "American Sectarian Medical Colleges Before the Civil War," *Bulletin of the History of Medicine,* II (1946), 148–65. Several books already noted, such as Starr's *Social Transformation,* also deal with the subject. For some interesting perceptions on southern medical education, see Harold J. Abrahams, "Secession from Northern Medical Schools," *Transactions and Studies of the College of Physicians of Philadelphia,* XXXVI (1968–69), 29–45, which describes the exodus of three hundred students from Philadelphia institutions in 1859; James O. Breeden, "States' Rights Medicine in the Old South," *Bulletin of the New York Academy of Medicine,* LII (1976), 348–72, arguing for the perceived distinctiveness of southern medical problems and setting in relief doctors' southern nationalism; and John Harley Warner, "A Southern Medical Reform: The Meaning of the Antebellum Argument for Southern Medical Education," *Bulletin of the History of Medicine*, LVII (1983), 365–81, which argues that southern doctors defended dramatic medical practice in order to enhance their status.

On quackery and domestic and alternative forms of medicine, see Martin Kaufman, *Homeopathy in America: The Rise and Fall of a Medical Heresy* (Baltimore, 1971); Jane Donegan, *Hydropathic Highway to Health: Women and Water-Cure in Antebellum America* (New York, 1986); James Harvey Young, *The Toadstool Millionaires: A Social History of Patent Medicines in America before Federal Regulation* (Princeton, 1961); Stephen Nissenbaum, *Sex, Diet, and Debility in Jacksonian America: Sylvester Graham and Health Reform* (Westport, Conn., 1980), on a leader in the vegetarian movement; and James O. Breeden, "Thomsonianism in Virginia," *Virginia Magazine of History and Biography*, LXXXII (1974), 150–80, a solid piece of research on this sect and its impact on at least one southern state.

For studies that deal exclusively with the South in the history of medicine, see Wyndham Bolling Blanton, *Medicine in Virginia in the Nineteenth Century* (Richmond, 1931); William H. Deaderick and Loyd Thompson, *The Endemic Diseases of the Southern States* (Philadelphia, 1916), which is old but still useful; Jill Dubisch, "Low Country Fevers: Cultural Adaptations to Malaria in Antebellum South Carolina," *Social Science and Medicine*, XXI (1985), 641–49, which has a sociological perspective; John Duffy, *History of Medicine in Louisiana* (2 vols.; Baton Rouge, 1958), a very positive view of Louisiana's contributions; Duffy, "Medical Practice in the Ante Bellum South," *Journal of Southern History*, XXV (1959), 53–72; Duffy, "A Note on Ante-Bellum Southern Nationalism and Medical Practice," *Journal of Southern History*, XXXIV (1968), 266–76; Martha Carolyn Mitchell, "Health and Medical Practice in the Lower South, 1845–1860," *Journal of Southern History*, X (1944), 424–46, which, although dated, emphasizes the frontier character of southern medicine; Darrett B. Rutman and Anita H. Rutman, "Of Agues and Fevers: Malaria in the Early Chesapeake," *William and Mary Quarterly*, XXXIII (1976), 31–60, covering the colonial period but giving an overview of malaria and its impact on early settlers; Richard H. Shryock, "Medical Practices in the Old South," in his *Medicine in America: Historical Essays* (Baltimore, 1966), 49–70, which is old but well written and informative; Joseph Waring, *A History of Medicine in South Carolina, 1670–1825* (Charleston, S.C., 1964); Waring, *A History of Medicine in South Carolina, 1825–1900* (Charleston, S.C., 1967); Waring, "The Influence of Benjamin Rush on the Practice of Bleeding in South Carolina," *Bulletin of the History of Medicine,* XXXV (1961), 230–37; and John Harley Warner, "The Idea of Southern Medical Distinctiveness: Medical Knowledge and Practice in the Old South," in Leavitt and Numbers (eds.), *Sickness and Health,* 2nd ed., 53–70. For the southern diet, see Edgar W. Martin, *The Standard of Living in 1860: American Consumption Levels on the Eve of the Civil War* (Chicago, 1942), which divides the subject by region; and Samuel Bowers Hilliard, *Hog Meat and Hoecake: Food Supply in the Old South, 1840–1860* (Carbondale, Ill., 1972).

Of importance to the study for comparative purposes were investigations into the health, childbirth, and infant-rearing practices of slaves. See Kenneth F. Kiple and Virginia Himmelsteib King, *Another Dimension to the Black Diaspora: Diet, Disease, and Racism* (New York, 1981), with interesting conclusions on slave diet, diseases, and environmental concerns, and on physiological characteristics that affected slave health; Todd Savitt, *Medicine and Slavery: the Diseases and Health Care of Blacks in Antebellum Virginia* (Urbana, Ill., 1978), with attention directed mainly to one state but with information applicable to other areas as well; Savitt, "Black Health on the Plantation: Masters, Slaves, and Physicians," in Leavitt and Numbers (eds.), *Sickness and Health,* 2nd ed., 313–30; Richard H. Steckel, "Birth Weights and Infant Mortality Among American Slaves," *Explorations in Economic History,* XXIII (1986), 173–98; Steckel, "A Dreadful Childhood: The Excess Mortality of American Slaves," *Social Science History,* X (1986), 427–65; Deborah White, *Ar'n't I a Woman? Female Slaves in the Plantation South* (New York, 1986); and Peter H. Wood, *Black Majority: Negroes in Colonial South Carolina from 1670 Through the Stono Rebellion* (New York, 1974), including his chapter "'The Soveraign Ray of Health.'" For primary source material on slaves, see John W. Blassingame, *Slave Testimony: Two Centuries of Letters, Speeches, Interviews, and Autobiographies* (Baton Rouge, 1977); Charles L. Perdue, Jr., Thomas E. Barden, and Robert K. Phillips (eds.), *Weevils in the Wheat: Interviews with Virginia Ex-Slaves* (Charlottesville, Va., 1976); George P. Rawick, *The American Slave: A Composite Autobiography* (41 vols. and index; Westport, Conn., 1972–81), which is important for its extensive collection of oral histories though having little information on childbirth, breast-feeding, causes of infant deaths, and slave participation in white deliveries and nursing; and

Dorothy Sterling, *We Are Your Sisters: Black Women in the Nineteenth Century* (New York, 1984).

Most historical works dealing exclusively with obstetrics, pregnancy, and female health concerns concentrate on changes in the urban Northeast but have been useful for conceptual orientation and for purposes of comparison. See Janet Bogdan, "Care or Cure? Childbirth Practices in Nineteenth-Century America," *Feminist Studies,* IV (1978), 92–99; Judith Chaney, "Birthing in Early America," *Journal of Nurse-Midwifery,* XXV (1980), 5–13; Irving S. Cutter and Henry Viets, *A Short History of Midwifery* (Philadelphia, 1964); Jane B. Donegan, *Women and Men Midwives: Medicine, Morality, and Misogyny in Early America* (Westport, Conn., 1978), which contends that forceps and education were central to the movement of physicians into obstetrics; Claire Elizabeth Fox, "Pregnancy, Childbirth, and Early Infancy in Anglo-American Culture" (Ph.D. dissertation, University of Pennsylvania, 1966); Sylvia Hoffert, *Private Matters: American Attitudes Toward Childbearing and Infant Nurture in the Urban North, 1800–1860* (Urbana, Ill., 1989), concentrating on women's experiences in the urban Northeast during the same decades that the present study concerns and including literary, medical, and feminine perceptions; Francis Kobrin, "The American Midwife Controversy: A Crisis of Professionalization," *Bulletin of the History of Medicine,* XL (1966), 350–63; Judith Walzer Leavitt, *Brought to Bed: Childbearing in America, 1750–1950* (New York, 1986), which, though dealing mostly with the post–Civil War period, convincingly argues that women played a key role in seeking changes in obstetric practice; James Mohr, *Abortion in America: The Origins and Evolutions of National Policy, 1800–1900* (New York, 1978), which shows changing political, legal, and medical ideas about abortion; Joyce Roberts and C. Mendez-Bauer, "A Perspective of Maternal Position During Labor," *Journal of Perinatal Medicine,* VIII (1980), 255–64; Catherine Scholten, *Childbearing in American Society, 1650–1850* (New York, 1985); Scholten, "'On the Importance of the Obstetrik Art': Changing Customs of Childbirth in America, 1760–1825," *William and Mary Quarterly,* XXXIV (1977), 426–45; A. Clair Siddall, "Bloodletting in American Obstetric Practice," *Bulletin of the History of Medicine,* LIV (1980), 101–10, which argues that bleeding became common when male attendants entered the birthing room; Harold Speert, *Obstetrics and Gynecology in America: A History* (Baltimore, 1980); Jill Suitor, "Husbands' Participation in Childbirth: A Nineteenth Century

Phenomenon," *Journal of Family History,* VI (1981), 178–93, which concludes that husbands took a larger role in the birthing process, a finding
that does not seem to reflect southern practices; and Richard Wertz and
Dorothy Wertz, *Lying-In: A History of Childbirth in America* (New York,
1977), a standard study with very little on the South.

For comparative purposes, see also William Ray Arney, *Power and the
Profession of Obstetrics* (Chicago, 1982), which outlines the role of mid-
wives in England and in the United States; Mireille Laget, "Childbirth
in Seventeenth and Eighteenth Century France: Obstetrical Practices
and Collective Attitudes," in Robert Forster and Orest Ranum (eds.),
Medicine and Society in France: Selections from the Annales (Baltimore,
1980), 137–76; Judith Schneid Lewis, *In the Family Way: Childbirth in the
British Aristocracy, 1760–1860* (New Brunswick, N.J., 1986); Ann
Oakley, *The Captured Womb: A History of the Medical Care of Pregnant
Women* (London, 1984), which contends that pregnancy was not considered a disease by British doctors but that poor health gave rise to a
dependence on physicians; and Oakley, *Women Confined: Towards a Sociology of Childbirth* (New York, 1980).

The works on antebellum women, their role in society, and the
situation of southern women are growing in number. For studies that
were particularly useful here, see Ann Boucher, "Wealthy Planter Families in Nineteenth Century Alabama" (Ph.D. dissertation, University
of Connecticut, 1978); Jane Turner Censer, *North Carolina Planters and
Their Children, 1800–1860* (Baton Rouge, 1984); Suzanne Lebsock, *The
Free Women of Petersburg: Status and Culture in a Southern Town, 1784–
1860* (New York, 1984), a sensitive and articulate examination of urban
women in the antebellum South; Jan Lewis, *The Pursuit of Happiness:
Family and Values in Jefferson's Virginia* (New York, 1983), which argues
for the deep affection in southern families and women's growing dependence upon their children; James Oakes, *The Ruling Race: A History of
American Slaveholders* (New York, 1982), which has an interesting outlook on southern migration during the antebellum period and on the
difficulties that women faced; Anne Firor Scott, "Women's Perspective
on the Patriarchy in the 1850s," *Journal of American History,* LXI (1974),
52–64; and Carroll Smith-Rosenberg, "The Female World of Love and
Ritual: Relations Between Women in Nineteenth-Century America,"
Signs, I (1975), 1–29 (reprinted in Michael Gordon [ed.], *The American
Family in Social-Historical Perspective* [2nd ed.; New York, 1978], 334–
58), a classic examination of friendship and bonding between women.

Index